*Museums and Silent Objects: Designing
Effective Exhibitions*

Cover image

Portrait busts of James Watt, on display in the Science Museum London. The two on either side are by the contemporary sculptor Peter Turnerelli, and the centre one is by Sir Francis Chantrey, the most eminent sculptor of the age. Chantrey also sculpted the full figure of Watt which was for a time in Westminster Abbey.

Watt's great interest in later life was the mechanical reproduction of sculpture, and he had a large collection of casts of various subjects, including Homer and Socrates. These are also in the collection of the Science Museum; they are surprisingly displayed in the middle of the workshop reconstruction, where there are also two large sculpture copying machines designed by him.

The interest in sculpture reproduction may account for Watt having so many of himself.

Museums and Silent Objects: Designing Effective Exhibitions

FRANCESCA MONTI AND SUZANNE KEENE

University College London, UK

Routledge
Taylor & Francis Group

LONDON AND NEW YORK

First published 2013 by Ashgate Publishing

Published 2016 by Routledge
2 Park Square, Milton Park, Abingdon, Oxon OX14 4RN
711 Third Avenue, New York, NY 10017, USA

First issued in paperback 2017

Routledge is an imprint of the Taylor & Francis Group, an informa business

British Library Cataloguing in Publication Data
Monti, Francesca.
  Museums and silent objects - designing effective
  exhibitions.
  1. Museum exhibits.
  I. Title II. Keene, Suzanne.
  069.5'3-dc23

Library of Congress Cataloging-in-Publication Data
Monti, Francesca.
  Museums and silent objects : designing effective exhibitions / by
Francesca Monti and Suzanne Keene.
    p. cm.
  Includes bibliographical references and index.
  ISBN 978-1-4094-0703-4 (hardback)
  1. Museum exhibits--Handbooks, manuals, etc. I. Keene, Suzanne.
II. Title.
  AM151.M566 2012
  069'.5--dc23

                                                                2012015709

ISBN 13: 978-0-8153-9951-3 (pbk)
ISBN 13: 978-1-4094-0703-4 (hbk)

CONTENTS

LIST OF FIGURES

LIST OF TABLES

PREFACE

We refer throughout this book to the authors and researchers as 'we', as this is easier for the reader. In this preface we wish to make our respective contributions clear.

The book is the product of a long and thorough research and authoring project. The theoretical review, the development of the key concepts and the practical research were all carried out by Francesca Monti for her doctoral thesis at UCL: *Allowing Objects to Speak, People to Hear: The Effective Display of Inconspicuous Objects from Egyptian Collections*. Monti was awarded her doctorate for this in 2007.

The research was supervised by Suzanne Keene and by Stephen Quirke, curator of the Petrie Museum. In the normal way, we discussed the research at length, suggested avenues to explore and methods to use, and advised on interpreting and writing up the results. The products of this stage of research are reported in Chapters 2–8, 10 and 11, and in the findings and conclusions in Chapters 13 and 14.

Chapters 9 and 12 are from other research that Francesca Monti undertook during and after the main research phase, which had not been written up or which existed only as internal reports.

During 2010–2011, Monti drafted a large part of this book. Suzanne Keene then took over as co-author. Keene substantially edited and re-organised the content, wrote Chapters 9 and 12 from Monti's research notes, obtained, drew or re-drew nearly all of the images and diagrams, and added material and references drawing on a number of pieces of current and new work.

Francesca Monti
Suzanne Keene

March 2012

CHAPTER 1

INTRODUCTION

Nothing is so poor or so trivial as not to have a story to tell us. The tools, the potsherds, the very stones and bricks of the wall cry out, if we have the power of understanding them.

(Flinders Petrie, 1892)

If during a museum visit we temporarily suspend our viewing of the collections to quietly observe other visitors, we notice that people's attention is not equally distributed among the objects on show. Rather, observation shows that some items are the focus of interest for many viewers, while others, which we term *silent objects*, are almost completely ignored, their presence barely acknowledged.[1] Perversely, objects with a more conspicuous and attractive appearance benefit from fuller interpretation and glamorous display, while others are relegated to the ranks of supporters.

This is problematic for museums for several reasons. By focusing on the most conspicuous and visually compelling objects, visitors may miss much of the interest of an exhibition and fail to appreciate the full richness and depth of a topic. They may go away with a false image of the collections and an incomplete or erroneous view of the past. In addition, from a practical perspective, an uneven viewing pattern creates congested areas where visitors converge, leaving other spaces empty.

From the visitor's viewpoint, an undue emphasis on certain objects restricts their freedom to identify where their interest truly lies and what they would appreciate seeing.

There are many reasons why some, silent, objects do not attract and hold attention. An inconspicuous appearance is a crucial factor. Overlooked objects are not exceptionally large or small, colourful, artistically noticeable, obviously ancient or precious looking, nor are they endowed with an iconic significance which makes them desirable to seek out. They are not as visually captivating as their more

---

1   We are not the first to light on the concept of silent objects, but we hope we have found some practical ways to enable their voices to be heard: Frank 2000: 93–104.

Figure 1.1   Three silent objects: shabtis at the feet of the gleaming gilded coffins of Henutmehyt in the British Museum. A few visitors look at the decorated shabti boxes, but the shabtis are ignored or even positively disliked (below, 8.5.3)

Source: © S. Keene, courtesy of the Trustees of the British Museum.

popular counterparts and, if they are not in a prominent location, people rarely even happen upon them by chance.

One might argue that this predicament could be simply resolved, for example, by placing the problematic objects in strategic positions within the room and by lighting them dramatically to increase their chances of being noticed. This stratagem could be employed effectively for some exhibits. However, if it were to be used to excess, it would cancel out the effect, which relies upon sensations of anticipation, on surprise, on the viewer's assumption that the museum is offering a selection of particularly worthwhile attractions. In addition, although such a display may initially lure visitors to the object, it does not necessarily increase the potential of the item to hold the viewer's attention for long enough for them to notice that it is interesting.

Research indicates that the appearance of objects contributes to the formation of split-second assumptions that visitors involuntarily or consciously make about the depth and quality of the experience that a specific object can provide.[2] In a perfect world, each museum goer would visit the galleries with full awareness of the narratives on offer and of the objects' roles in relation to these. However, this is rarely the case. When visitors are immersed in an environment in which display and interpretation is inadequate for them, they tend to retreat to contingent modes of selection and meaning-making strategies. They look at the most striking objects in view and they make sense of them using their pre-existing knowledge. They rely on the visual magnetism of some exhibits and on casual encounters with what is in their path. For these reasons, many objects are ignored during museum visits.

For example, one of the objects on display in the Horniman Museum's *Music room* display, *Listen to order*, a glittering array of musical instruments organised according to type (see below, Figures 3.3 and 6.11), is a tiny pair of arms with hands, neatly fashioned out of bone. Only the meticulously organised or targeted visitor would notice these insignificant items. The label states that they are a pair of clappers from ancient Egypt, collected by the archaeologist Flinders Petrie (they may be the oldest item on display in that gallery). Those intrigued by the trajectory of an object's history might discover from the online catalogue that these were acquired from Petrie by the son of the founder of the Horniman Museum. But what we don't learn, which would be poignant indeed given the great attraction of the gallery for families and children, is that 3,500 years ago this pair and another were placed in the burial of a child for them to use on their onward journey and to console the survivors – a specific person, specific because they lived at a specific time in a specific place.[3]

Again, visitors to the spectacular *Egyptian death and afterlife: mummies* gallery overlook or even express boredom with the number of shabtis[4] included in the displays (Figures 1.1 and 8.9). Were they to read one of the many informative text panels (considered to be too numerous by many visitors), they would learn that these little figurines were placed in burials from about 2000–2030 BC. Often inscribed with a magic spell, they were intended to carry out work on behalf of the dead person, who might otherwise have to labour in the fields or do other menial tasks. While at first only one or two were included in a burial, they were subject to shabti inflation, eventually to over 400 – one for each of the 365 days in the year plus 36 overseers.[5]

---

2   E.g. Alt and Shaw 1984; Bitgood 2006; Csikszentmihalyi and Hermanson 1995; Shettel 1973.

3   S. Quirke, UCL, personal communication. For further information on these intriguingly silent objects, see www.ucl.ac.uk/silent-objects.

4   Shabtis are small figures representing servants that were included in ancient Egyptian burials.

5   Source: text panel in British Museum Room 63, *Egyptian death and afterlife: mummies* gallery.

1.1   NEW RESEARCH

This book reports the findings from extensive research aimed at identifying the key factors which can transform the display of a silent object into an exciting and interesting encounter for the visitor. Ideally, all objects on show to the public would be exhibited so that their potential interest is evident. Yet, despite a wealth of information on the museum experience in general and on visitor interaction with objects in particular, museums still have not found optimal ways to exhibit less visually attractive objects. It is clear from the extensive published research into exhibition techniques that there is no magic solution that will cover all situations.

This unsatisfactory state of affairs stems from a focus on the core elements of the museum experience in isolation: visitor and exhibits; visitor and environment; visitor and visitor; environment and exhibits. Instead, any strategic intervention aimed at displaying silent objects effectively and hence rebalancing viewing patterns requires a combination of solutions based on the characteristics of the object, the exhibition setting, the nature of the museum and its visitors.

The visitor–object encounter is framed and encompassed by the nature and quality of three main parameters: the setting, which includes the gallery or museum and the other visitors present in the space; the visitor: their prior knowledge, experience of museum visits, whether they are on their own or with others, and their physical and mental state – fresh or tired, young, old, etc.; and the object or exhibit. Figure 1.2 depicts the transection of the three dimensions.

A comprehensive approach requires an analysis of the three aspects in combination: the physical and symbolic characteristics of objects; visitors' cognitive and affective responses to them; and visitors' responses to the setting and environment – all in the broader spatial and contextual scale of the museum visit. This process is comparable to the way in which one responds to a cinema scene, where the eye in turn focuses on different details of the picture, each individual element contributing to a facet of the scene, but with the overall background view always in sight.

Therefore, a programme of research addressed the challenge of enabling the *voices* of silent objects to be heard by conveying to the visitor the existence of interesting stories and creating the conditions for a rewarding experience. It addressed these specific questions:

- why do people choose or neglect specific exhibits?;
- what causes them to act in this way?; and
- what are the characteristics of the observed interactions?

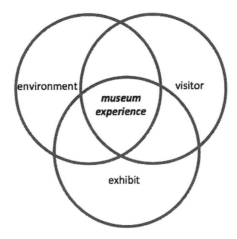

Figure 1.2   Setting–exhibit–visitor: the combined elements of the museum experience
Source: © F. Monti/S. Keene.

A better understanding of these issues can inform a treatment of museum objects that increases visitor awareness of the rewards concealed behind their appearance. By studying people's reactions to such objects in different display and interpretation scenarios, it is possible to understand the causes of their actions and lack of engagement, and consequently to address them.

The research has indeed helped us to understand the reasons for some objects' silence. Further, it enables us to offer a range of techniques and practical guidelines on how to display and interpret them to better advantage. This could help to re-balance viewing patterns in museum galleries and enable people to make an informed choice of what they want to see and interact with.

The results are widely applicable to the display of objects in general rather than only silent objects. Instead, a set of general concepts and tools have been developed and are presented here that can be applied to the design and evaluation of any object display, showcase or gallery. This can provide a far deeper and more holistic understanding of the object-based information landscape of the museum than current tools can offer. This approach facilitates a re-balancing of the 'attracting, holding and communicative power of objects', whatever their visual qualities.[6]

We are encouraged in this by finding in two of the galleries we investigated a viewing pattern evenly distributed between spectacular and inconspicuous objects.

---

6   Bitgood 2000.

Whether by chance or as a consequence, audiences spent longer in these two galleries than in other comparable ones, and those interviewed expressed great satisfaction and pleasure with their experience (Chapter 13).

1.2   ATTRACTIVE VERSUS SILENT OBJECTS

The hypothesis in this research is that the way something looks greatly influences our behaviour towards it. In this respect, museum objects fall into two categories.

To the first group belong objects that easily attract and hold the viewer. This may be due to their material qualities, such as colour, size, shape, symmetry and fabric,[7] or to their non-physical attributes, such as age, iconicity,[8] sense of past, magical significance,[9] material value and familiarity.[10] The latter qualities are nevertheless signalled by physical characteristics. In the second category are the objects whose inner qualities and stories are buried deeper within their appearance. Because at a first glance they do not seem very interesting, they are often overlooked by museum visitors.

This attention deficit relates to the 'general value principle' set out by Bitgood. He argues that during a museum visit, visitors tend to (normally unconsciously) calculate the value of an experience as the ratio between the benefits and the costs: 'We attend to things which are perceived as beneficial (such as satisfying curiosity, enjoyment) only if the costs are perceived as low in relation to the benefits.'[11] Objects whose appearance does not suggest sufficient cost-effective rewards are more likely to be ignored. They remain silent.

This dichotomy is accentuated by two museum customary practices. From the early modern period, museums have been predominantly institutions of the visible, where exhibitory practices prioritise sight over other senses.[12] The customary *in the glass case* display model is heavily reliant on the presentation of the physical appearance of objects. However, visually prominent objects are frequently accompanied by others of less striking appearance that nevertheless represent important parts of the complete narrative. Exhibitions can benefit from a visually enticing treatment that engages the viewer; but then, artefacts which were not originally created to be admired but which have practical uses lose meaning and

---

7   Csikszentmihalyi and Hermanson 1995: 37.
8   Csikszentmihalyi and Hermanson 1995: 37.
9   Morphy 1992: 10.
10   Csikszentmihalyi 1993.
11   Bitgood 2006: 464.
12   Bennett 2006: 263, where exhibitory practices prioritise sight over other senses.

significance when only experienced through sight. It is difficult, for example, to appreciate a prehistoric hand axe without carefully touching its sharp edges and feeling how its ergonomic design fits the hand. Conversely, a painting's impact is intended to be visual: it involves perspective, in the sense that everything represented in a picture is represented from a point, or points, within represented space and is therefore created with the eye in mind.[13]

Although for most visitors sight and written interpretation are an acceptable method of presentation, exhibits can be experienced in many other ways and at many levels. The traditional case and text arrangement is not best suited to promoting novel and personal interactions, and leads to objects that are not visually exciting being disregarded. This display paradigm reinforces the gulf between visually enticing and problematic, between eloquent and silent exhibits. Objects can be encountered through touch, sound, smell, evocative images and poetic contemplation, according to setting, display and individual preferences. Of course, both the terms of an interaction and the selection of objects are defined by the museum's display and interpretative choices. These are informed, in turn, by the need to illustrate, through the artefacts themselves, the narratives to be conveyed to the viewer, while at the same time complying with practical and theoretical considerations. The supremacy of sight over other senses therefore operates at two levels. Firstly, it subtly exerts its influence during the process of object selection for exhibitions, when artefacts with a presumed better visual impact are favoured over less striking ones because of their potential attracting power and ability easily to convey elements of the narrative. Secondly, sight-centred exhibitions increase the popularity of visual objects and diminish the chance that less visually striking ones will be appreciated, thus reinforcing the likelihood that visitors will be offered only fragments of the collections and their stories.

The second museum custom is the distinction between art and artefact (below, 5.1.3), with the consequent different treatment of objects on display. The desire to seek the extraordinary and the beautiful is very deeply rooted in modern culture and is not a sole prerogative of the Western world. In Japan, for example, the privately owned Miho Museum by the architect I.M. Pei, nestled among the verdant mountains south of Kyoto, aims to create a spiritual and aesthetic experience through the contemplation of spectacular pieces from Egyptian and Greek antiquities, among others, in a dreamlike and awe-inspiring setting.[14] Therefore, the grandstanding of *beautiful* museum objects feeds market demands and public expectations.

---

13   Hopkins 2004: 149.
14   Miho Museum website: www.miho.or.jp [accessed 16 July 2012].

BOX 1.1   THE *JAMEEL GALLERY OF ISLAMIC ART* AT THE VICTORIA & ALBERT MUSEUM – BEAUTY AND DAZZLING OBJECTS

A typical review of the *Jameel Gallery of Islamic Art* at the Victoria & Albert Museum (V&A) (Figure 1.3) praises this 'magnificent showcase' for art which displays '400 of the most spectacular 10,000 Islamic artefacts in the V&A's collection'. The emphasis here is on art, beauty and dazzling objects. Although this is undoubtedly a fundamental characteristic of the material culture of Islam, this journalistic piece highlights our hunger for the wonderful and the eye-pleasing, which is fed and intensified by current exhibition practice. Even bearing in mind that the V&A is a museum of art and design, one still wonders whether the *Jameel Gallery* offers a complete and fair representation of the cultural production of Islam and of the people behind it. By omitting less striking examples from the gallery, the museum presents solely one face, albeit an attractive and crowd-pleasing one, of this culture.

Museums are subject to intense and conflicting pressures. The search for the extraordinary is seen every day in our approach to and expectations of them. The *Jameel Gallery*, as an example, opened in 2006 and is indicative of the Museum's need to please sponsors and stakeholders alike and to attract as many visitors as possible through its doors (visitor numbers being one of the main sources of vital sustenance for such institutions) (see Box 1.1 and Figure 1.3). Another requirement is the need to satisfy funding agents, whether public, corporate or private benefactors. Yet another pressure is to shake off accusations of past colonialism by fairly and fully representing the cultures of other countries, and here the *Jameel Gallery* is arguably less successful. However, with many of the UK's heritage institutions growing ever more dependent upon money from the private sector to support their exhibitions and public programmes,[15] the preferences of these stakeholders are always likely to trump considerations of equality. The ability to compromise, negotiate and discern among conflicting pressures is now a necessary requirement of the museum professional.

An uneven distribution of attention among exhibition objects is also influenced by other factors, such as the personal preferences of the curator, the characteristics of a particular museum, the qualities of objects, design solutions and practical factors. A variation in attraction is particularly noticeable with ethnographic and archaeological collections, where objects of unassuming appearance share museum space and compete with striking ones for visitors' limited attention (Figure 1.1).

---

15   Davies 2006: 37; Bailey 2011.

Figure 1.3   The *Jameel Gallery* at the Victoria & Albert Museum, London
Source: © F. Monti, courtesy of the Trustees of the Victoria & Albert Museum.

1.3   THE BASIS FOR RESEARCH: ANCIENT EGYPT

Displays of notable Egyptian collections were used for most of the investigation, in displays in the British Museum, the Horniman Museum and the Petrie Museum. Galleries in the V&A and Horniman Museums were also analysed in order to research specific issues. Ancient Egypt enjoys a particularly high profile in the European reception and construction of ancient history, historiography and archaeology.[16]

Displays of Egyptian antiquities mostly include sharply contrasted objects: the extraordinary and the exotic (such as colossal statuary and funerary material) and modest and everyday objects (such as documents in cursive scripts and pottery). Humble domestic material remains have attracted widespread interest among audiences since their first debut in 1837 in the British Museum Egyptian Room for the glimpse they offer into the Egyptian household of 3,000 years ago. However, when exhibited, they are displaced from their original domestic context,

---

16   For example, Neal Ascherson's review (2004) of the set of volumes *Encounters with Ancient Egypt* (Ucko 2003).

which would be a source of familiar appeal to the viewer, and are juxtaposed with dramatically visual colossal statuary, with bizarre and mysterious religious items or with funerary objects of irresistible ghoulish appeal.[17] However interesting they might be to the viewer should they pause to look, these modest everyday remains are overshadowed by their more enticing counterparts. Hence, Egyptian antiquity displays are well suited for investigating the range of visitor preconceptions and reactions to different object characteristics and exhibition contexts. The findings are likely to be applicable and adaptable to a wide range of collection types.

1.4   THE VISITOR–OBJECT ENCOUNTER

It is not to be expected that all visitors will engage with all objects on any one occasion. Visitors have a limited attention span and tire mentally and physically during a museum visit: they are constantly deciding how to invest their time and energy in line with the 'general value principle'.[18] Individuals have different preferences and interests. The museum should aim to facilitate the visitor in choosing and defining the terms of their interaction with all of the objects on display according to their personal parameters. In other words, the objective is to create the *circumstances* for an ideal encounter with every object, hence allowing gallery goers to identify, focus on and enjoy what they are interested in.

1.4.1   The Atomic Theory of the Museum Visit

The *atomic* level of engagement, between one visitor and one object at a time, was used as the unit of experience in this research. The visitor–object interaction is only one dimension of the museum visit: interactions between visitors, whether children, friends or family members, play a large part in framing the experience. However, our focus was highly specific to the visitor–object interface, influenced by space but not by social interaction. We argue that the atomic one–visitor–one–object encounter is the starting point in the construction of a museum experience. Even at this atomic level, the visitor–object interface has multiple complex facets. Visitor education level, personal sensibilities, taste, self-perception, expectations, object types, object characteristics, communication strategies and contingent situations constitute the fabric of each visitor–object relationship.

Using the atomic level of engagement enables us to anticipate that in a given situation people's behaviours can, in general terms, be predicted.[19] This, we are confident, would mean that our results could be replicated and hence that our

---

17   Moser 2006: 228, 277.
18   Bitgood 2002: 8; 2006: 464.
19   Norman 2004: 54.

recommendations could be adopted with confidence that they would result in improved visitor experiences.

We acknowledge that visitors are far from being a homogeneous body and that there are endless differences at an individual level. Nevertheless, the advertising and marketing industries clearly trade on their ability to influence behaviours despite the enormous variety among individuals.[20]

The atomic theory of the museum visit is a step towards a better understanding of the museum experience as the product of converging influences. Once the modes and mechanisms of the one–visitor–one–object stance are understood, this knowledge can be employed to better understand the experience of a whole gallery or exhibition (Chapters 8 and 12). A number of variables come into play during social visits, with a major distinction being drawn between intentional interactions between people visiting as part of a group and chance encounters between individuals who move around in the same space.[21]

The duration of a successful experience, which will vary according to visitor, object and environment, is to an extent irrelevant. What matters is for an object to convey the existence of interesting information or stories. When this communicative link is established, the viewer can choose whether to interact, to briefly look, to glance, to return to it subsequently or simply to ignore it.

We have defined the visitor–object interaction as a four-stage model. Each stage of the model is used to explore a different aspect of the visitor–object interface. This four-stage model will be used as a point of reference throughout this book.

Stage 1 is about the 'attracting power' of an exhibit: its ability to draw attention.[22] In this stage, the issues relate to how to attract the visitor's attention to an object with little or no visual impact: of how to make them aware of its presence. This is a necessary condition for any of the following steps and for any object interaction, whatever the extent and depth. Once the visitor is aware of the existence of an item, it is up to them to determine the terms, modes and duration of the contact. What for various reasons may not develop into an interaction may one day blossom into a more rewarding connection if the conditions are met. Csikszentmihalyi believes that there are two necessary requirements: 'the object must contain a set of visual challenges that engages the interpretative skills of the beholder' and 'the environment must be conducive to a centering of the attention on the object and to a screening out of distractions'.[23]

---

20   Alexander, Crompton and Shrubsole 2011.
21   Stephens 1989: 61.
22   Bitgood 2000.
23   Csikszentmihalyi 1990: 19.

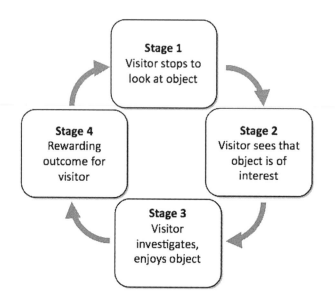

**Figure 1.4   The four stages in a visitor–object interaction. A positive
outcome will encourage more interactions in the future**
Source: © F. Monti/S.Keene.

Stage 2 centres on an exhibit's 'holding and communicative powers': on its ability
to maintain the viewer's attention and to communicate basic information.[24] It deals
with the question of how to suggest the existence of rich cultural contexts and
interesting narratives behind the humble appearance of silent objects. The stories
which visitors may find appealing are related to their perception and expectations
of the museum, their socio-cultural background, life circumstances and personal
preferences. An interesting question arises at this point: should the museum
present the object so that the visitor relates it to their own experience or existing
knowledge, should it simply suggest the existence of interesting and valuable
information or should it aim to upset preconceptions by suggesting controversial
and unexpected connotations? It can be argued that any of these would serve the
purpose. Familiarity with certain themes is a powerful magnet, as demonstrated, for
example, by the results of the study in the *Egyptian death and afterlife: mummies*
gallery (Room 63) at the British Museum (below, 8.5.2); however, some viewers
want to acquire new knowledge and so deepen their understanding of the subject;
and then again, deeper involvement and long-lasting memories are generated when
notions are challenged and questions posed.[25]

---

24   Bitgood 2000.
25   Sandifer 2003.

Stage 3 concerns ways to assist the visitor in investigating the object and conveying information about it. The holding and communicative qualities of the exhibit are the focus in this stage. Once the main themes have been signalled to the viewer, more detail and complex aspects can be offered. If the visitor is sufficiently intrigued by the object, the actual investigation can be thorough, or if the proposed object is not at the time of interest to the individual, it may be brief.

Stage 4 addresses the rewards the visitor gains from the encounter: enjoyment, inspiration, learning, recollection of memory or even outrage or horror. At any moment during this stage, people can choose to turn their attention away from the object and yet they will still be enriched by knowing that it exists. Irrespective of the outcomes of the experience, the return operates at two levels. The visitor may develop and increase their cultural capital: they would be able to discuss with others what they have seen and learned, and be able to derive greater benefit and enjoyment from subsequent reading or further cultural experiences.[26] Or, even if the visitor decides that the object is not of particular interest to them in the current circumstances, they will nevertheless be enriched with that very knowledge and with the awareness of the existence of the object, which may become of interest in the future. For these reasons, any of the potential outcomes of Stage 4 are regarded as knowledge gain. This stage also relates to questions of how visitors link objects in constructing narratives and the ways such connections are developed and elaborated beyond the visit.

1.5   RESEARCH STRATEGY: WHO DID WHAT

We have set out in the Preface our respective responsibilities for this research project. In general, Francesca Monti conceived, organised and undertook the research itself; Suzanne Keene organised and edited the text of this book. However, although the work was divided in this way, 'we' is used throughout for readability.

1.6   THEORY DOMAINS

The research strategy stems from the belief that the three central elements of the museum visit – *visitor, object and environment* – are indivisible (Figure 1.2).[27] On a micro level, these three components are the inseparable units that define the visitor–object encounter on which this investigation focuses.

---

26   Keene 2005: Chapter 10.
27   Falk et al. 1985.

We looked widely for the conceptual foundations for this work. Visitor studies have brought extensive understanding of particular aspects of the museum experience, but often there is a strong emphasis on learning modes and outcomes.[28] Yet there are other important indicators of positive experiences which cannot be defined in educational terms. These have been expressed in various ways (see Box 1.2).

BOX 1.2   EXPERIENCES WITH OBJECTS

Cathartic: objects purge the audience's feelings by reliving hidden impulses, sorting them out and bringing them into harmony with more conscious aspects of life.[29]

Aesthetic: 'A sense of awe and exhilaration people feel upon seeing or hearing something "beautiful".'[30]

Poetic: opposed to the categorical or didactic experience, it 'draws out the profounder, more elusive meanings inherent in so many artefacts from our past'.[31]

Introspective: the exhibition and the objects are a looking glass for visitors, who experience what they are capable of experiencing and who they are.[32]

Flow: a specific form of enjoyment with a deep involvement and opportunity for people to use a wide range of knowledge, emotional sensitivity and skills.[33]

Sensory: our brains are naturally programmed to draw from a range of sensory information on our environment, including vision, touch and hearing.[34]

Memorial: as memory voice, exhibits play an active role in constructing memories and identities.[35]

Therapeutic: museum objects have recently been explored for their potential in therapeutic work: for instance, object handling as an enrichment activity for patients and hospitals.[36]

---

28   E.g. Durbin 1996; Falk 2002; Falk and Dierking 2000; Hooper-Greenhill 2008, among others.
29   Csikszentmihalyi 1990:14.
30   Csikszentmihalyi 1990: 5.
31   Spalding 2002: 9.
32   Ohta, cited in Weil 2002: 69.
33   Csikszentmihalyi 1990.
34   Ernst and Bülthoff 2004.
35   Keene 2005: Chapter 6 and p. 98.
36   Chatterjee 2008.

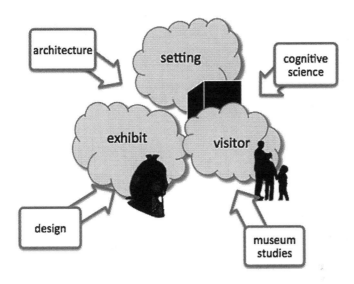

Figure 1.5   The relationships of the main theoretical sources and the elements of the visitor–object encounter
Source: © F. Monti/S. Keene.

The visitor's encounter with an object is a product of the effect of space on the viewer, the qualities of the object, the design and interpretative strategies of the exhibition, the viewer's aesthetic, emotional, affective and cognitive reactions to the exhibits, their socio-cultural background and, besides this, their interaction with other visitors.

Fields that we found relevant to exploring this plethora of variables and on which to ground the theoretical and subsequent observational enquiry are: *architecture, design, cognitive science* and *museology. Architecture* addressed aspects of visitor behaviour in the exhibition space. *Design* afforded an understanding of issues of display techniques and the effect of design features on users. Within the realm of *cognitive science*, notions of perception, affect and cognition, beauty and multi-sensory experiences were considered, and concepts from semiotics and aesthetics were encountered and explored. Notions from *material culture*, such as object biographies, were drawn on in conjunction with *museology* to probe deeper into certain aspects of the visitor–object interplay. *Museology* also facilitated an exploration of the elements of the museum experience, the cultural value of objects and institutional and curatorial authority.

The relationship of these to the elements of the visitor experience are shown in Figure 1.5.

1.7   THE KEY CONCEPTS

From these disciplines, a number of key concepts were selected that would enable us to dissect and analyse the visitor–object encounter so as to understand it in the round as a compound of variables: *space syntax, design idioms, beauty and usability, flow, learning models* and *object biographies.* They are summarised in Box 1.3 and are shown in Figure 1.6.

BOX 1.3   CONCEPTUAL SOURCES AND KEY CONCEPTS

Space syntax, born out of architectural theory, is a technique employed to analyse visitor movement patterns and behaviour in relation to the configuration of space.[37]

Design idiom is a concept from exhibition design that comprises a tool to explore and assess exhibit characteristics and to understand visitor reactions to key design elements of museum displays.[38]

Beauty and usability need to be in balance according to many who work in the fields of interactive design and cognitive sciences. This concept is a useful way to assess the cognitive and affective reactions of a visitor to a system.[39]

Flow is a concept from the field of cognitive psychology that throws light on aspects of the visitor's reactions with objects and on potential positive outcomes.[40]

Object biographies is the idea, borrowed from anthropology, that objects have life histories just as people do, which can help visitors to make connections with exhibits.[41]

Learning styles, the subjects of open debate within museology, are utilised to further explore visitors' rapport with objects and the outcomes of the interaction.[42]

1.8   RESEARCH METHODS

The key concepts we identified are ideas or notions that are key to the visitor experience. These were used to create research tools for analysing and evaluating galleries and exhibits so as to understand the visitor experience.

---

37   Hillier 1996: ix.
38   Hall 1987: 127.
39   Norman 2002: 42.
40   Csikszentmihalyi 1990: 7.
41   Csikszentmihalyi 1990: 7.
42   Serrell 1996: 51.

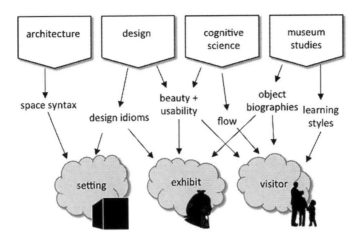

Figure 1.6   Theory domains, key concepts and the elements of the visitor experience

Source: © F. Monti/S. Keene.

For the concept of space syntax, sketches of the gallery layout were used to record circulation patterns and static snapshots of visitor placement in relation to exhibits, together with a gallery observation record sheet (for examples, see particularly Chapter 6, Figures 6.4, 6.5, 6.8 and 6.12; galley observation record sheet, Appendix 1).

To apply the other concepts, the principles for each were organised into a series of opposing statements (semantic differentials). Semantic differentials are the product of research into social science methodology in the 1950s; they reflect the suggestion that we use adjective pairs to organise our thinking about the world and are considered to be a good way to capture affective information.[43] The respondent's response is recorded on a scale that indicates whether it is closer to one statement or to the opposing one.

Formatted as tables in *concept checksheets* (Appendix 2) each pair of statements can be rated on a scale, 5 indicating a high level of correlation with the criterion, 1 indicating little or none. This allows the characteristics of an exhibition or gallery to be quantified and compared (as in Chapter 7). In our case the concept checksheets were used to record the responses and opinions of the researcher, but they could be administered in a (lengthy) visitor questionnaire survey. We found that even when used by the researcher alone, they created a uniquely detailed insight from

---

43   Punch 2005: 100.

multiple perspectives into the qualities and characteristics of the exhibit or gallery as they affect the visitor.

Our approach was predominantly qualitative, based on case studies of a number of galleries. In each case study, a variety of investigative methods were employed. This approach provided a comprehensive picture of all the aspects of the investigated gallery. This was also a means of triangulation: each of the methods checked the findings from the other parameters used to investigate the same phenomenon.[44]

The research process is described in 1.10.

Different kinds of museum were selected for the research, allowing investigation with a range of contexts and audiences. This variety of galleries meant that site- and context-specific variables could be compared, which achieved a depth of understanding. Silent objects require different display approaches according to the contexts in which they are found and their audiences. But, as we shall see, a number of commonalities were observed across this heterogeneous range of venues. This enabled us to draw conclusions that we think will be widely applicable.

1.9   ETHICAL CONSIDERATIONS

This enquiry raises some important ethical considerations. Museum displays have a pervasive power and the ability to touch, through the creation of knowledge, a heterogeneous range of visitors and non-visitors alike. Hence, the research presented here has a wider resonance. We argue that offering a more balanced and comprehensive appreciation of the collections and affording visitors a chance to draw enrichment from a variety of objects contribute to the creation of a new understanding of the collections, the characteristics of which will eventually reach those outside the museum walls. However, we are aware that there are some caveats to be considered.

One issue is the relationship between visitors and the authority of the museum. Another is the question as to whether it is justifiable consciously to alter established viewing patterns. Will museums be manipulating their audiences by adopting new, more effective ways of diverting attention to objects or information that they had decided were important?

1.9.1   Visitors and the Authority of the Museum

The first displays of Egyptian antiquities were opened at the British Museum between 1759 and 1880. The reception and reaction among audiences and researchers

---

44   Berg 2004: 5; Korn 1989: 229.

alike exemplified how, to different extents, we are all susceptible to the subtly pervasive powers of museums in the creation and formation of knowledge and public opinion, and in the construction of a set of identities for ancient cultures. At that time, audiences were, inevitably, uninformed about the civilisation of ancient Egypt. In a fascinating journey of discovery into the relationship between display making and the creation of identities for ancient Egypt in the context of the British Museum, Moser challenges the common belief that knowledge is simply created by researchers and then filtered down to the masses. He proposes, instead, that knowledge 'is also created by many other types of discourse which in themselves shape the ideas of researchers'. The early Egyptian displays at the British Museum therefore had a wider resonance. They played a crucial role in the formation of visitors' perceptions of ancient Egypt and contributed to the formation of the discipline of Egyptology. Ultimately they reached a wider audience and defined the public understanding of the Egyptian past.[45]

Museums are well aware that visitors in general hold them to be authoritative. In every display or exhibit they create, they influence the behaviour of visitors. The extent to which a visitor accepts or questions the influence of a museum depends on variables such as education, self-perception, cultural background and character traits. However, this does not remove the roles of museums as author and text and visitors as receivers and readers.[46] This research creates a greater understanding of these influences so that museums can take fuller responsibility for what they do.

1.9.2   Control of Viewing Patterns

A second caveat is raised as to the possible ethical and moral implications of manipulating established viewing patterns. To acquire the means to steer attention and curiosity at will towards particular objects seems an alarming proposition: this ability could be employed for unethical reasons. The present situation with attention seized by visually striking objects is at least transparent. Such issues have been debated concerning advertising and marketing since 1957, when Vance Packard published *The Hidden Persuaders*, and more recently by the Public Interest Research Centre under the banner of the World Wildlife Fund and other organisations concerned about the manipulation of the public towards unrestrained material consumption.[47]

In defence of our project, we argue that all museums are by definition places of subtle indoctrination, where predetermined narratives are offered to willing viewers.[48] After all, any authority-invested institution is in the privileged position of swaying

---

45   Moser 2006: 4–8.
46   Bennett 2006: 278.
47   Packard 1956; Alexander, Crompton and Shrubsole 2011.
48   Bennett 2006: 263, Preziosi 1996: 100.

current thought and public opinion. What is important in such circumstances is the overall objective and the ethical conduct and intentions of those involved in the project. The pursuit of enriched visitor encounters with inconspicuous objects is a means to a higher end: to place each visitor, whatever their prior knowledge or socio-cultural background, in a position to leave the museum with a knowledge gain, intended not as an accumulation of notions, but as a full appreciation of the potential of the collections and a better understanding of themselves.

1.10   STRUCTURE OF THE BOOK

In a society where split-second decisions about the value of things are grounded on visually derived characteristics (which can either relate to the physicality or to the non-material attributes of things)[49] museum viewing patterns often consist only of a series of interactions with visually striking, iconic or crucially positioned objects. It may be desirable to re-balance this viewing pattern by demonstrating that all objects, whatever their visual qualities, potentially embody interesting cultural contexts and content. In this way, visitors, whatever their previous knowledge and their understanding of museum-going codes, will be better placed to appreciate the full range of interest that objects can offer. Within that spirit, the details and outcomes of this investigation are described in the following chapters.

In Part 1, Chapters 2, 3, 4 and 5 set the scene by reviewing the fields of knowledge that were drawn on for this project and identifying from each the key concepts that could be applied to understanding the visitor–object encounter. Chapter 2 deals with architecture and the concept of *space syntax*. Chapter 3 discusses the broad range of ideas, highly relevant to museum displays, that are found in the field of design, and identifies *design idioms*: colour, lighting, placement and spatial organisation and text, as a key concept. Chapter 4 takes *cognitive science* and finds the concepts of flow, and beauty and usability. In Chapter 5 the more familiar ground of *museology (museum studies)* is examined and the concepts of object biographies and learning styles are found. For each concept, the semantic differential statements are set out (1.8) that are used in the concept checksheets (Appendix 2).

Part 2 moves on to test the application of these key concepts: are they effective tools for investigation? Three well-known and very different galleries in three London museums are evaluated and analysed using them. These are the *Enlightenment* gallery in the British Museum; *Understanding objects*, part of the British Galleries suite in the V&A and the *Music room* in the Horniman Museum. Observations are reported in Chapter 6, and the three galleries are compared within the framework of key concepts in Chapter 7. In Chapter 8 we move on to apply them to analysing

---

49   Monbiot 2011.

the famous *Egyptian death and afterlife: mummies* gallery (Room 63) in the British Museum.

In Part 3, Chapters 9, 10 and 11 take the research beyond the familiar museum visually focused display. Chapter 9 reports the evaluation of the *Hands on* desks in the British Museum. At these, visitors can handle selected objects from the past and talk about them to trained volunteers. In Chapters 10 and 11 experimental exhibits were created to focus on a number of display factors that influence visitors in engaging with objects: line of sight and strategic placing, colour and sound, graphic display of information and moving images. We found in the studies above that these were significant, so in these experiments we aimed to determine whether they might contribute to a better understanding of the optimal display techniques.

Part 4 sums up the findings and presents conclusions. First, Chapter 12 reports the investigation into the *Tomb-chapel of Nebamun* (Room 61), another of the ancient Egypt galleries in the British Museum. A serendipitous encounter suggested that in this gallery silent and spectacular objects worked in harmony to create an enjoyable experience for visitors, who paid as much attention to the everyday objects from ancient Egypt as to the beauty of the wall paintings from the tomb. Chapter 13 offers practical guidance for museum professionals. It discusses the overall findings in the context of the original research question as defined by the visitor–object interaction model (Figure 1.4). Drawing from the research evidence, it highlights practical approaches to exhibition design in order to include silent objects. Chapter 14 then sets out a comprehensive critical summary of the practical tools developed and a reflection on the benefits and limitations of this investigation and its implications for museums. Future research developments are considered and proposed.

PART 1

EXHIBITING OBJECTS – THEORIES AND CONCEPTS

A person's experience with an exhibit is the product of the space where the encounter takes place; the characteristics of the object; its placement and presentation within the gallery; the viewer's emotional, aesthetic, affective and cognitive reactions to the exhibits; their socio-cultural background; and their interplay with other visitors.

THE ELEMENTS OF THE VISITOR EXPERIENCE

These variables group into three general areas: the visitor (and their cognitive and affective processes), the object (its qualities, perception and presentation) and the setting (with emphasis on its impact on the individual).[1] Falk, Koran, Dierking and Deblow identified three main factors that forge visitor behaviour, similar to those used by Bitgood and Patterson[2] (Figure 1.2).

FRAMEWORK OF THEORY

In order to explore these elements, this research programme drew on four main theoretical domains:

- Chapter 2: architecture – the science of building design and construction and the spaces within buildings.
- Chapter 3: design, a very broad range of applications, the most relevant of which are exhibition and interaction design, product design and visual merchandising.
- Chapter 4: cognitive science, meaning the study of the brain and mental processing, including how information is processed in perception, language, memory, reasoning and emotion.
- Chapter 5: museology, in particular, object biographies, learning theory and styles and over- and under-interpretation.

---

1   Falk et al. 1985.
2   Bitgood and Patterson 1988.

KEY CONCEPTS

We identified a number of key concepts – one or more from each of the theory domains. To apply the concepts of space syntax, sketches of the gallery layout were used to record circulation patterns and static snapshots of visitor placement in relation to exhibits, together with a gallery observation record sheet (Appendix 1).

We developed *concept checksheets* to apply the other key concepts. Using opposing statements, semantic differentials, each pair of statements can be rated on a scale, 5 indicating a high level of correlation with the criterion, 1, little or none.[3] For the concept checksheets, see Appendix 2.

TESTING THE CONCEPT CHECKSHEETS

To test the validity of the array of theories and concepts, we used these research tools first to analyse and compare three famous galleries in London museums (Part 2, Chapters 6, 7 and 8), and the *Hands on* desks in the British Museum (Part 3, Chapter 9), before employing them to develop a variety of experimental exhibits (Chapters 10 and 11). We then applied our developing understanding to try to fully understand what worked and what did not in exhibiting silent objects in further well-known galleries (Part 4, Chapters 12, 13 and 14).

USING THE CONCEPT CHECKSHEETS

In the chapters below, the opposing statements for each key concept will be displayed as tables following its discussion. For the concept checksheets, see Appendix 2. The concept checksheet scores were employed to compare the three galleries used to validate the concepts – see Chapter 7.

---

3   Punch 2005: 100.

CHAPTER 2

ARCHITECTURE AND SPACE SYNTAX

There is a close relationship between museums (as containers of collections) and the objects they accommodate and exhibit for the public.[1] Ideas and cultural movements have determined the architectural features of museums, and in many cases their buildings have been moulded to accommodate particular assemblages of objects and their display.[2]

2.1 ARCHITECTURE AND THE VISITOR EXPERIENCE

Iconic buildings play a major part in attracting large audiences.[3] As many have noted, the architectural style, spatial layout and physical qualities of a museum convey meaning to visitors and are central to the formation of a visit.[4] Psarra emphasises that individual displays are also important in determining the pattern of visits.[5] Spatial features are responsible for circulation patterns and also influence the reception of the exhibition message and even the way that visitors attach meanings to things.[6]

Thompson suggests that a visit is defined and influenced by both the physical environment and the social environment.[7] He identifies a number of aspects of the physical, architectural environment: accessibility, the ambient environment, the circulation route, the relationship between architecture and exhibits, spatial relationships and symbolic variables (building configuration, spatial configurations, materials, illumination and colour) and the non-visual environment. The setting for the visit, one of the three inclusive elements that determine its nature, is greatly influenced by the architecture of the building (above, 1.1 and Figure 1.2).

---

1   Pearce 1992: 107.
2   Parry and Sawyer 2005: 39, 40.
3   Psarra 2005: 78.
4   Bitgood 2000; Psarra 2005: 78; Psarra 2009: Chapter 1; Psarra and Grajewski 2002; Thompson 1993.
5   Psarra 2005: 78; Psarra and Grajewski 2002: 38.
6   Peponis and Hedin 1982; Popova 2001; Psarra 2005: 79.
7   Thompson 1990: 72.

2.2   MUSEUM BUILDINGS AS EXHIBITS

Some museum spaces are exhibits in their own right. For example, Sir John Soane's Museum in London is a place of space, light and artefacts that has remained unaltered since Soane's death in 1837. The building, as well as being designed as the abode and workspace of the architect, was from the beginning intended as a backdrop for his collections and as a living demonstration of some of the principles of his architectural thoughts.

A modern example of a museum as exhibit is the Jewish Museum in Berlin by the architect Daniel Libeskind. Its vast spaces, at first devoid of any tangible content, invite visitors to reflect on the destruction of Jewish life in Germany at the times of National Socialism, creating a physical parallel between the emptiness of the space and the state of things in Germany after the Second World War.[8] Skolnick cites this museum as an example of the ultimate embodiment of Louis Sullivan's notorious notion that *form follows function.*[9] This concept is not necessarily to be interpreted as a subordination of appearance to pragmatic purposes. Instead, just as in Daniel Libeskind's construction in Berlin, museum spaces are interpretative of the subject rather than being unrelated. The Jewish Museum, however, has been criticised for its highly architecturally specific places, which make exhibitions redundant and difficult to mount, and for its abstract and complicated intrinsic narrative.[10]

2.3   ARCHITECTURE AND SOCIAL POLICIES

Architecture can help, hinder or even at times ignore the role of museums as places of social inclusion.[11] For a long time, museums delivered hierarchical arrangements of objects to represent biased histories in which the absence of cultural diversity contributed to the exclusion, alienation and disempowerment of certain groups.[12] In the current climate of political awareness, the constant building, re-modernising and creation of new museums is inevitably characterised by an attempt to promote inclusiveness, accessibility and cultural diversity. The creation of London's South Kensington museums in the Victorian era was fuelled by the desire to inform and to construct cultural meaning;[13] in the present, developments such as the interactive Darwin Centre at London's Natural History Museum, the transformed British Galleries at the V&A and the Great Court at the British Museum are examples of the aspiration to ensure that museums are spaces for all. For example, in the British

---

8   Stiftung Jüdisches Museum Berlin 2001: 4.
9   Skolnick 2005: 124; Sullivan 1956: 258.
10   Fleming 2005: 54, 57.
11   Fleming 2005: 53.
12   E.g. Bennett 1995; 2006: 263.
13   Psarra 2005: 89.

Museum's Great Court, a vast agora-like space, people can congregate and, feeling exonerated from the rigid code of conduct of traditional museums, can casually converse, shop, dine and rest (see below, Figure 14.2). The very awareness of such a place helps to define what Fleming calls the 'psychological space' of a museum, a place which exists in our minds and is fostered by media, marketing, publicity, word of mouth and previous experiences.[14]

The challenges of modern museum architecture are significant. Contemporary museum design 'is trying to serve many needs and wants to be all things to all people'.[15] At its best, it is about creating an aura of 'nobility' around the museum without making the visitor feel alien to the space.[16] It can deliver orientation, exciting interpretative sequences, subtle and effective lighting and ventilation complying with conservation standards and can address a range of other practical issues. It also has to offer to diverse audiences a context for objects that is so well structured and remarkable that the visit leaves a long-lasting memory.[17]

The museum space is now not restricted to the museum edifice, but can happen anywhere and at any time through websites and social software (Flickr, Facebook, Twitter and suchlike). This global outreach helps to shape audiences' expectations and experiences of the museum. A successful example comes from the Brooklyn Museum in New York, which is considered by many to be a model of how to create a working online community.[18]

2.4   SPACE SYNTAX

BOX 2.1   SPACE SYNTAX ANALYSED IN THE ART GALLERY AND MUSEUM IN GLASGOW

Despite constant changes in architectural trends requiring new approaches to the crafting of experiences, certain aspects of visitor behaviour are more predictable and fixed than others.[19] Psarra and Grajewski's space syntax analysis of the displays at the Art Gallery and Museum in Kelvingrove, Glasgow combined visitor observation techniques with computer analysis to reveal a detailed picture of how people's behaviour is influenced by the layout of space. The evaluation, commissioned by the Kelvingrove as part of a large project for the re-development of its new galleries, informed the museum's strategy for improving the accessibility and functionality of the new displays.[20]

---

14   Fleming 2005: 55.
15   Jacob 2009: 17.
16   Fleming 2005: 60.
17   Psarra 2005: 93.
18   Billings 2009: 41.
19   Sklonick 2005: 119.
20   Economou 2004: 38.

Their analysis showed clearly how visitors used the museum space, with many galleries being ignored due to their location and configuration as 'segregated spaces'.

Visitor-centred studies of this type allow museums to be transformed from containers of knowledge to spaces fitted to the educational and leisure needs of contemporary audiences.

Architecture therefore plays a crucially important part in shaping the experience of museum visitors. Hence, a way was sought to understand this influence separately from that of the exhibit components – exhibition design, text and other communication media and objects.

Spatial layout in museums is part of the enunciation and transmission of knowledge; it can be influential in structuring social relations.[21] In order to understand spatial forms, we must also understand the underlying rules and constraints that generate it. *Space syntax* is both theory and method that can be employed in the analysis and description of a built environment. Originally conceived by Bill Hillier and Julienne Hanson at the Bartlett Faculty of Built Environment at University College London, space syntax techniques are tools of configurational analysis which allow 'how things are put together' to be quantified in architecture and urban design.[22] The social dimension of complex geometrical networks can be understood through a mathematical approach.

A strength of space syntax is that it is both a concept through which to explain some of the most elusive issues in architecture and a tool of analysis. Patterns of movement and static activities can be recorded and systematically analysed in order to improve spatial layout: the way that parts fit together is more important than any of the individual spaces.[23]

This technique can be used on a micro or a macro scale to address a variety of social issues (for example, retail vitality, crime, traffic, the effect of space on hospital accident and emergency departments and, indeed, museum visit patterns)[24] and to offer highly visual graphical representations of results which make the findings easy to understand and interpret – all highly relevant to the visitor experience in museums.

---

21   Peponis and Hedin 1982: xi.
22   Hillier and Hanson 1984; Hiller 2007: Introduction, 1.
23   Hillier 2007: 17; Space Syntax website: www.spacesyntax.com [accessed 18 June 2012].
24   Intelligent Space Partnership 2003. This publication has particularly good examples of the use of space syntax analysis.

The full employment of space syntax analysis involves using complex technical calculations and specialist computer-based design software: advanced tools limited to space syntax cognoscenti. However, some of the principles at its core can be borrowed to assess patterns of use in museums.

2.4.1 Applying Space Syntax Analysis

Space syntax analysis is undertaken in three stages. In the first stage, the spatial components of a plan are identified (Figure 2.1).

- A diagrammatic representation of the building's layout is divided into *convex* elements (a).
- The axes of sight and access throughout the building are drawn: the longest that link convex spaces without interruption (b).[25]
- Then the *integration* and *segregation* of spaces is calculated (c).

Integration can be defined as the degree of connection between a given space and the layout of the whole building.[26] An integrated space is easily accessible from every other space in the same area and requires few changes of direction to enter it. Conversely, a segregated space may be distant from the rest of the layout and require a considerable number of detours to enter it.

In space syntax theory, each of these three steps relates to a particular aspect of the use of space. The convex spatial configuration focuses on static activities, such as the presence of other individuals and in relation to spatial characteristics. The axial dimension measures the movements of people within an area.[27]

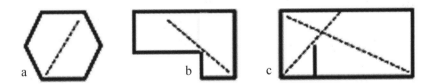

Figure 2.1 a) A convex space in which any two points are joined by a line that does not cross the space's boundaries (after Psarra and Grajewski 2002: 37); b) two convex spaces with axial lines of movement and sight; c) a space including a segregated space, often created in galleries by showcases or installations

Source: © F. Monti/S. Keene.

---

25   Psarra and Grajewski 2002: 36.

26   Psarra and Grajewski 2002: 36.

27   Hillier and Hanson 1984: 17.

In the second stage of the analysis, a range of observation techniques is employed to capture the patterns of visitors' movements through the building and how they use the space. These include a record of movements and activities, snapshot observations and tracking to create a precise picture of spatial movements and visitor counts at room entrances to determine the flow in and out of museum spaces.[28]

To complete the analysis, the data from observations in relation to the special layout are analysed by computer. The results suggest the spatial characteristics that influence visitors' use of the museum spaces.

Space syntax analysis can provide a wealth of information about patterns of use of museum space. In galleries and exhibitions, space is deployed as a physical realisation of curatorial classifications that aim to aid understanding.[29] The treatment of circulation has for a long time been considered crucial to the cultural functions of the museum.[30] Spatial arrangements can make certain objects more accessible than others, and viewing sequences can be imposed on visitors by means of spatial restrictions.[31]

2.4.2   Limitations of Space Syntax Analysis

With some exceptions, most of the observational studies of visitor movements in museums have been conducted in individual exhibition galleries or in confined areas.[32] These studies have focused on local and room-specific aspects of layout and visitor behaviour, and have not always taken into account the larger space in which the rooms are located and its influence on movement patterns. Also, our understanding of the influence of architectural space upon patterns of visits is restricted by the lack of a systematic method for describing either the overall configuration of the museum setting or the pattern of visitors' movement on a larger scale.[33]

In addition, the visitor–object encounter is not the only form of dialogue taking place in museums; the visitor–visitor interaction is equally important and may in fact be the main motivation for the visit.[34] The dynamics of these social events can take different forms according to the layout of the room and variables such as levels of crowdedness and the purpose of the visit. For example, visitors may queue or bunch in front of displays (exacerbated by technologies such as audio

---

28   Psarra and Grajewski 2002: 36.
29   Jordanova 1989; Markus 1987; Peponis and Hedin 1982; Pevsner 1976; Vergo 1989.
30   Gilman 1923; Levine 1982.
31   Hall 1987: 130.
32   E.g. Tzortzi 2007. Studies for individual exhibition areas or spaces: Bechtel 1967; Borhegyi 1968; Lakota and Kantner 1976; Screven 1969; Shettel 1973.
33   Choi 1999: 241.
34   Stephens 1989: 61.

Figure 2.2 The *African worlds* gallery in the Horniman Museum: this
gallery has a complex structural layout with a central raised
walkway resulting in segregated spaces. With terracotta coloured
divisions, it uses colour to suggest an African ambience

Source: © S. Keene, courtesy of the Trustees of the Horniman Museum.

guides) or may pursue independent routes. Our understanding of the role of
architectural configuration needs to be able to account for the social variables
present in museum visits and to reflect upon the relationship between the layout
of museums and the pattern of social awareness and encounter that they permit
or promote. There is some disagreement as to the extent to which the nature of a
space determines the extent and nature of social interaction, some arguing that it
is a fundamental factor and others that space syntax modeling is not a valid way to
throw light on the social activities of the people inhabiting a space.[35]

Space syntax techniques neglect the effects of the *content* of the space.[36] As we are
not all equally spatially aware, some of us may respond primarily to content (of
galleries and objects), not context, and message, not medium.[37] This point is critical

---

35   Hillier and Hanson 1984: 24; Leach 1978: 397.
36   Boast and Evans 1986.
37   Boast and Evans 1986; Fleming 2005: 54.

in museums, where the nature of specific objects, their relevance to the viewer and the appearance of displays greatly affect people's movements within the galleries. A comprehensive assessment of visitor movements within a gallery must account not for interaction with a hypothetically empty shell, but for the product of experiences within a configured space which accommodates a variety of objects.

2.5   SPACE SYNTAX: A KEY CONCEPT FROM ARCHITECTURE

We have selected space syntax as one of the *key concepts* for evaluating, analysing and creating exhibitions and exhibits. Some of the practices can usefully be borrowed. When movement patterns and space usage are carefully observed, recorded and analysed, this reveals a wealth of information which can be employed to maximise and improve gallery usage.[38]

Space syntax can be employed to gauge the attracting power of objects and their visual qualities (Stage 1 in the visitor–object interaction; see Figure 1.4) against the configuration of the exhibition space. Once patterns of visitor movement within the layout of the space have been mapped, the influence of the arrangement of objects can be explored. This may make it possible to determine the extent to which the qualities of objects are or are not the primary factor in viewing patterns, and whether their influence on visitors can be modified by the layout and design of the exhibition space.

2.5.1   Space Syntax Diagrams

In this study, the applicability of space syntax analysis, used without the computerised analysis stage, was tested in the three museum venues at the British Museum, the V&A and the Horniman Museums (Chapters 6 and 7). Each venue was assessed against the three elements central to space syntax – convex spaces, axial lines of movement, and integrated and segregated spaces. Some examples of movement flow diagrams can be found in Figures 6.4, 6.8 and 6.12, while examples of static snapshot diagrams can be found in Figures 6.5 and 8.5.

2.5.2   Concept Checksheet

Although the main space syntax tools are diagrammatic, we also developed opposing statements (semantic differentials) that can be used in concept checksheets, as we did in Chapter 7 when comparing the British Museum *Enlightenment* gallery, the V&A *Understanding objects* gallery and the Horniman Museum *Music room*.

---

38   E.g. Psarra and Grajewski 2002.

Table 2.1   Space syntax: opposing statements for concept checksheets

The layout of exhibition elements in a space and the configuration of the space influence the behaviour of visitors		
Clear intentional viewing path	– or –	No clear intentional viewing path
Visitors follow intended viewing pattern		Visitors ignore/don't follow intention
Spaces in gallery integrated		Separate spaces, secluded corners
Vista over all areas of gallery		Some parts not visible from entrance/all areas
One or more large prominent exhibits dominate the exhibition		Attention is evenly spread among exhibits

CHAPTER 3

DESIGN AND DESIGN IDIOMS

In museum exhibitions, design determines the layout, appearance and placing of every physical element, including the selection and placement of objects. Design is always linked with and expressive of the culture in which both designers and users function.[1]

3.1   EXHIBITION DESIGN

The design of an exhibition works together with museum architecture in shaping the experience of a space and its content, often in ways not apparent to the visitor. The first systematic studies of the impact of exhibit design on visitor behaviour were conducted around the 1920s and 1930s by Robinson and Melton.[2] Since then, visitor studies have highlighted the multitude of diverse, and at times contradictory, responses of different audiences to a space.[3] Spatial configurations can signal and shape people's encounters with collections and privilege certain readings of them. For example, one study of policies of exclusion practised in the eighteenth and nineteenth centuries identified the compensatory, the celebratory and the pluralistic models of display organisation.[4]

3.1.1   Messages through Design

Museums would do well to consider the messages they are conveying to their visitors at these subliminal levels. Devotees of the TV series *Mad Men* (about a 1950s marketing company in Madison Avenue, New York) will know that advertisers have for decades been developing an indepth understanding of how people receive messages from design and visual communication. In 1957 Vance Packard's fascinating and entertaining book *The Hidden Persuaders* described the psychological tricks used to influence us.[5] Advertisers have only become more adept

---

1   Buchanan and Margolin 1995: ix, xix.
2   Robinson 1928; Melton 1935.
3   E.g. Ohta 1998.
4   Sandell 2005: 186, 189–93.
5   Packard 1957: 6.

at this since then. The president of the communications agency Engine went as far as to call for the use of brain scanning as it was more effective than focus groups in understanding how messages are processed. Although this recommendation has been widely condemned,[6] the temptation to discern people's reactions directly has been too great and some agencies are now adopting brain scanning as a more accurate and truthful indication than focus groups in determining what people think of their products or branding.[7] In any case, unconscious processing is a standard offer of advertising research agencies: 'Our new tools are ideally suited to categories which are more emotional than rational, those where "political correctness" taints responses and those where the real reasons for choice are deeply embedded in the unconscious mind.'[8]

The cultural specificity of design has significant implications for museums. The creation of an exhibition is the product of the cultural and social setting of a given society, and so visitors operating within that same cultural frame will more readily decode the messages embedded in the design and will proceed more fluidly through the visit. This cultural familiarity adds a dimension of emotional reward for the viewer.[9]

3.1.2   Implicit and Explicit Messages

Human responses to everyday things are complex and defined by a variety of factors. Some come from outside the person, originating from the designer of an object or its physical characteristics. Other responses originate within the viewer, the result of personal experiences or preferences. People and situations differ in what is an optimal design for them.

Research into the effects of design on human perception and mental processing has suggested that perception and reception operate at three levels: visceral, behavioural and reflective, involving, first, emotions and, subsequently, cognition.[10] Visceral design refers to the initial impact, to appearance, when affective processing leads to rapid, barely perceived judgments on what is good or bad. Behavioural design is about look and feel, the total experience of using an object. Reflective design is about thoughts and feelings afterwards and the image it leaves with the user.[11]

---

6   Alexander, Crompton and Shrubsole 2011: 4.1.

7   Neate 2011.

8   Two Minds Research Co. website: www.twomindsresearch.co.uk [date accessed 18 July 2012].

9   Wagensberg et al. 2006: 38

10   Ortony, Norman and Revelle 2005.

11   Norman 2004: 22.

It is suggested that this same rationale can be drawn on to explain some of the mechanisms of visitor engagement with exhibits. Objects can attract and hold a viewer's attention on visceral, behavioural and reflective levels (Table 3.1). At the visceral level, the physical features – look, feel and sound, its total impression on the viewer – dominate. The behavioural aspect relates to the function, performance and usability of an exhibit, and to its ability to communicate, through visual clues, how effective and pleasant it would be in use. Finally, the reflective level invokes the public status or image of an object.[12]

Table 3.1   Norman's emotional design theory in the context of museum objects

Communication level	Object qualities	Effect on viewer	Example of object (ancient Egyptian)
Visceral	Appearance	Visual gratification	Nebamun tomb painting
Behavioural	Function/usability	Pleasure/usability	Minoan vessel
Reflective	Status	Personal satisfaction	Rosetta stone

An object can make an impression in more than one dimension, or alternatively the viewer may not make a connection at any of the three levels. For example, Tutankhamun's gold death mask has both visual appeal and reflective appeal derived from its status. When an exhibit does not obviously qualify for any of the three categories above, it will not engage visitors. Since an object's visceral appeal cannot be directly manipulated or changed (other than through its display setting), the behavioural and reflective dimensions can be accentuated in an attempt to establish a conversation between object and viewer.

3.1.3   Form versus Function

The debate around form and function is recurrent within design discourse. It is believed by some that an object can acquire beauty from being designed to function perfectly to meet users' needs.[13] To achieve this, designers need to put aside personal taste and style in pursuit of a true understanding of the challenge they face and reclaim their role as 'visionary generalists and coordinators in the product development process'.[14] Conversely, others condemn a functionalist approach and

---

12   Norman 2004: 22.
13   E.g. Norman 1988; Zaccai 1995.
14   Zaccai 1995: xv.

Figure 3.1   Communication level: reflective; object quality: status; effect on viewer: personal satisfaction. The must-see Rosetta Stone at the British Museum

Source: © Trustees of the British Museum.

believe that form should not be subordinated to function, as all works should be the result of choices, not mere necessity.[15]

There are a number of arguments against design that is driven by aesthetics alone. It can distract the designer from an understanding of the communicational and social significance of their work; some advocate a shift from an emphasis on the relationship of visual elements to one on the relationship between user and design. Designers' work should be evaluated according to the changes it induces in audiences and should be grounded on a solid understanding of human communication and cognition.[16] This argument is particularly relevant to visitor–object interaction, where the main concerns are not the visual qualities of the exhibits, but the feelings, reactions and emotions they evoke on the viewer.

Deep design is proposed as the way to reconcile engineering and aesthetics within design, as a means of reviving engagement. This term is used to stress the symmetry that links humanity and reality. Only a product that embodies usability and aesthetic needs fully recovers the depth of the design activity and offers a physical setting capable of provoking and rewarding engagement.[17]

3.1.4   Information, Graphic and Visual Display

Museums are visual environments that rely almost exclusively on the sense of sight. And yet displays are often dominated by words and text, neglecting the visual potential of objects. This is a limiting practice that distances object from viewer. Words are still the focal point in museums to the detriment of other senses, such as touch, hearing and even sight. By leaving the 'cool web of language' behind and embracing a multi-sensory approach with emphasis on the visual, people's cognitive and emotional experiences can greatly improve.[18] Ethnography and archaeology displays in particular are badly served by a text-heavy approach: archaeology is better experienced, like many scientific objects, through a combination of sensory inputs or through more inventive display strategies.[19]

Graphically driven design strategies address both the arrangement of objects and the communication of information (see Box 3.1 and Figure 3.2). Objects can be effectively displayed so that they put across the exhibition message without the need for much additional interpretation. The very choice of artefacts, their juxtaposition, their spatial arrangement and the object-to-space ratio can spark ideas or suggest meanings.

---

15   Pye 1978: 85.
16   Frascara 1995: 44.
17   Borgmann 1995: 15–16; Ekuan 2002; Norman 2002, 2004.
18   Robertson 2002.
19   See e.g. Wagensberg et al. 2006: 44.

BOX 3.1   DO VISITORS MISS TEXT?

When text is not used in exhibitions, visitors can be baffled. For example, the *Enlightenment* gallery in the British Museum displayed objects in an exhibition devoted to discovery and learning in the age of George III.[20] The gallery consciously re-created the object rich and interpretation meagre style of the Enlightenment era. The effect on a modern visitor of this highly visual display, with minimal written interpretation, is remarkable. Although visitors initially appear puzzled by this display format, it has the potential to allow viewers to process and organise the information independently within their own cultural and interpretative framework.

The *Psychoanalysis* exhibition at the Science Museum in London (October 2010–April 2011) adopted an object-centred design approach (Figure 3.2). Historical, artistic and archaeological artefacts were displayed so as to encourage visitors to draw connections and, in a psychoanalytical fashion, trace hidden associations and unconscious meanings between the objects. Labels were absent from the cases and information was offered instead in the form of handouts.

The British Museum has been researching visitors' use of text panels such as those introducing exhibitions. They found that although very few visitors (less than ten per cent) read them, they still said they wanted them. The Museum is replacing some with 'gateway objects'.[21]

In a successful design of exhibits, object representation, layout, colour, production techniques and visual principles are all in balance. Such components encourage criticism and revision in the viewer. Some principles of visual information which have interesting implications for museum practice are:

- the presentation of information in small repeated multiples;
- the combination of information on a micro and macro level;
- the role of shape, value, size and colour in defining individual items of information; and
- the principle that in design one plus one equals three or more.[22]

Tufte suggests that by presenting small multiples in association with each other, visual reasoning is facilitated. The repetition of a unit of information in the same visual display enables the viewer to perceive and contrast within their active eye span, rather than relying on recall. A high-density strategy can allow viewers to select, compare, narrate, re-cast and personalise data, whereas sparse, low-density displays that continue over several exhibits or panels require viewers to rely upon visual memory in order to make a comparison and to develop a full understanding.[23]

---

20   Sloan 2003:14.
21   Slack, Francis and Edwards 2011: 159.
22   Tufte 1990: 35.
23   Tufte 1990: 32, 35.

**Figure 3.2   The *Psychoanalysis* exhibition at the Science Museum in London
– no labels**
Source: © F. Monti/Trustees of the National Museum of Science & Industry/Science & Society.

However, a high-density presentation approach needs to be treated with caution because it can overwhelm the senses and bury the message under layers of stimuli.[24] We found an example of this in the *Egyptian death and afterlife: mummies* gallery at the British Museum (Chapter 8). Also in this gallery, displays of shabti (small figurines in burials representing servants) were little appreciated by interviewees (below, 8.5.3; Figure 8.9), but on the other hand, the object-rich case displaying over 1,500 musical instruments in the Horniman Museum had considerable holding power for viewers (below, 6.3; Figure 3.3).

Information can be presented simultaneously at a micro and a macro level. When macro-information (for example, overviews and time scales) and micro-information (such as a detail of the overview) are harmoniously integrated, immensely complex information can be conveyed and easily understood.[25] This principle finds multiple applications in museums. In the Horniman's *Music room*, the *Listening to order* display consists of an object-rich typological arrangement of musical instruments (Figure 3.3). When seen as a unity, it gives an indication

24   Tufte 1990: 35; Wittlin 1971: 144.
25   Tufte 1990: 38.

Figure 3.3   Repetition of design elements: part of the wind section in the Music room *Listening to order* display in the Horniman Museum

Source: © S. Keene, courtesy of the Trustees of the Horniman Museum.

of the sub-divisions of musical instruments. But if the eye selects one unit of information, a specific musical instrument, details can be found. In this instance the combination of small units of data (individual instruments) within a larger conceptual scenario (the typological classification of objects) offers information at both a micro and a macro level. However, successful micro-macro displays are expensive, and if not carefully implemented the result can be clutter and confusion.

BOX 3.2   VISUAL DISPLAY IN A HYPERCUBIC SHOWCASE

A novel visual display of information is found at the CosmoCaixa Museum of Science in Barcelona. Here, a hypercubic showcase is employed as a solution to overcome the limitations of conventional showcases. Within a 'hypervitrine', a large number of objects are visually and physically connected on a grid so that each link between any pair of objects acquires meaning. Essential to the success of this strategy is a choice of objects with common themes, such as tools of human creativity. Three relevant quantifiable concepts were assigned to each one of the three axes of the cubic showcase.[26]

---

26   Wagensberg et al. 2006: 46.

Simpleness is a general aesthetic preference, although not necessarily a guide to clarity.[27] For example, in typography the more the letters differ from each other, the easier they are to read, although such characters are not necessarily the most aesthetically pleasing: in closely packed text, serif letters are preferable because 'they bring order, character and fluidity to the text and help the eye along'.[28]

Another notion to consider is that layers of information can be distinguished by means of distinctions in shape, value (light to dark), size and especially colour. The relationship between layers of information is crucial if the viewer is to be able to decode the data.[29] Colour (3.2) has many applications in information design: it can be used to label (as noun); to measure (as quantity); to represent or imitate reality (as representation); and to decorate (as beauty).

One of the key principles of information design is that in design one plus one sometimes equals three or more, as in Figure 3.4, due to the way in which visual elements interact and contextualise each other.[30]

Figure 3.4   **Example of Albers' design law: '1+1=3 or more'. Six separate shapes can be perceived, although the image has only two components**

Source: © F. Monti/S. Keene.

---

27   Tufte 1990: 51.
28   Verlarde 1988: 64.
29   Tufte 1990: 54; Verlarde 1988: 61.
30   Albers 2006; Tufte 1990: 61.

3.1.5   The Role of the Designer

Just as the architect requires cross-disciplinary knowledge in their approach to museum building,[31] the effective designer needs to use a number of skills from a variety of disciplines. For the most effective outcome, the professional designer works with the user in mind, is a member of an interdisciplinary team comprising engineers, computer scientists, psychologists, sociologists and anthropologists, and has an understanding of the fundamental concepts.[32] For buildings that are venues for people, such as museums, a good designer must be acutely interested in people and their use of space, even an amateur psychologist.[33]

3.2   DESIGN IDIOMS: A KEY CONCEPT FROM DESIGN

As one of our *key concepts*, we have identified certain design idioms as being major determinants of the nature and quality of the visitor's encounter with an object. The display of objects is an art in its own right, by no means only in museums.[34] As such, it elicits a reaction from the viewer: instinctive, emotional, aesthetic or intellectual. These design idioms are elements of display that are common to all exhibitions, whatever the approach. Also important in retail and shopping, they are colour, lighting, text and use of space and juxtaposition of objects.[35]

Hall uses the term *design idioms* to discuss elements of exhibition design that can be employed for emphasis, punctuation, direction or to alert the visitor's attention. They are of two types: atmosphere, to set the mood of the whole exhibition; and action, to prompt a desired action, to suggest the pacing within the space or a desired itinerary.[36] Idioms of action include alerts which signal to the visitor, such as a banner at the entrance or on the street.

Capturing the visitor's attention is easier if the objects are arresting or attractive, unusual or paradoxical. And placing them in a meaningful sequence can suffice to convey a story about them. However, attracting attention to inconspicuous objects is undeniably hard, and it is equally taxing to create an attentive audience for their stories. Hall suggests that a series of design idioms are employed to lead the visitor: 'feelings and impulses must be transmitted to aid appreciation of the objects and understanding of the information which accompanies them'.[37] Many

---

31   Fleming 2005: 60.
32   Buchanan and Margolin 1995: x.
33   Verlade 1988: 11; Hall 1987: 91.
34   Portas 1999: 14.
35   Black 1950; Hall 1987: 127; Portas 1999; Velarde 1988; Belcher 1991; Dean 1994.
36   Hall 1987: 128.
37   Hall 1987: 127.

expedients are employed to attract and hold visitors' attention, lead the eye to key points and guide them through the exhibition: a crucial part of the designer's agenda.[38] For example, an eye-catching vista can be laid out ahead, dramatic lights can instil a sense of anticipation, or text and display which is only partially visible through slits in the wall can draw visitors forward through curiosity.[39]

A successful exhibition is magic: it enlightens and entertains people simultaneously.[40] Exhibition design can be viewed as a selling process, using displays to attract visitors, hold their attention and inform them about products or concepts and ideas.[41] Museum displays, like shop windows, are communication activities that should aspire to 'sell' their products, but also to 'offer an interpretation, to propose a new angle on the familiar, to produce something brighter, loftier and more controversial than the mundane that we know and live through'.[42]

3.2.1   Limitations of Assessment Using Concepts from Design

Some design idioms are culturally specific, which is a possible limitation for their use as an evaluation tool. For example, certain colours have different associations among different cultures: black is the colour for mourning in Western cultures, while it is yellow in China and white in India. In Europe (reflecting writing and reading customs) people tend to move from left to right, and assume that the most significant objects will often be encountered at the end of their itinerary. But in Japan, among other countries, the principal exhibit will be placed in the centre of the room, with the surrounding material being subordinate.[43] Therefore, when considering the effect of a design solution on audiences, it must not be forgotten that the same solution may be received and experienced differently by visitors from different cultural backgrounds and different educational frames.

However, due allowances can be made for these variations. Colour, light and text are factors that have a major influence on how visitors perceive and relate to objects in displays. They are relevant at all stages of the visitor–object model (Figures 1.4 and 11.3). The skilful use of these display techniques can direct visitors' attention so that they notice silent objects. By analysing visitor responses to different applications of these design elements, the display requirements that will draw and hold the viewer can be isolated.

---

38   Dean 1994: 56.

39   Hall 1987: 130.

40   Velarde 1988: 9.

41   Black 1950; Velarde 1988; Belcher 1992: 649.

42   Portas 1999: 15.

43   Hall 1987: 134.

Figure 3.5   Colour: in this harmonious display in the British Museum's
***Tomb-chapel of Nebamun* gallery, the humble objects displayed,**
some 3,200 years old, are mainly a rusty brown colour. Pale
duck-egg blue and creamy limestone colours create a delicate
contrast so that they look their best

Source: © S. Keene, courtesy of the Trustees of the British Museum.

3.2.2   Colour

Colour creates its own space and environment and creates a body of wholeness
and containment, rendering it an important tool for compact display areas, such as
windows or museum showcases.[44] A valuable tool in display design, colour catches
peoples' imagination, draws their attention and can be employed to create a certain
atmosphere or to elicit specific behaviour in the viewer. It can be used to brand a
company, like Selfridges' yellow. It interacts with fabric and display surfaces to
accentuate a desired effect.[45]

Colour is a property inherent to all materials. When light strikes an object, certain
wavelengths are absorbed and others reflected. The reflected wavelengths determine
the colour of the object.[46] Colour is a mixture of three attributes: hue, lightness and

44   Portas 1999: 78.
45   Dean 1994: 33–5.
46   Lamb and Bourriau 1995.

saturation. Hue describes the colour that one experiences when looking at an object: red, blue, yellow, etc. Colours can be light or dark when their lightness (how bright they are) is compared. Saturation refers to the relative purity of a hue. It depends on the percentage of grey added to a hue of a determined lightness.[47]

Colour, more than any other physical characteristic, can be employed to send specific messages to people about objects on display and to influence their emotive response to them. It is widely accepted in the scientific world that different colours elicit different physiological responses. For example, the eye reacts most quickly to bold colours, such as orange and red.[48] Different cultures, religions and superstitious have endowed colour with widely divergent significances and associations as a catalyst for emotions.[49]

Individuals vary in their preferences for colour, as research both from the design perspective[50] and from an aesthetics framework[51] has demonstrated. Nevertheless, there are general trends. For example, McManus et al. noticed that most people have a preference for blue hues and dislike yellow.[52] Portas has found that colour qualities in a defined space are important; in particular, if a single colour is used to convey a message, the hue is pivotal.[53]

Table 3.2   Design idioms: opposing statements for concept checksheets: colour

Colour can be used to accentuate a desired effect, to draw people's attention, to delimitate a space		
Colour used to highlight sections	– or –	Sections are not colour-themed
Evokes feelings/impressions		Not evocatively used
Draws attention to collection features		Not related to collection features

3.2.3   Light

Traditionally, lighting has been employed in retail displays to highlight the quality and texture of materials, particularly when the colours of these are grey or dull-

47   Minolta 1998.
48   Dean 1994: 52.
49   Portas 1999: 78.
50   Dean 1994; Portas 1999.
51   McManus, Jones and Cottrell 1981.
52   McManus, Jones and Cottrell 1981: 651.
53   Portas 1999: 78.

Figure 3.6   These objects represented accessories for the clothing and possessions of well-off people in medieval times, with an ivory bishop's crozier head with gilt decoration. More even lighting, a closer grouping of objects and perhaps text with graphics might release them from silence

Source: © S. Keene, courtesy of Winchester City Council.

looking.[54] Light can also be used to emphasise the shape of products – an approach favoured, for example, by Prada stores, where the quality of products emerges from this minimalist approach.

Poor lighting is a major reason why some objects are almost literally invisible to visitors. Light can draw attention to particular objects or, if they are poorly lit, distract from them. This is not necessarily due to low light levels: all too often, light is misdirected and misses the object or label, or shines almost vertically from above. Many examples of unevenly lit displays demonstrate that excellent lighting for museum exhibits can be hard to achieve, while others equally demonstrate that it is possible.

There are generally recognised limits to light exposure in museum displays to avoid objects fading and deteriorating,[55] but this is not a reason for poor lighting. A

---

54   Portas 1999: 142.
55   Thomson 1978: 2.

more valid excuse might be technical constraints – an existing lighting installation may have to be used – or budgetary constraints, since lighting equipment is very expensive.

As in colour, different qualities of light can evoke specific moods and enhance the qualities of different subjects. Marketing material for interior design distinguishes between mood or ambient lighting and task lighting. The most flattering light for people is a warm, yellow light similar to candlelight. Incandescent bulbs emit a similar light spectrum, which is doubtless why people are reluctant to forgo them in favour of more energy-efficient alternatives. Fabric qualities are emphasised by a cool white light that will render colours accurately.[56] This dilemma highlights the importance of variety and flexibility in light positioning, a freedom which is seldom available within the physical specifics and conservation frame of the museum.

Different qualities of light are achieved by using a variety of light sources: spotlights, fluorescent tubes, fibre optics, light emitting diodes, halogen sources and even carefully controlled daylight. Many of these are new, developed in response to the need to reduce energy use: there is a plethora of research into the effects of these light sources on objects and on visitors.[57]

Light exposure can be limited instead by carefully managing the length of time the object is lit: changing displayed items for others or by movement-sensitive lights, moveable covers, etc. However, this is a very complex subject, the one undeniable fact being that exposing light-sensitive coloured materials to light, however limited, will result in their fading, which must be a concern for museums.[58]

Table 3.3   Design and design idioms: opposing statements for concept checksheets: lighting

Lighting can be employed to highlight quality, texture, shape and specific features of objects		
Appropriately lit	– or –	Too dark/too bright
Objects enhanced by lighting		Object viewing worsened by lighting
Additional lighting tools		No additional lighting tools used
Lighting creates or enhances atmosphere		Lighting does not contribute to atmosphere

---

56   Portas 1999: 143.
57   For material, search the web for 'museum lighting sources'.
58   Michalski 1990.

3.2.4   Text and graphic information

Wall panels, titles, subtitles, labels: text is a primary means for informing visitors about objects. Depending on the in-house style, museum professionals may choose to supply only the most basic identifying information for an object or they may offer additional levels of interpretation or connect numerous objects, facts and ideas into a thematic exhibition. As well as the issues of text design, discussed below, exhibits may, intentionally or unintentionally, be under-interpreted, with too little textual explanation, or over-interpreted, with too much (below, 5.5).[59] Effective labels go hand in hand with clearly conceived ideas about how exhibits are organised and presented. Ideally, they should be an integral part of the exhibit design rather than an addition to an exhibit after the fact. Exhibition labels need to make sense within the organisation of the whole. On the other hand, due to the ways visitors tend to encounter them out of sequence, each label needs to function independently. Possibly upsetting this tidy concept, in the British Museum the whole question of exhibit text is being re-visited.[60]

Labels may be interpretative, non-interpretative or labels for interactive exhibits.[61] Interpretative labels provide organised information and help to convey the rationale for the exhibition. They comprise the following types:[62]

- Exhibition titles (1–7 words): to attract the visitor attention and to inform about the theme to identify. This is an important piece of visual and written information which sets the tone of the exhibition and helps to define its general parameters.
- Subtitles (10–20 words): to help the visitor follow the flow of information and connections between the displays.
- Introductory labels (20–300 words): to introduce the big idea, to orientate visitors to the space rationale.
- Group labels (20–150 words): to conceptually unify a specific object group or to introduce a sub-theme.
- Caption labels (20–150 words): to interpret individual objects.
- Non-interpretative labels consist of identification labels, or ID labels, donor plaques, way findings and prohibitive signs, as well as credit panels. They also include distributional material, such as gallery notes, brochures and catalogues. Labels for interactive exhibits need to be customised in order to serve the specific design of the interactive they explicate and the ways visitors may use it. They are often characterised by phrases such as 'what to do; what to notice; what's going on; so what?'.

---

59   Wittlin 1971.
60   Slack, Francis and Edwards 2011.
61   Serrell 1996.
62   Serrell 1996: 33, 167; Dean 1994: 109.

A tawny cat catches birds among the papyrus stems. Cats were family pets, but he is shown here because a cat could also represent the Sun-god hunting the enemies of light and order. His unusual gilded eye hints at the religious meanings of this scene.

EA 37977

Figure 3.7   Text and graphic information in the *Tomb-chapel of Nebamun* gallery in the British Museum. A detail is picked out and explained, which encourages closer attention to the painting itself, displayed above (see also below, Figure 12.4)

Sources: Painting © Trustees of the British Museum. Text panel © S. Keene, courtesy of the Trustees of the British Museum.

The two main concerns with text design are legibility (easy to see and read) and readability (easy to comprehend).[63] Legibility is dependent on the typography of the

---

63   Serrell 1996: 192.

labels: typeface (the type family: serif, sans serif, etc.), font (plain type, italic, bold, etc.), type size and contrast between text and background. Legibility is also determined by the position of the text: knee level is seldom a good position for labels. Readability is influenced by the reader's familiarity with the subject, how interested they are, the writing style, the length of sentences and the vocabulary level.[64]

The typeface and font selected should allow the reader's eyes to glide smoothly in a horizontal sweep across the lines of type, while finding the beginning of each line with ease.[65] As a rule of thumb, sans serif fonts are more effectively employed for titles, while serif typefaces facilitate reading for body text.[66] Good contrast between text and background is also fundamental to legibility: the viewer's attention is much more easily attracted by legible text with good contrast, which is comfortable to read, with high contrast between the letters and the background.[67] When it comes to size, 18 point type is the minimum size that is easily legible at 20 inches away from the reader. However, bigger is not necessarily better, as the type needs to fit comfortably in the reader's retina.[68]

Table 3.4   Design and design idioms: opposing statements for concept checksheets: text

Text (exhibition titles, introductory labels, group labels, object labels) should be readable, legible and enrich the visitor's experience		
Clear delivery of key messages	– or –	Key messages don't come across
Effective visual display of information		Ineffective visual display of information
Good graphics (typography, colour)		Ineffective graphics
Appropriate register		Inappropriate register
Appropriate use of terminology		Excessive use of specialist terminology
Appropriate text length		Text too long/too concise

3.2.5   Use of space and exhibit layout

There are no fixed rules for the use of space and display properties: there is a constant trade-off between items and space. Although in many cases less is more – and sometimes 'emptiness can create a great sense of expectation' – Portas, like

---

64   Bitgood 2006: 5.
65   Serrell 1996: 194.
66   Verlarde 1988: 64.
67   Bitgood 2000: 5.
68   Serrell 1996: 138.

Tufte, is equally supportive of the *more is more* approach: 'sometimes you can do a slightly chaotic window where the eye is distracted over many areas and it's a feast of layers and elements of surprise – every time you come back you see something new' (see also below, Figure 14.3, a small part of a very object dense display in the Science Museum).[69] This is a method which relies very heavily on ad hoc styling to ensure that it doesn't create visual, and conceptual confusion.

In retail window displays, props are used to give hints to consumers about how the goods on show would enhance their life; in museums, they provide a link between an exhibit and the visitor. These can be photographs or additional objects and can be conveyed by different media. One approach to an effective display is to highlight the link between the everyday (the visitor's tangible experience) and the exquisite (the item available for purchase).

**Table 3.5   Design and design idioms: opposing statements for concept
checksheets: space and layout**

Space and object layout: there are no fixed rules as to the use of space and object layout, as long as objects are visible		
Objects are visible to all	– or –	Objects are too high, low or hidden
Objects are mounted to be visible, at the correct inclination		Key object details are not visible
Juxtaposition of objects increases interest		Inappropriate object juxtaposition
Objects laid out with sufficient space		Objects too crowded/sparse to appreciate

---

69   Portas 1999: 57; Tufte 1990: 32, 35.

CHAPTER 4

COGNITIVE SCIENCE, FLOW AND BEAUTY

Cognitive science concerns the psychological processes that enable us to make sense of the environment and decide what action might be appropriate, such as attention, visual perception, learning, memory, language, problem solving, reasoning and thinking.[1] In particular, the fields of visual perception, attention and memory are relevant to visitor–object interaction. The effects and perceptions of design are largely determined by cognition.

4.1 VISUAL PERCEPTION

Visual perception covers, among other factors, the way things are visually organised, colour, space and object recognition.

Perceptual organisation relates to our ability to work out which elements of visual information belong together. Gestalt psychologists initially raised many of the questions still studied today by vision scientists. The Gestalts defined six main laws describing the mechanisms of perceptual grouping, perceiving things as related in some way, which have implications in the design of exhibitions. These laws are:

- proximity: the objects closest together are more likely to form a group;
- similarity: objects similar in size and shape are more likely to be perceived as a group;
- closure: our brains add missing elements to complete a pattern;
- symmetry: symmetrical items are more likely to be grouped;
- common fate: objects moving in the same direction are more likely to be seen as a group;
- continuity: once a pattern is formed, it is more likely to continue even if the elements are distributed.[2]

---

1   Eysenck 2001: 2.
2   Eysenck 2001: 21–2.

4.1.1   Attention

Cognitive psychologists disagree on the processes of attention.[3] However, there is agreement on three of its fundamental characteristics:

- Attention is selective. This means that we focus on one thing at a time, to the neglect of others. Only in very specific circumstances are we capable of dividing our attention.[4] In a display of objects, only the features capable of attracting attention have a communicative chance. The salience or distinctiveness of an exhibit and patterns of movement in the environment have been identified as the most obvious factors that contribute to drawing attention to a feature.[5]
- Attention requires motivation, which depends on cognitive emotional arousal and minimal perceived effort and distractions.[6]
- The resources of attention are limited and they deplete over time as efforts are expended. These reserves can be renewed through rest periods or, more quickly, by cognitive-emotional arousal. For example, when visitors are tired of a specific display type, a change of subject and objects may renew their interest.

There are a number of key implications for attention in museums. In densely stimulating environments such as exhibitions, with many items competing for attention, only the most distinctive elements are likely to succeed, and the capacity for attention is likely to be exhausted before many are viewed. Design and interpretation need to take account of the limitations and characteristics of our cognitive system.

4.1.2   Memory

Theories of memory are concerned with the structure of the memory system and with the processes operating within that structure.[7]

Many different theories have been developed within the study of memory, but there is a consensus on the three main stages involved in memory processes. These are encoding, the processes occurring during the presentation of information; storage, when the results of encoding are stored within the memory system; and retrieval, recovering an item of information.[8]

---

3   Bitgood 2000: 32.
4   Bitgood 2000: 32.
5   Bitgood 2000: 43.
6   Bitgood 2000: 43; Bitgood, Dukes and Abbey 2006: 464.
7   Eysenck 2001: 157.
8   Bitgood 1994: 5; Eysenck 2001: 157.

A multi-store model of the architecture of memory has been proposed.[9] In this paradigm there are three main type of memory stores:

- sensory stores: each holding information briefly and solely in relation to one sensory modality;
- short-term stores: with very limited capacity, often referred to as working memory;
- long-term stores: with unlimited capacity and capable of holding data over an unlimited period of time. This type of memory is better for storing information which has been deeply processed when acquired. In other words, we are more able to remember what we understand.[10]

An understanding of the mechanism of memory has many benefits. It can inform the design of effective exhibits, illuminate the modes of viewing, explain the short- and long-term impacts of a visit and develop more realistic expectations of viewing patterns. Many visitor studies have focused on recall of museum experiences.[11] These observational studies suggest that visual information is remembered better than semantic or non-visual content. Also, different exhibitions elicit different rates of memory for the visual, semantic and non-visual sensory categories.[12] Memory of objects is clearly superior to other types of memories.[13] Several types of memory of the museum experience can be solicited by prompting associations with specific elements, for example, objects or subject matter.[14] (It is important to note that the type of memory recalled is influenced by the methods used by the researchers to produce specific types of recollections.)

The multiple exposure theory of memory has interesting implications for the museum experience. In this model, in an information-rich environment, if similar events (or objects) are repeated, the tendency is to remember them as a unit of information.[15] In contrast, a museum display of visually and semantically similar exhibits, with one object that stands out, will be recorded as two main memory units:

- the collective memory of similar objects (for instance, a room full of pottery);
- the dissimilar element (the blue vase).[16]

If objects do not possess intrinsically distinguishing qualities, design can intervene to make an object stand out.

---

9   Atkinson and Shiffrin 1968.
10 Eysenck 2001: 158.
11 E.g. Bitgood and Cleghorn 1994; McManus 1993.
12 Bitgood and Cleghorn 1994: 11.
13 Stevenson 1992.
14 Bitgood and Clerghorn 1994: 12.
15 Norman 1988: 117.
16 Norman 1988: 117.

4.2   AFFECT AND COGNITION

Affect and cognition are relevant to the museum experience because together they contribute to one's perception of an exhibit. Both concern information processing. The affective system is judgmental and rapidly attributes positive or negative valences to the environment, while the cognitive system interprets and makes sense of the world.[17] Each has an impact on the other; often some affective states – emotions – are cognition-driven, but cognition is in turn influenced by affect. We are all different in the way in which we elaborate external stimuli and, further, we may receive the same object differently on different occasions. The characteristics of objects, the context and external circumstances – all these variables account for the affective and cognitive outcomes of the visitor–object interaction.

4.3   VISUAL AND AESTHETIC VALUES

Aesthetic taste and visual values are different concepts, but they cannot always be neatly separated. Visual values are not the product of individual perceptual stimulation, but rather are the result of social consensus. In all societies, art institutions and critics serve to create meanings; they construct value criteria that eventually become associated with particular visual elements. For instance, during the Enlightenment, the classical style set the artistic fashion. What we define as public taste is hence the result of an association of visual qualities with the values ascribed to them.[18]

Each museum visitor comes with a set of visual values and subjective aesthetic taste, which are largely culturally determined. It is widely thought that aesthetic values are the product of social class and acculturation and that people from higher social strata are more likely to spend time on cultural pursuits.[19] This is not because of innate inner sensibility; rather, it is a social faculty either acquired during upbringing or otherwise explicitly learned.[20]

It is a valuable role for museums to create an environment that facilitates the viewer in forming their own independent perspectives and opinions. In arts, as in other fields, individuals are capable of creating their own meanings, but it is difficult to detach oneself completely from the values one grew up with, and those of authority figures. The museum should attempt to be clear about the possible multiple readings of objects rather than presenting one universal interpretation, to encourage a critical approach to object viewing.

---

17   Norman 2002: 38-9.
18   Csikszentmihalyi 1995: 125.
19   Bourdieu 1984.
20   Wacquant 2007.

4.3.1   The Perception of Beauty

Perception and looking are two distinct processes: what one looks at is not necessarily what one perceives. Different cells in the brain select and admit to consciousness different features of the optical image.[21] Perception is strictly related to experience, with consciousness of what the seen things signify. It depends on memory and is usually unconscious. Aesthetic taste, personal sensitivity and the fashion of the time also influence the way we look at things. One may therefore maintain that the eye is part of the mind and that, during a museum visit, looking and seeing are by no means the outcome but are the starting points of a holistic experience.[22]

Beauty, a subjective perception, is not directly transmittable. Pye argues that to say that something is beautiful is a statement both about an object seen and also about the seer of it, and it is also about the impact of that vision on many others too. As such, a judgment of beauty is an expression of a collective sentiment, which cannot directly be taught and which is arguably culturally bound, as well as being an individual aesthetic experience.[23]

In museums the sight of numerous objects with similar visual qualities, however individually beautiful, can desensitise the viewer. The mind labels them as a unit of information and reduces them to a collective entity. In such circumstances, the exhibits are not individual things, but assemblages of paintings, busts and statues sharing similar visual characteristics. Additional signals are needed to prompt the viewer's attention. How can this be reconciled with the valuable design idiom concept of repeated multiples discussed above (3.1.4)? Repetition creates visual information in layers: that there is a general type of object or information (the group) which can, if the viewer wishes, be examined in detail (by comparing and contrasting individual objects).

A comparison between the experiences of beauty in music offers an insight into the mechanisms governing the perception of beauty.

The experience of beauty does not arise from direct sensations but from a subtle relationship with them and the remembered context and the indistinct field of peripheral vision.[24] Thus, a visitor's encounter with an exhibit is the product of what they actually see, plus its broader visual and conceptual context. By carefully planning and designing the peripheral field (display context) of an exhibit, we may be able to affect the visitor's experience of it.

---

21   Pye 1978: 116.
22   Weil 2002: 72.
23   Pye 1978: 99.
24   Pye 1978: 153.

4.3.2   Meanings from Objects

People's choices of things in daily life are not necessarily driven by aesthetic values. Instead, they are often related to the objects' significance to a person's life. Csikszentmihalyi conducted a study designed to challenge the Aristotelian notion that art helps to bring order into life, which offered an insight into how 'normal' people respond to art objects and design qualities in their environment.[25] The results suggested that art pieces played a very marginal role in people's lives, yet the respondents treasured some artefacts not because of their aesthetic value (which they largely lacked) but because they were charged with meaning for the owners.[26] Aesthetic or formal qualities were rarely mentioned as reasons for liking an object; rather, objects were selected because they conveyed memories, because they referred to family members or friends, or in connection with a special function. As Baudrillard has it, they had become 'household gods, spatial incarnations of the emotional bonds and the permanence of the family group'.[27]

Even our colour perception is founded on an understanding based on the Western science of colour as the result of the physical properties of light; having learned these properties, we find it difficult to see things otherwise. For example, research among Uzbeks in the Soviet Union revealed that the quality of colour is not an abstract but is seen as part of specific objects: the brownness of a piece of wool is different from the one of dung.[28] This evidence appears to challenge the theories advanced by critics to explain the effects of visual stimuli as universal and objective.

Displayed objects can affect us on two main levels: perceptually and symbolically. Museum objects acquire symbolic power because they are validated by an elite. The things we surround ourselves with are the physical expression of principles that order our lives. A family photograph can be a reminder of our happy life and, as such, is highly valuable to us. 'The creation of meaning in everyday life often uses trite symbols – kitsch rather than originality. Yet, our lives are held together by the strands of meanings these worn forms convey.'[29]

The viewer's attention can be directed to a silent object by suggesting its potential relevance to them. This would establish a relationship between viewer and object. Then, the individual may forget the visual qualities of the object (just as in their home) and be drawn into a symbolic relationship with it because it is significant to

---

25   Csikszentmihalyi 1995.
26   Csikszentmihalyi 1995: 118–26.
27   Baudrillard 1968: 16.
28   Csikszentmihalyi 1995: 122.
29   Csikszentmihalyi 1995: 126.

them. A powerful source of enjoyment in museums is the surprise of recognising a familiar object from our past.

4.4   DRAWING ON MULTIPLE SENSES

Our brains are naturally programmed to draw from a range of sensory information on our environment, including vision, touch and hearing.[30] Data are selected and merged from all the different senses.[31] Research in cognitive neuroscience has suggested potential benefits from such a strategy.[32] For example, a listener derives information not only from auditory inputs but also from visual clues from the lips, face and physical gestures of the interlocutor.[33]

To make sense of multi-sensory information, the individual combines input from the different senses to maximise information about the environment. In addition, sensory integration is used to reduce variance. However, one sensory dimension can be weighted more heavily than another during such processes if this reduces uncertainty.[34]

The brain's natural tendency to employ a range of sensory information has an impact on museum display and interpretation procedures. As Robertson explains, an approach that uses more than one sense can facilitate learning and memory processes, because more areas of the brain are involved in capturing the experience.[35] Further, such an approach can make exhibits accessible to a wider range of visitors, including challenged audiences and those with disabilities.[36]

4.5   BEAUTY AND USABILITY

The concepts of beauty and usability, founded on an understanding of cognitive psychology, can greatly assist in the design of a successful museum experience. True beauty is the sum of many elements; it is not merely skin deep and it does not merely relate to the façade connotations of an object or of its display surroundings.

To illustrate this concept, Ekuan employs the example of the Japanese Lunchbox, *makunouchi bento*, a sectionalised wooden lacquered container within which small

---

30   Ernst and Bülthoff 2004: 162.
31   Driver and Spence 1998: 13–19.
32   Driver and Spence 2000; Stein and Meredith 1993; Vroomer and de Gelder 2000; Welch and Warren 1986.
33   Driver and Spence 1998: 13–19.
34   Driver and Spence 2000: 731.
35   Robertson 2002: 131.
36   Davidson, Heald and Hein 1991: 273.

amounts of carefully prepared selections of food are arranged (Figure 4.1). The *makunouchi bento* symbolises many elements ordered as one, the spirit of form and aesthetic reconciling functionality and beauty.[37]

The usability concept was popularised in the human–computer interface and design communities through Donald Norman's book *The Psychology of Everyday Things.*[38] We must distinguish between usability and usefulness. Usability is related to the actions that a user perceives an object being capable of performing. The notion of usefulness is instead intrinsically linked to its functionality. In museum displays, the focus is on usability rather than usefulness: the visitor's perception of the functions and characteristics of an exhibit rather than its actual functions.[39]

In his seminal work of 1988, Norman placed the concept of usability centre stage in the design world, neglecting the topic of aesthetics, since, as he later apologetically explained, he 'thought it already well covered elsewhere'.[40] This omission was interpreted by many as advocating the supremacy of usability and functionality over beauty. The tension between aesthetics and usability in design, as well as those between affect and cognition, have been exhaustively explored and reconciled by Norman in his later work, *Emotional Design*, where he explains how on a rational level products should be functional but be beautiful and have an emotional impact as well.[41]

Usability is today regarded as one of the pillars of design practice. Others, however, argue that appearance should be the first preoccupation of a designer and form should never be subordinated to function.[42] However, successful product design requires all the design elements to be in harmony. Usability, aesthetic appeal, marketing considerations and manufacturability must be accounted for throughout all the stages of the design process.[43] The immense commercial success of Apple's products is held to be because they are both beautiful and usable, and hence desirable to own on both counts.[44]

In recent years the emotional impact (affect) that beauty and aesthetic qualities play in our cognitive system has started to be understood. It is now believed that the emotional response to the way something looks deeply affects cognitive tasks on a neuropsychological level.[45] For a long time, it was erroneously assumed that

---

37   Ekuan 2000: x–xi.
38   Norman 1988.
39   Gibson 1979.
40   Norman 2002: 38.
41   Norman 2004.
42   Black 1950: 124; Pye 1978: 12.
43   Norman 2002: 42.
44   Turner 2007.
45   Norman 2002: 39; Ashby, Isen and Turken 1999; Isen 1993.

only negative feelings (such as anger) and strong emotions could have an impact on cognitive processes. However, an ever-growing body of research testifies that even mildly positive states of emotions have a definite influence on thought processes.[46]

Individuals, when they are experiencing positive affect, find it easier to categorise material more flexibly, to notice similarities or dissimilarities among items, to make associations among ideas, to observe multiple relations among stimuli and to elaborate the material.[47] Positive affect plays a fundamental role in memory storing and retrieval, and promotes creativity, efficiency and thoroughness.

Figure 4.1   The Japanese lunchbox, an example of a successful combination of usability and beauty, as a metaphor for the ideal museum display

Source: © S. Keene.

4.6   BEAUTY AND USABILITY: KEY CONCEPTS FROM COGNITIVE SCIENCE

Research suggests that the benefits of positive affect play an important role in visitor satisfaction in museums.[48] In art museums, it has been demonstrated that objects can affect us on perceptual, cognitive, emotional and communicative

---

46   Isen 1993: 261.
47   Isen 1993: 263–4.
48   Caldwell 2001; Legrenzi and Troilo 2005.

planes.[49] The same rationale can be extended to any museum object. A display engendering positive feelings in visitors is likely to facilitate a number of cognitive processes and hence contribute to the visitor's appreciation and understanding of the exhibits. Conversely, negative affect will partly inhibit the visitor's experience. However, we should note that the circumstances of the individual and the specific visit will have an overriding effect on the outcome of the visit.[50]

An exhibit can be intended to inform, to surprise, to create a reaction, to stimulate people's imagination or to be aesthetically satisfying. In the exhibition context, beauty and usability relate to both the object and its display surroundings. Usability relates to the potential of both to communicate their intended function. Both can influence visitor behaviour and the realisation of the exhibit's aims.

Concerning unassuming objects, an assessment of the beauty and usability of display design can contribute to a better understanding of how to convey their cultural richness (Stage 2 of the object–visitor encounter). It can also help us to understand how to encourage an object investigation (Stage 3).

4.6.1   Beauty and Usability in Concept Checksheets

Table 4.1   Cognitive science: opposing statements for concept checksheets: beauty and usability

BEAUTY

The overall visual and physical dimension of a design system affects the visitor experience		
Harmonious	– or –	Incongruous
Welcoming		Unwelcoming
Relaxing atmosphere		Solemn and overwhelming
Design consistency		Inconsistent
Visually appealing		Visually dull
Colour coordinated/themed		Colour mixed
Attention to detail		Detail overlooked
Vista into gallery		Fragmented view
Well maintained		Run down
Adequately lit		Inadequately lit
Appropriate number of visitors		Overcrowded/empty
Comfortable temperature		Cold/hot/stuffy

---

49   Csikszentmihalyi 1990.
50   Isen 1993: 263, 265.

USABILITY

Usability is equally crucial – it refers to a user's perception of how easily they can relate to an exhibit		
Clear topographical orientation	– or –	Absence of topographical orientation
Conceptual guidance		Absence of conceptual guidance
Proximity of object to interpretive medium		Object separated from interpretation
Exhibits at comfortable height/ distance		Too high, low, far
Engaging		Not engaging
Intuitive to use		Difficult to use/interact
Friendly interactive interface		Unfriendly interface

4.7 FLOW: A KEY CONCEPT FROM COGNITIVE SCIENCE

Flow is a state of full involvement, of complete immersion in a task or an activity.[51] The term originated in interviews with artists and other creative individuals who described their experiences in this way.

4.7.1 Requirements for a Flow State

The main requirements for an activity that will engender a state of flow are:

- the activity has clear sets of goals that require appropriate responses;
- the activity provides immediate feedback;
- the person's skills are fully involved in overcoming a challenge which is just about surmountable (Figure 4.2);
- the person is completely focused because of the total demand on mental activity.[52]

Flow appears to be similar to the state described in philosophy as an aesthetic experience: a comparison suggests that they share similar requisites.[53]

Csikszentmihalyi's work is founded on observational data collected through surveying people about the activities they were undertaking and their feelings about these. The results suggested that individuals are generally unhappy doing nothing and are happy when engaged in occupations of some kind, although they

---

51   Csikszentmihalyi 1997: 29.

52   Csikszentmihalyi and Robinson 1990: 8; Csikszentmihalyi 1997: 29–31.

53   Beardsley 1982.

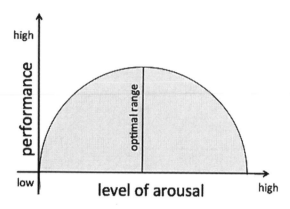

Figure 4.2   Diagrammatic representation of the Yerkes–Dodson law of arousal

Source: © F. Monti/S. Keene.

could not always pinpoint the reasons for their feelings. Csiksentmihalyi's research began with artists; he found that many described how an ecstatic (from the Latin to stand aside) state was achieved when they disconnected from the surrounding reality and experienced only the creative flow.[54]

The quality of an experience has been described as a function of the relationship between the level of challenge and the skills of the individual. This concept is founded on a principle known in psychology as the Yerkes-Dodson law of arousal (Figure 4.2).[55]

Arousal plays a central role in mental states such as anxiety, attention, agitation, stress and motivation. The optimal level of arousal varies from task to task and from individual to individual. It has also been observed that the optimal level is lower for more difficult or intellectually challenging tasks (because of the need to concentrate on the material) and higher for tasks requiring endurance and persistence (which require greater motivation).[56] Experimental psychology has also shown that the higher the level of arousal, the better the memory performance.

In order to understand flow states, Csikszentmihalyi explored different mental states resulting from the combination of various degrees of challenge and skills. Too high a level of challenge will cause stress or frustration, whereas challenges that are too low in relation to skills lead to relaxation and often boredom. As

---

54   Csikszentmihalyi 1975, 1988, 1990, 1997: 49–63.
55   Csikszentmihalyi 1997: 31.
56   Clark 1999.

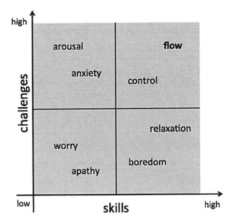

Figure 4.3   **The quality of experience expressed as the relationship of**
degree of skills and the level of challenge (adapted from
Csikszentmihalyi 1997: 31)
Source: © F. Monti/S. Keene.

seen in Figure 4.3, optimal experience, flow, is achieved when both variables
are high.[57]

To enable optimal museum experiences, displays should ideally keep each
visitor motivated and engaged in terms of arousal, but not to the point of causing
stress or frustration: they should offer enough stimuli to capture interest and
offer a sense of personal achievement. Clearly, this is a challenge where there
is a broad spectrum of audiences, with different skills, knowledge, expectations
and characteristics. A multi-layered approach is a possible solution, as it will
allow each person to select the level of arousal and motivation necessary to fully
concentrate on the exhibit.

A considerable challenge for a museum is to create the flow conditions
that will transform initial curiosity or attraction into an intense encounter.
Csikszentmihalyi has examined the application of his research to museums and
suggests a set of guidelines that may facilitate flow-like experiences in visitors.[58]
Among these are:

- promoting mindfulness: 'an open, creative, probabilistic state of mind
  in which the individual might be led to finding differences among things
  thought different';

57   Csikszentmihalyi 1997: 31.
58   Csikszentmihalyi 1995.

Figure 4.4   Visitors concentrating on putting music to instruments at one of the sound benches in the Horniman Museum *Music room*

Source: © S. Keene, courtesy of the Trustees of the Horniman Museum.

- encouraging deep absorption by soliciting engagement thorough sensory, intellectual and emotional faculties;
- satisfying the need for clear rules and goals, for an awareness of what is to be accomplished; and
- offering information that allows the museum goer to compare their cognitive and intellectual responses to other standards.

A display that asks the viewer to guess, to evaluate and to respond complies with these guidelines. The Art Gallery of Ontario, Canada, for instance, acquired in 2008 a new wing to house a remarkable bequest of 2,000 works of art and eclectic objects. The additional collections have been displayed imaginatively and provocatively, offering surprising encounters and exciting juxtapositions, rather than a traditional exploration of themes born out of a predefined narrative.

The Science Museum, London refers to the people involved in engineering and invention at the birth of the Industrial Revolution by juxtaposing marble busts with the tools from James Watt's workshop (below, Figure 13.2; both are types of object that would often be overlooked).

The most successful visitor–display interaction is one that generates creative flow in the visitor. Visitors do not always expect an intellectual experience when visiting a museum: 'What the audience expects from an art museum is above all a magical transformation of experience', to momentarily escape the predictable confines of the daily routine. The pleasure derived from such an experience will be the visitor's highest personal reward.

4.7.2   Criticism of Flow Theory

An early criticism of flow was that the theory is too deeply rooted in the Western mindset.[59] Carl's answer to this objection was that since Csikszentmihalyi does not precisely describe the dynamics of flow, whatever is necessary to achieve it can be extracted in any relevant circumstances. As such, there is not a cultural bias.[60]

A practical issue is that the content of flow is specific to the individual and the situation; it can be as various as the possible activities we engage in. It is therefore not possible to prescribe what will be most likely to engender a state of flow in museum visitors. Indeed, Csikszentmihalyi's basic description of flow was in artists, musicians or athletes using skills they had attained through years of practice and who were aware only of the process they were engaged in, while being oblivious to the mechanics of their actions. Only the most dedicated museum critic is likely to be in this situation.

4.7.3   Flow and Museum Exhibitions

Flow and the four conditions characterising flow states can be employed to identify the characteristics of an exhibit that would intensely engage visitors and create a favourable setting for a rewarding encounter with an object (Stages 3 and 4). In particular, our research suggests ways to provoke curiosity about an object. This would enable the visitor to choose their favoured outcome of the object encounter (Stage 3).

---

59   Sun 1987, cited in Carl 1994: 21.
60   Carl 1994: 21.

Table 4.2   Cognitive science: opposing statements for concept checksheets: flow

FLOW

The activity has a clear set of goals		
Aims of the displays are clear	– or –	Aims are unclear
The interactives' goals are evident		The interactives' goals are unclear
Guidance on use of interactives		No guidance on use of interactives

The activity provides unequivocal feedback		
Feedback available at all viewing stages	– or –	Feedback not always available
Feedback on extent of exhibition		No feedback available
Feedback on duration of interactive		No feedback on duration of interactive
Each visitor's action with interactive causes a visible change of state		No obvious change of state noticed

The person is completely focused because of the demands of the mental activity		
Full absorption in interaction	– or –	Distracted by the outside world
Prolonged time spent interacting		Brief time spent interacting

The person's skills are adequate to the challenge of the activity		
Relaxed	– or –	Anxious/uneasy
Sense of achievement/progress		Inadequacy
Engagement		Boredom
Enjoyment		Frustration

CHAPTER 5

MUSEUM STUDIES: OBJECT BIOGRAPHIES, LEARNING STYLES, LEVELS OF INTERPRETATION

Museum studies (also termed museology) reflect the significance of museums for national and cultural identity, education and enjoyment as well as for reflective and spiritual purposes. There is a wealth of literature attesting to the value and purpose of museums: to give three examples, in 1857, J.C. Robinson reflected on the value of the newly established South Kensington Museum; in 1929, John Cotton Dana discussed the role of the museum in art collection; and in 1967, Bazin in *The Museum Age* reflected on the purpose of the museum and identified a manifest and widespread wish to escape from the present time and to seek representations of earlier ages.[1]

Museum studies encompass all the multiple aspects of museums, from collecting and collections, the visitor experience, their buildings, management, social and economic significance and educational function, drawing on a wide range of theoretical fields from learning studies to anthropology, art history, social science, cultural economics and many others.

In this book we drew particularly on visitor studies, in which an understanding of how visitors experience museums has been developed over many years, and education and learning theory, a well-researched aspect of this. However, the museum visitor carries with them a level of expectation about the museum itself, which importantly influences the visit experience, so we will also discuss this.

5.1 THE MUSEUM AND THE OBJECT

5.1.1 Preconceptions and Expectations

The importance of people's perceptions and expectations in their decision on whether to visit a specific institution has been demonstrated by observational research.[2] For example, Perry, studying the Children's Museum of Indianapolis,

---

1   Bazin 1967: Foreword; Cotton Dana 1929; Robinson 1858.
2   Hood 1993; Vaughan 2001.

identifies three expectations that people have: interactions, needs and outcomes. 'Interactions' refer to visitors' desires to participate in their visit physically, socially and intellectually. 'Needs' encompass six psychological requirements in order for visitors to appreciate their experience: curiosity, confidence, challenge, control, play and communication. 'Outcomes' refers to the change visitors undergo as a result of their experience, whether it is learning new information, a new skill or a change in attitude.[3] Although this model could be criticised because of its dependence on just one study, it constitutes a useful reminder of the importance of including visitor expectations and psychological needs when gauging the quality of museum experiences.

5.1.2   The Cultural Values of Objects

Museum objects constitute repositories and sources of cultural capital.[4] Throsby proposes two definitions of cultural value: anthropologically as 'a set of attitudes, beliefs, mores, customs, values, and practices which are common to or shared by any group' or, more specifically, as 'certain activities ... and the products ... which have to do with the intellectual, moral, and artistic aspects of human life'.[5] Cultural value, it is suggested, is the result of the relationship between objects and society and their ability to convey an insight into issues of social organisation, political structure and power.[6]

Throsby identifies six cultural characteristics that are sources of cultural value for objects: aesthetic value (beauty); spiritual or religious value; symbolic value (the extent to which cultural objects act as repositories and conveyors of meaning); social value (a thing may provide people with a sense of connection to others); historical value; and authenticity.[7] Museums are places where the cultural value of objects is maintained, through appropriate documentation, conservation and storage, and can be increased through research, adding to what is known about an object. At a basic object sustenance level, physical preservation alone increases cultural capital because older objects increase in capital value.[8]

Following the same rationale, when a visitor has a rewarding experience with objects, this enhances the cultural value of museum objects in general, since the visitor will better appreciate the worth of objects in collections. To maintain the value of their collections is arguably the main duty of a museum. Such experiences

---

3   Perry 1993: 43–7.
4   Keene 2005: 160.
5   Throsby 2001: 4.
6   Keene 2005: 162.
7   Throsby 2001.
8   Throsby 2001: 161, 168.

are the means by which visitors can benefit from this store of value and increase their own cultural capital.[9]

5.1.3   Culture and Aesthetics

Museum exhibitions cannot be discussed without considering the many cultural and aesthetic issues that are intrinsic to them. Aesthetics in material culture refer to the quality of physical characteristics of objects: the effects on the senses and on their perception.[10] Such qualities include physical properties, such as colour, size, symmetry and balance, and non-material attributes, such as age, sense of distant place and magical substance. While many of the physical attributes are understood cross-culturally, the non-material attributes presuppose cultural knowledge. For example, although a particular material used to make an object can have an impact on the perceptual system irrespective of the cultural background of the viewer, the way one looks at that object may be influenced by knowledge of the properties of the raw materials used and their cultural significance[11] – gold would be a good example, imbued as it is with many cultural significances. It is this in-depth knowledge of the full qualities of an object that makes it attractive and significant to those equipped to read its material signs.

The idea of aesthetics as a cross-cultural concept is open for debate.[12] Those in favour of the motion maintain that a category is cross-cultural if it is a tool of cross-cultural analysis; furthermore, aesthetics is an essential aspect of our lives, and if we neglect it, we neglect much of the human essence.[13] Opponents claim that the concept of aesthetics is a product of bourgeois philosophy and therefore does not allow us to step outside it 'as though it were a set of clothes we could discard'. However, the very notion of the aesthetic does not easily lend itself to cross-cultural analysis because it is too deeply embedded in our Western analytical terms, through which it may be unfair and dangerous to assess the values of other peoples.[14]

This issue especially pertains to the display of objects from ethnographic and archaeological collections. Should objects of other cultures be presented as aesthetic forms of art? To what extent, when offering them as art, are we guilty of a distortion or appropriation of value? We need to analyse the relationship between the aesthetic qualities of the object as perceived by its Western public and the viewpoint of the producer of the object.[15]

---

9   Throsby 2001: 161, 168.
10   Morphy 1996: 258.
11   Morphy 1992: 10.
12   Ingold 1996: 255–91.
13   Morphy 1996: 255–91.
14   Ingold 1996: 290–291.
15   Morphy 1992: 2.

Aestheticisation of the works of other cultures can mask the practice by which the object was acquired and separate them from their human, historical and political provenance, so that they lose much of their cultural value. Ascribing a variety of objects to a homogeneous category, art, within which objects are expected to be appreciated solely for their aesthetic effect can be seen as a process of appropriation of their cultural values and subordination to the West. To avoid this, aesthetics could be considered a dimension that any object can potentially possess, rather than something belonging to arbitrary groups of objects.[16] In this conceptual framework, the role of museums is to engender people to see for themselves the qualities of each object, regardless of its attributes. This would lead to a cross-cultural view of the aesthetic potential of each object, regardless of provenance or visual qualities. Kingery proposes a conciliating view, suggesting that all objects, even those created for a specific function, are to some extent art and thus require consideration of both form and content.[17]

5.1.4   Museum Authority and Visitor Choice

One of our concerns is visitor autonomy and choice. The authoritative role of curators and educators has to be acknowledged and understood. It transcends the curation of a particular exhibition. Once in a museum, objects become statements, elements of a newly found narrative. An exhibition confers a further meaning on objects.[18] Different sequencing of exhibits has an impact on the message one receives and can also alter visitor behaviour and learning.

The choice of which objects to place in an exhibition can in itself be used to suggest meaning or to spark questions in the visitor's mind. The presence or absence of objects is an authorial assertion, affecting the final readings of the exhibition as well as perceptions of the role that museums in general play in fully representing society (or not).[19] Curatorial choices, even if outside conventional practices, are bestowed from above and conferred on the audience. What may at first appear as a more open exhibition structure is instead perhaps just a comforting thought for museum professionals, offering an illusion of visitor empowerment. Choice is considered democratic, a tool to allow the visitor, rather than the exhibition-maker, to make the final decisions. However, the choices have, of course, been preconfigured, thus eliciting the question of 'what the choices were to be made between'. Furthermore, by feeling capable of choosing, visitors may be encouraged into a less critical approach.[20] This is the essential nature of any exhibition, which is the physical expression of an exhibitor's

---

16   Morphy 1992: 3; Handsman 1987: 147.
17   Kingery 1996: 14.
18   Vergo 1989: 46.
19   MacDonald 2004: 167; Sandell 2007: 147.
20   MacDonald 2004: 168.

choices, but always leaves the viewer free to receive and interpret it according to their personal choice.

5.2   THE BIOGRAPHY OF THINGS: A KEY CONCEPT FROM MUSEOLOGY

A way to redress the balance of representation in favour of the full narrative that the object represents is to draw on this concept, which can revolutionise our view that 'things have no meanings other than those that human transactions, attribution and motivations endow them with'.[21] Instead, according to the anthropological concept of object biographies, the meaning of things is inscribed in their forms, uses and trajectories.[22]

In museums, the practical application of object biographies to the treatment of problematic exhibits could provide communication channels between the visitor and the object. By seeing the object's role in somebody else's life, the observer could relate such a situation to their own experience and appreciate the stories embodied in even the most mundane thing, regardless of its physical appearance.[23]

There are inherent challenges. This type of approach is difficult to repeat for more than a handful of objects in the context of permanent galleries. Replication across too many objects could nullify the impact of the display's originality and increase the rate of depletion of attention. Further, this preferential treatment might be interpreted as a declaration of the worth of the selected objects and stories at the expense of others.

However, there are definite advantages. Not only can objects which are themselves mute tell their stories and convey a great deal of information about their many cultural contexts, but this interpretative model promotes a visitor-centred and reflective viewing. The dynamics of the object's existence in a museum – the relationships between collectors, manufacturers, curators, scientists, conservators and visitors – can be unveiled. An example of this is the explanatory panel placed beside the Piranesi vase in the British Museum's *Enlightenment* gallery (Figure 5.1).

---

21   Appadurai 1986: 3–5.
22   Appadurai 1986: 5; Kopytoff 1986; Hoskins 1998.
23   Alberti 2005: 96.

PIRANESI VASE
Roman, 2nd century AD fragments of
a decorative vase and several other
monuments incorporated into Italian
18th-century composition.

Ornamental vase with relief decoration
showing satyrs at vintage, on a triangular
base. Designed by Giovanni Battista
Piranesi (1720–78) and restored in
his workshop. According to Piranesi
discovered at the villa of the Roman
Emperor Hadrian at Tivoli in 1769.

Acquired by Sir John Boyd for his country
mansion Danson House before 1778.

Figure 5.1   **The Piranesi vase, displayed in the British Museum's *Enlightenment* gallery (but ignored by most visitors). The text panel tells its story: created using classical Roman fragments by the famous eighteenth-century Italian artist Piranesi, acquired for an English country house in 1778 and purchased for the Museum in 1868**

Source: Vase © Trustees of the British Museum. Text panel © S. Keene, courtesy of the Trustees of the British Museum.

5.3   MUSEUMS AS PLACES FOR EDUCATION AND LEARNING

Are education and learning the most important functions of museums? Although proposed by some, this is far from universally accepted. Arguments that these services are so vital to society that museums should adopt them as being of overriding importance are countered by claims that this leads to 'dumbing down' and purely instrumental roles that are in any case the proper responsibility of institutions of education and learning.[24] Nevertheless, the learning/education style of a gallery strongly influences the visitor experience, whether they come to learn or simply to enjoy, and is a valuable diagnostic tool.

---

24   Holden 2006; Keene 2005: Chapter 10.

Table 5.1   Museum studies: opposing statements for concept checksheets: object biographies

OBJECT BIOGRAPHIES

Are the following portrayed: key moments? Changes in status? Significant ages? Differences from similar objects? Impact of socio-economic context?		
Key moments conveyed	– or –	Not conveyed
Changes of status put across		Not put across
Significant ages conveyed		Not conveyed
Comparison with similar objects		No comparison with similar objects
Overview of the socio-political contexts		Not conveyed

Do objects appear in their own right or as symbols, to convey a predetermined projection of the past in the present and future?		
The object moves/arouses/excites	– or –	The object leaves us indifferent
The object narrates the past		The past is not conveyed by the object
Object is not a symbol but a part of the past		Object is used to convey a predefined story
Multi-sensory experience of objects		Only experienced visually and verbally

Objects are both art and artefact and need reflection of both form and content		
The physicality of objects comes across	– or –	An arbitrary meaning comes across
Displays convey agency/effects of objects		Displays solely elicit admiration of beauty
Cultural contexts of origin are conveyed		No cultural contexts come across
Both visual qualities and uses are conveyed		Bias on art or artefact side of the object

5.3.1   Knowledge in the World and Knowledge in the Mind

Museums are seen as repositories of knowledge as much as of objects. Theories of knowledge are pertinent to museum education and learning: there are differing theories on where knowledge can be said to reside.

Knowledge in the world assumes that much everyday information resides in the world and is interpreted through mental processes. To create knowledge in their heads, people rely upon the placement and location of objects, texts and artefacts of a society to interpret the knowledge in that world. Objects offer clues in terms of physical constraints, semantic constraints, cultural constraints and logical constraints. Knowledge in the head, internal knowledge, corresponds to human memory and to the ability to retrieve information and make connections.[25]

In museum displays, unless the object is of great significance or personal relevance to the viewer, the learning and remembering process is facilitated if some of the efforts of remembering are transferred to the outside world (the displays).[26] For example, if information about an exhibit is related to easily recognisable physical features of it, the burden of remembering is transferred onto the objects themselves, which, as we have seen above, are more readily recalled than text (4.1.2).

There are numerous theories of education, but any one has at its core a theory of knowledge and also a theory of learning. On knowledge, Hein describes the two opposing theories outlined above: knowledge, following the Platonic idea, exists independently of the thinker; or knowledge exists only in the mind of the knower. Regarding learning, there are again two positions: learning consists of an incremental assimilation of information (the behaviourist position) or the mind constructs schemata, and learning consists of selection and organisation from the sensations present in the environment, as in the work of Pepper and Piaget (drawn on by Hein).[27]

Table 5.2   Four categories of education models as defined by Hein[28]

Didactic Knowledge independent of learner Learning by incremental assimilation	Discovery Knowledge independent of learner Teacher arranges knowledge in forms to be discovered
Behaviourist Knowledge not independent of learner Built incrementally	Constructivist Knowledge not independent of learner Learners enabled to construct knowledge as the process of learning

From these positions, four models of educational approaches in museums have been identified (Tables 5.2 and 5.3).[29] Each model suits one of the main types of personal learning style, discussed below in 5.4.

---

25   Norman 1988: 84–6.
26   Norman 1988: 73.
27   Hein 1995: 1, drawing upon the work of Dewey (1938) and upon Pepper's (1981) four world views on how knowledge is constructed.
28   Hein 1995, 1998.
29   Hein 1995, 1998.

Table 5.3   The four museum educational models identified by Hein,[30] with associated learning styles

Educational model	Characteristic of model	Exhibition type/ learning style	Characteristics of exhibition
Didactic: traditional lecture and text	Teaching occurs in a linear and systematic way	The systematic museum *Suits analytical learners*	Systematic display of collections
Behaviourist	Knowledge is acquired brick by brick	The orderly museum *Suits common sense learners*	Structured, gives rewards and provides motivation
Discovery	Enquiry-based learning	Discovery museum *Suits experiential learners*	Provides rich experiences, but negates social influence
Constructivist	Knowledge dependent on the learner's mind	The constructivist museum *Suits imaginative learners*	Personal knowledge is constructed from the exhibits

5.3.2   The Didactic Model

The didactic or traditional 'lecture and text' model combines the beliefs that knowledge exists independently of learners and that it can be passively assimilated by them. Didactic museums are those that focus on the systematic organisation of their collections and the associated knowledge.[31] In museums, knowledge and information transmission are determined *a priori* by a figure of authority, which can correspond to the curator, and people are seen as vessels needing to be filled with knowledge.[32] Didactic exhibitions adopt a linear sequential order of exhibits, which it is difficult to avoid following. Exhibits tend to be organised in a strict hierarchical order, with labels detailing what is to be learned from the displays.[33] The beginning and end are clearly defined.

---

30   Hein 1995, 1998.
31   Hein 1995: 22.
32   Hooper-Greenhill 2001: 4.
33   Popova 2001: 21.

5.3.3   The Behaviourist Model

When learning is incrementally created in the mind of the learner, it results in a stimulus–response educational approach known as the behaviourist model.[34] This approach creates orderly museums which, although sharing many characteristics of the systematic museum, tend to concentrate on the method of teaching rather than on the subject to be taught.

Behaviourist exhibitions would have reinforcing components that repeatedly impress the stimulus on the learner and reward appropriate responses. Some exhibits do this by providing a positive written or computer-screen response, perhaps with a sound, ('Yes, that's the right answer!') when the visitor pushes the correct button, lifts the appropriate flap or arranges items in the correct sequence.[35]

Visitors to the orderly museum are encouraged to participate in this preconstructed learning process, which is determined by curatorial and educational staff.

5.3.4   The Discovery Model

In this model it is assumed that although knowledge exists outside the learner, the individual has to construct their own version. Learning is an active process, as the learner 'discovers' knowledge through participation, which transcends the mere accumulation of facts. In the discovery museum, visitors are presented with information that requires mental (or even physical) activity in order to receive it. Emphasis is on exploration, so that the individual has to discover what is to be assimilated rather than passively learn the given material. Hein argues that whatever the methods employed, 'the learners will only learn those things we wish them to learn', leaving little room for true discovery.[36]

Spatially, exhibits and their interpretative methods will encourage mental and physical participation, taking the form of touch-screens, levers and buttons accompanied by clear labelling which will encourage the visitor to find out the answer to the posed questions.[37]

5.3.5   The Constructivist Model

The constructivist museum is grounded on the principle that knowledge is created in the mind of the visitor using personal methods. It is said to:

---

34   Hein 1995: 22.
35   Hein 1998: 29.
36   Hein 1998: 30–31.
37   Popova 2001: 22.

- provide for all ages and stages of learning;
- be highly visitor-orientated;
- provide maximum freedom of movement and circulation for the visitor; and
- allow the visitor to explore a range of topics according to their personal interest and to draw personal conclusions.[38]

Figure 5.2   **A discovery display – the panoramas in the Canadian Museum of Nature in 2009. There are a range of activities below the panorama window, including AV screens, lift the flap, handle fur and so on**

Source: © S. Keene, with kind permission of the Canadian Museum of Nature.

In the constructivist museum, visitors are facilitated in their own intellectual enquiry. Open-ended questions are posed and time is allowed to foster reflective thought. High-level thinking is encouraged: visitors are motivated to go beyond factual assimilation. The museum–visitor experience is not top down; the displays promote a dialogue with the exhibits. Raw data, physical and interactive materials are offered and the visitor is encouraged to partake in practical activities.[39]

Much is claimed for this model. It is widely accepted today that each of us processes information in different ways; as such, a flexible educational stance

---

38   Hein 1995: 23.
39   Brooks and Brooks 1993.

can accommodate a wider range of visitors.[40] People do not have a fixed single IQ and there is a range of learning styles among individuals (discussed below, 5.4). And, according to Gardner's multiple intelligence theory, there are at least seven or eight different forms of intelligence; individuals tend to develop some of these intelligences over others.[41]

From a critical viewpoint, it is argued that with this educational model (as in other learner-centred approaches) visitors can be trapped within the domain of what they already know. The individual draws from personal resources within the boundaries of the belief systems, bodies of knowledge and behavioural possibilities they have assimilated since childhood,[42] so 'what if the learner does not have the basis on which to construct new knowledge and challenge preconceptions?'.[43] In addition, although the constructivist paradigm aims to empower visitors, the process of knowledge making is nevertheless still mediated and, to an extent, shaped by the museum. Some argue that it gives people the illusion of actively partaking in the meaning-making process, while, deep down, the museum remains the puppeteer of their thoughts.

5.4   PERSONAL LEARNING STYLES: A KEY CONCEPT FROM MUSEOLOGY

People take in information in different ways and with a variety of outcomes. Research undertaken in the past 30 years in the field of learning theories proposes a fourfold subdivision of museum learners, which relate to the different educational models described above:[44]

- *Analytical learners* assimilate by thinking and observing. They favour interpretation that offers facts and sequential ideas, and want sound logical theories that allow for consideration and intellectual comparison. The traditional object and label-rich art and design museums cater well for this group.
- *Common-sense learners* learn by thinking and doing. They prefer first-person experience, trying out theories and testing them for themselves.
- *Experiential learners* assimilate by doing and feeling. They enjoy imaginative trial and error, and prefer hands-on experiences while searching for meanings.
- For *imaginative learners*, feeling and watching, listening and sharing ideas are essential; they prefer interpretation that encourages social interaction while they search for personal meaning.

---

40   Museums, Libraries and Archives Council 2004.
41   Gardner 1985.
42   Brookfield 1986: 124.
43   Sachatello-Sawyer et al. 2002: 99.
44   E.g. Honey and Mumford 1982; Kolb 1984; Serrell 1996: 51.

Therefore, a successful exhibition would be a complex construction capable of addressing a range of learning modes. The Museums, Libraries and Archives Council suggested that in order to create inspiring places, the following points need to be addressed:

- Emphasise intuition, feeling, sensing and imagination as well as the traditional skills of analysis, reason and sequential problem solving.
- Connect with all four learning styles using various combinations of experience, reflection, conceptualisation and experimentation.
- Refer and make connections with people's everyday experiences when introducing concepts or themes that may be unfamiliar.
- Involve a range of people in developing the resources for learning, including the learners themselves. In this way the displays will be more likely to appeal to a wide range of learning styles.[45]

Table 5.4   Museum studies: opposing statements for concept checksheets: personal learning styles

PERSONAL LEARNING STYLES

Each visitor has a particular learning style preference (or may combine them), and different types of museum exhibitions and exhibits will appeal to those with the relevant style

Criteria: didactic exhibition style/analytical learning
- Objects are systematically arranged in displays
- Interpretation is mainly facts and sequential ideas
- No allowance for personal interpretation
- Specialist language used
- Logical theories invite comparison and thinking
- Topics progress from simple to complex

Criteria: behaviourist exhibition style/common-sense learning
- Displays designed to motivate viewers
- Interpretation gives a linear set of goals
- Interaction by individual encouraged
- Visitor physically responds (e.g. press a button, tick a box)
- Feedback from one action used to create next
- Positive/negative feedback provided for responses
- Interactives removed from exhibition space to avoid distractions

---

45   Museums, Libraries and Archives Council 2004.

Criteria: discovery exhibition style/experiential learning

- Exhibits lead to a gradual understanding of museum's narratives
- The visitor plays an active role
- The displays are highly interactive with clear feedback
- Hands-on experiences employed to promote first-person discovery
- Interactives are integrated in the exhibition space
- Enjoyed by children due to participation
- The gallery is a lively place

Criteria: constructivist exhibition style/imaginative learning

- Exhibits not presented in linear, predetermined sequence
- Exhibits offer different entry points
- Information offered via various media, uses more than one sense
- Social interaction encouraged
- Listening and sharing of ideas is important in the search for meaning
- Visitors can make connections with familiar concepts and objects
- Physical involvement to promote independent thinking
- Places for contemplation encourage time with the exhibits

5.5   LEVELS OF INTERPRETATION

Allied to learning styles are issues of over- and under-interpretive exhibits. Three categories of exhibit have been defined by Wittlin – *under-interpretive, misinterpretive* and *interpretive*.[46] Under-interpretive exhibits either provide too little written interpretation and object-sparse displays or impose an intellectual overload due to too much. Misinterpretive exhibits may be due to a profusion of objects and visually driven presentation, which leads to sensory over-stimulation coupled with an intellectual deficit. As a result of this combination of elements, the viewer may be overwhelmed by the excess of text and objects, and may lose sight of the exhibition's message. Object-dense displays, with little interpretation belong to the first category, while over-designed displays may camouflage their meaning, distracting the viewer from the message.[47]

This finding is supported, for example, by research commissioned by the Department of Learning and Information at the British Museum,[48] which suggested that people spent longer and were more deeply engaged when a limited number of objects were on show.[49] Re-distribution of attention in relation to the number of exhibits was also demonstrated in studies by Melton in 1935 and Robinson in 1928, in which the number of art works in a gallery was systematically varied to

---

46   Wittlin 1971: 145.
47   Wittlin 1971: 145.
48   Summarised in Morris Hargreaves McIntyre 2005.
49   Mazda 2006.

reveal that a decrement of attention (as measured by average viewing time per object) occurred as the number of paintings increased.[50]

Table 5.5   Museum studies: opposing statements for concept checksheets: levels of interpretation

LEVELS OF INTERPRETATION

a) Under-interpretive/intellectual overload		
Adequate ratio of object/space	– or –	Overcrowded displays
Adequate interpretation		Too little/too much interpretation
Intellectual stimulation		Intellectual overload
Displays intelligible to all		Intelligible to experts
Visitor takes time looking		Visitor hurries by

b) Sensory over-stimulation and misinterpretive exhibits		
Objects enhanced by design	– or –	Objects as ornaments
Presentation is visually pleasing		Presentation is aesthetically overloaded
Object visually enjoyed and understood		Spectacle distracts from meaning

c) Text, layout and design work together – interpretative		
Interpretation complements object	– or –	Interpretation doesn't explain object
Information is effective		Information is confused
Design enhances the message		Design confuses the message

---

50   Melton 1935, 1972; Robinson 1928.

PART 2

FROM CONCEPTS TO PRACTICE

Following the review of relevant theory and the selection of key concepts that could be used to understand the visitor–object interaction, the next step was to test the applicability of the concepts we identified. To do this, we used the tools we developed from the concepts described in Part 1: space syntax diagrams, observation records and concept checksheets. We developed and employed these tools to evaluate major galleries in three London museums and to compare the visitor experience in them. We applied them further in a detailed investigation into visitor interaction with silent objects in the spectacular and highly popular *Egyptian death and afterlife: mummies* gallery at the British Museum, where we added visitor interviews to develop a deeper understanding.

THEORY DOMAINS AND KEY CONCEPTS

The Toolkit

Architecture: Space syntax

Design: Design idioms – colour, light, text, use of space and layout

Cognitive science: Beauty and usability; flow

Museum studies: The biography of things; personal learning styles;
               levels of interpretation

The toolkit consisted of:

- gallery observation record sheet (Appendix 1) – to record the general behaviour of visitors in relation to the exhibition and exhibits;
- space syntax diagrams – using a gallery layout plan as the basis, diagrams of the paths most commonly taken by visitors;
- snapshot diagrams – again using a gallery layout plan as the basis, snapshot records of where visitors commonly stood, taken at predetermined intervals;
- concept checksheets (Appendix 2) – for recording scores against the

opposing statements under each of the key concepts;
- and this time we added we added questionnaire-based interviews with visitors to our previous evaluation and research tools (Appendices 3–5). As such, we were able to find out much more about visitors' reception of and interaction with these exhibits.

Using these tools, we evaluated major galleries in three London museums and compared the visitor experience in them. These were the *Understanding objects* gallery, part of the British Galleries suite in the V&A, the Egyptian scripts section of the *Enlightenment* gallery in the British Museum and the *Music room* in the Horniman Museum. In each gallery, we observed and recorded circulation flow and visitor attention using space syntax techniques and then evaluated the gallery using concept checksheets (Appendix 2). Results for the three galleries are set out first in Chapter 6 and the applicability of the concepts is discussed in Chapter 7, where they are used to compare the galleries.

We took these further, investigating how visitors choose which objects to engage with and whether they develop narratives and stories from their viewings, in a world-famous gallery, *Egyptian death and afterlife: mummies*, Room 63 at the British Museum, for this research (Chapter 8).

From this exercise, we identified some display techniques that would assist the display of silent objects, which we were able to test in experimental exhibits described later in Chapters 10 and 11.

The gallery observation sheet will be found in Appendix 1 and the concept checksheets in Appendix 2. For the *Egyptian death and afterlife: mummies* gallery, Appendices 3–5 contain the observation results, interview questionnaire and interview responses.

Data for these studies are available on the website, www.ucl.ac.uk/silent-objects.

CHAPTER 6

TESTING THE CONCEPTS IN THREE LONDON MUSEUMS

The concepts presented in Part 1 constitute a theoretical framework that covers the key elements of the visitor–object connection. They are also the basis for a set of practical tools that could be used to evaluate and analyse visitor interaction with exhibitions and exhibits. To explore their use, we used them to evaluate three different galleries, with the kind permission of these museums, in the British Museum, the V&A and the Horniman Museum.

In this chapter we report our results for each of the three galleries. In Chapter 7, we compare the galleries against each concept as a group.

In each venue, the first exercise was to track and observe visitors. A gallery observation sheet was used for each (Appendix 1) and gallery layout plans were the basis for recording observed visitor movements and where they stood, so as to apply space syntax analysis. Observations are set out below. To use the other concepts, the concept checksheets that had been constructed were used to assess each gallery (Part 2: Introduction; see Appendix 2 for a template for these).

Silent objects are the focus of our research, but by applying these concepts, we learned much about the visitor experience and use of galleries in general as well as about interactions with objects.

We had in mind at all times the framework for the visitor–object interaction (Chapter 1, introduction, Figure 1.4 and Chapter 7, Figure 7.7):

Stage 1: the visitor stops to look at the object.

Stage 2: the visitor perceives that the object is of interest.

Stage 3: the visitor investigates and enjoys encountering the object.

Stage 4: the outcome is rewarding for the visitor.

6.1   RESEARCH PROGRAMME

The objectives of this research programme were:

- to assess the extent to which the concepts (Table 6.1) can be effectively employed as investigative tools;
- to create a comparative analysis of visitor responses to different display approaches in three settings; and
- to extrapolate information about effective object display in exhibitions, especially for silent objects.

Table 6.1   Theory domains and the key concepts that were tested in the three galleries. Object biographies and interpretation levels were not used at this stage

Theory domain	Key concepts
Architecture (Chapter 2)	*Space syntax* Techniques employed to analyse visitor movement patterns and behaviour in relation to the configuration of space[a]
Design (Chapter 3)	*Design idioms* – colour, light, text, use of space and layout A tool to explore and assess exhibit characteristics and to understand visitor reactions to key design elements of museum displays[b]
Cognitive science (Chapter 4)	*Beauty and usability* Derives from the fields of interaction design and cognitive science. This concept is a useful way to assess the cognitive and affective reactions of a visitor to a system[c] *Flow* Throws light on aspects of the visitor's reactions with objects and on potential positive outcomes[d]
Museum studies (Chapter 5)	*Object biographies* The life trajectories of specific objects and their relationships with other objects and people can be used to understand how different individuals encounter and make sense of objects[e] *Personal learning styles* Used to further explore visitors' rapport with objects and the outcomes of the interaction[f] *Level of interpretation* To quickly assess whether too much or too little, or confusing, information is offered to the visitor[g]

Notes: [a] Hillier 1996: ix. [b] Hall 1987: 127. [c] Norman 2002: 42. [d] Csikszentmihalyi 1990: 7. [e] Alberti 2005; Appadurai 1986. [f] Serrell 1996: 51. [g] Wittlin 1971: 145.

6.2   RESEARCH METHOD

Three varied galleries were chosen from the different museums. The evaluation was carried out during the months of July, August and September 2004. The total sample size for the structured observation study in the three museums was 105 visitors, and the movements of 212 visitors were tracked.

In each venue the following data were collected:

- Visitor movement patterns (visitor flow count, visitor movement tracking and snapshots of visitors' static placing relative to key features). Records of visitor movements are shown in the discussion of each gallery.
- Structured observation of visitor behaviour.

For the forms employed, see Appendix 1 for spatial analysis; for assessment of the galleries against the concepts using checksheets, see Appendix 2.

Fuller details of the methods employed are given in the discussion of each gallery. Additionally, in some cases, visitor conversations and comments in visitor books were noted, which supplemented observations. At this stage of the research, visitors were not interviewed.

6.3   THE *ENLIGHTENMENT* GALLERY IN THE BRITISH MUSEUM

The *Enlightenment* gallery (Figure 6.1) is housed in a magnificent neo-classical space, the former King's Library, constructed in 1823–1827 to hold the scholarly library of George III. The *Enlightenment* gallery itself was opened in 2003 in celebrating the 250th anniversary of the British Museum.

Architecturally, the room has a central section and two long end sections, each with three sub-sections (Figure 6.2). It is adjacent to the Great Court. Conceptually the exhibition reflects the architectural sub-divisions, each of the seven spaces corresponding to one aspect of the Enlightenment. The effect on visitors of the vista of this magnificent room and the object-rich displays is one of wonder, curiosity and intellectual stimulation. As a result, this is considered an exhibition that invites visitors to think about how the objects are organised and presented, and why they are organised in that way.[1]

There are three types of display case in the *Enlightenment* gallery (Figure 6.3): floor cases including table-top displays of materials, wall presses and traditional free-

---

1   Lord 2005: 150.

**Figure 6.1   The *Enlightenment* gallery in the British Museum: vista over the
            whole gallery**
Source: © Trustees of the British Museum.

standing upright glass-fronted cases.[2] The objects in the floor cases are presented
according to the traditional object and label format, with labels of unusual design.
The walls are lined with cabinets full of objects which further illustrated the seven
thematic sections; these wall presses (which previously housed books for the
King's Library) are reminiscent of the first cabinets of curiosities, where objects
from different natural and human contexts are showcased as *oggetti di meraviglia*
(objects of wonder), with the purpose of engaging and touching the imagination
and spirit of the observer in different ways.[3] Here text is minimal; generic group
labels offer a summary of the cases' contents.

The gallery is large, 300 feet long, 41 feet high and 30 feet wide,[4] so this study
focuses on the *Ancient scripts* section. This space comprised four table-top
display cases, a portion of the wall presses and a facsimile of the Rosetta Stone
which can be touched by visitors. A *Hands on* desk is also in this area; this is a
table staffed by trained volunteers where a selection of objects, some purchased
specially for the desk and some replicas, can be handled by visitors (Chapter 9;
Figure 9.3).

2   Sloan 2003.
3   Lugli 1996.
4   Sloan 2003.

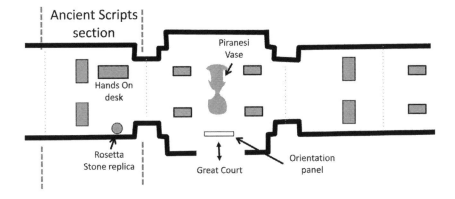

Figure 6.2   The *Enlightenment* gallery in the British Museum: plan. The
Ancient scripts area is within the dotted rectangle. The positions
of the *Hands on* desk and facsimile of the Rosetta Stone are
indicated

Source: © F. Monti/S. Keene.

6.3.1   Analysis of Visitor Movement Patterns

Flow count to measure movement types in the space   At the time of the study, the
gallery was relatively quiet. As noted by McManus, no one hour or day is exactly
like another in a museum, 'however, visitors are doing a fairly similar range of
things when visiting a particular exhibition and the proportion of people following
a particular pattern of behaviour was likely to be repeated over time'.[5]

There are over 90 rooms to visit in the Museum and the average visit time for the
over six million visitors is two hours 14 minutes.[6] Many prefer to visit a range
of galleries; some wish to concentrate on a few or even one. Therefore, for this
exercise, two minutes was set as the minimum time for interaction. During the
hour, 239 people entered and left the space. Of these, 132 moved rapidly and
directly from one section of the gallery to another. In other words, 55 per cent of
visitors entered, gazed round the space and left again. A total of 107 (45 per cent)
came into the *Ancient scripts* section and interacted with the displays for at least
two minutes.

Tracking visitor movements in the space   Over a two-hour period, the movements
of 19 visitors were observed in and out of the Ancient scripts section. Two
imaginary lines were drawn at the extremities of the Ancient scripts area – one
bordering the Classifying the world section and one at the Magic and rituals section.

5   McManus 2003: 26.
6   S. Frost, personal communication, 2012.

Figure 6.3   The *Enlightenment* gallery in the British Museum: three types of display: wall presses, a traditional upright case and table-top displays

Source: © Trustees of the British Museum.

Adults visiting on their own were randomly chosen at their point of entry in the Ancient scripts space. To detect variations in behaviour that depended on where the visitor was coming from, the two entry points were alternatively targeted as the starting point. For each visitor, the following data were recorded on a plan of the gallery: movement within the space, approximate time with exhibits, and type of interactions with individual exhibits (looking, reading labels, taking photos and so on). Once the subject left the space, the next single adult entering the Ancient scripts area was similarly observed.[7]

Two distinct viewing patterns were observed (Figure 6.4). Many visitors (16 out of 19) did not look at the whole section; rather, they moved along the room on its long axis either clockwise or anticlockwise. A tendency to move in a circular pattern has been recorded in numerous visitor studies.[8] However, three people in the sample viewed this exhibition space as intended in the curatorial plan, examining the showcases on both sides of the *Ancient scripts* area.[9] These visitors spent longer with the displays than those individuals who took a circular route around the gallery. These findings suggest that those engaged in deeper interaction were aware of the thematic sub-divisions of the gallery and wanted to complete the story told by the four cases comprising a gallery section before moving on to the next one.

---

7   E.g. Sandifer 2003.
8   Bitgood 2000; Underhill 2000: 76.
9   Sloan 2004.

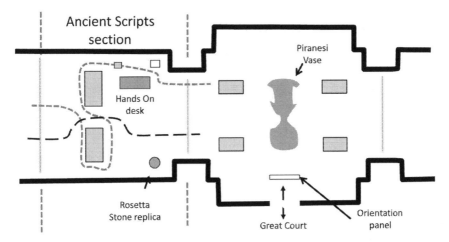

Figure 6.4   The *Enlightenment* gallery in the British Museum: two typical movement patterns observed in the *Ancient scripts* section: a circular motion around the gallery (dotted grey) and the 'by section' viewing model (black dashed)

Source: © F. Monti/S. Keene.

Static snapshots of visitor placing   During an hour, the locations of 64 people were recorded at 10-minute intervals (Figure 6.5). The modern facsimile of the Rosetta Stone is a focal point in this space: 33 per cent of static locations were recorded around this exhibit. Despite its unprepossessing appearance, this copy of the ancient Egyptian object is extremely popular among tourists, who enjoyed being able to touch it and to be photographed with an iconic object. Beard suggests that the Rosetta Stone perfectly symbolises the British Museum's fame and indecipherability.[10] It is one of the key attractions in the British Museum that many visitors come specifically to see. The replica offers the chance of a close inspection of this iconic object,[11] but this exhibit's popularity may partly be because, according to conversations overheard and to visitors' body language, not everybody realises that this exhibit is a copy. (The original, displayed in Room 4 opposite the entrance from the Great Court, in a secure showcase, is equally if not more popular – see above, Figure 3.1.)

6.3.2   Structured Observation of Visitor Behaviour

Over three two-hour periods, 39 visitors were monitored. Structured observations of their behaviour were recorded on an observation sheet (Appendix 1). The visitor profile was analysed by gender and visually inferred age group. There was a balance of male and female visitors. Overall, 23 subjects were male (59 per cent)

---

10   Beard 1992: 519–27.
11   MacDonald 2003: 95.

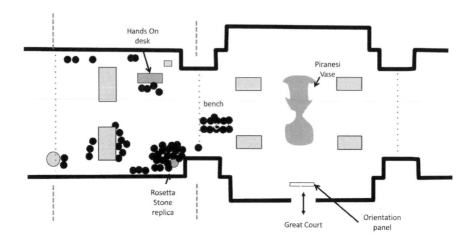

Figure 6.5   The *Enlightenment* gallery in the British Museum: static snapshot of the distribution of visitors in the *Ancient scripts* area
Source: © F. Monti/S. Keene.

and 16 were female (41 per cent). The sample comprised adult visitors from all age ranges, with a predominance from the 50–59 age group and the 20–29 age group.

The time spent with the displays varied considerably (Figure 6.6). If we look at the data in terms of broad time ranges, the results show that about a third of the 39 individuals spent between two and four minutes in the assessed area, a further third spent between four and seven minutes, and the rest spent longer. Two visitors who spent around 20 minutes in the area also used the *Hands on* desk. This result was particularly significant considering the extent and nature of the room in a museum with so many other compelling attractions.

6.3.3   The British Museum Enlightenment Gallery: What We Observed

Exhibit layout and visitor movement   Records of visitor movements confirmed that most people are initially drawn towards what is on the path they are following; during this observation exercise, only two visitors appeared to stop and look around to choose what to view. The propensity of visitors to interact with objects encountered in their path rather than consciously seeking others that might be more interesting to them has been detected in other studies.[12]

The nature of interactions   The findings from the structured observation exercise showed two kinds of interaction by single adult visitors. The first was typical of

12   Choi 1999: 249.

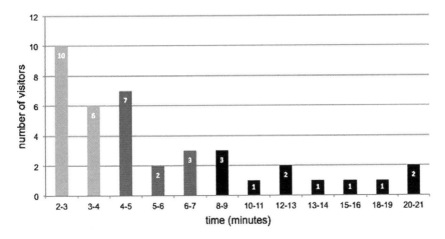

Figure 6.6 The *Enlightenment* gallery in the British Museum: duration
of interactions in the *Ancient scripts* section. Darker shading
corresponds with longer interaction

Source: © F. Monti/S. Keene.

shorter visits. These visitors demonstrated awareness of the spatial and architectural
environment; they looked around them at the gallery as a whole and occasionally
glanced at the exhibits and labels.

The second interaction type was characteristic of longer visits: the visitor explored
case contents, looking at the objects and reading labels to a varying degree of
intensity and duration. It may be hypothesised that while the latter model is
observed with independent learners,[13] the first is more prevalent among tourists
and first-time visitors. Nonetheless, there are other possible motives: for example,
patterns of conduct may be defined by the reason for the visit, learning styles or
simply passing circumstances.

From conversations overheard among foreign visitors, including comments on the
gallery by users of the *Hands on* desk (Chapter 9), it was noted that individuals
who could not fully engage with the narrative of the gallery were nonetheless able
to connect visually by looking at objects which were eye-catching or curious and
finding out what they were or by admiring the room for its architectural and design
qualities.

Two additional kinds of interaction which transcend language and culture barriers
were observed. The first was at the *Hands on* desk or with the facsimile of the
Rosetta Stone. In both of these, visitors can handle the objects. The second was
the performance of a ritual in a 'liminal' space, where visitors adopt patterns of

13   Durbin 2002.

behaviour according to cultural conventions and the context of the visit.[14] The act of taking photographs can be interpreted as an expression of this ceremonial agenda, around the Rosetta Stone replica in the foreground in Figure 6.1, but often elsewhere in the gallery as well.

Effects of case design   A range of behaviours was recorded in relation to different types of showcase (see Figure 6.3).

The wall presses, reminiscent of the display typology of the cabinet of curiosities, are intended as a three-dimensional reference gallery to complement the key objects in the central cases and to tell the story of the main collectors of the eighteenth century. They are also meant to indicate the existence of the collections themselves, the far greater body of information and knowledge that validates any display.[15] They were the least closely inspected of the three types.

Observations of behaviour and body language detected two broad responses to the wall presses. On the one hand, we observed an initial difficulty in relating to this display style. Visitors were noticed searching around for clues about the wall cabinets, appeared at times perplexed in front of such an abundance of objects and did not spend long with any particular exhibit. Some individuals walked slowly along the displays, glancing mostly at objects at eye level and occasionally venturing deeper exploration of their contents. Rarely did they complement their viewing of the floor cases with a comparison and detailed inspection of individual exhibits in the wall presses. Conversations between foreign visitors, comments in the visitors' book and personal communication with museum professionals confirmed this difficulty.

On the other hand, visitors often paused and stepped back to admire the vista over the tall wall displays or to photograph their contents, suggesting that they had visual appeal on a different level, as if they were architectural or decorative features.

As such, these results should not be interpreted as negative. In fact, the puzzlement raised by the object-dense cabinets, together with the strong aesthetic appeal of the gallery, promoted a novel mode of exploration among visitors: a journey of visual discovery and amazement. Moreover, this display method allows children and wheelchair users to comfortably view objects on the same basis as any other visitor.

Floor cases are of two types, upright and tabletop. Visitor behaviour differed. Many exhibits in the upright cases are large and eye-catching, and can be seen from a distance. In contrast, artefacts in the table-top displays are smaller and

---

14   Duncan 1995.
15   Sloan 2003.

less visually attractive and can only be seen on close inspection. The upright stand-alone cases and their contents can be experienced in three dimensions as an integral part of the room, while objects in the table-top displays are separated from the room in a two-dimensional environment. Thus, these exhibits encouraged a more intimate viewing experience.

More people stopped at the upright displays, but for shorter periods, while the table-top displays attracted the more engaged people. People could lean on these horizontal cases: a comfortable position for prolonged viewing. Both types of cabinets had a lower-level section where exhibits were on show. Few adult visitors paid attention to these, although small children enjoyed the selection of curious objects.

6.3.4   The Attraction of the Visual

In general, the horizontal floor displays in the *Ancient scripts* section attracted more detailed viewing than the wall presses, particularly the central section of Case 15, with a selection of Babylonian seals, and Case 16, containing, among other exhibits, an Egyptian funerary statuette. The colourful ceramics on the eastern wall presses were also magnets for visitors, overcoming their tendency to focus on items in their path. This might be due to the objects' central position in the cases, but their vibrant and interesting appearance must be a factor. The observation that after an initial glance, visitors neglected a prominently positioned yet visually unattractive object supports this hypothesis. The preference for visually attractive objects is often discussed in museum literature. For example, Baxandall writes that a key condition for the effective visual display of objects rests in the pleasing appearance of the things.[16] Evidence in support of the importance of visual characteristics in attracting and holding attention emerged from the research carried out in the *Egyptian death and afterlife: mummies* gallery, also at the British Museum (Chapter 8), and during the assessment of the *Hands on* desks (Chapter 9).

6.4   UNDERSTANDING OBJECTS IN THE BRITISH GALLERIES AT THE V&A

The British galleries in the V&A were opened in 2001. The suite of 15 rooms on two floors display the best of British art and design from 1500 to 1900 in a variety of ways, including study rooms, interactive kiosks and discovery areas, as well as object-rich visual displays.

The focus of the research at the V&A was Room 123: *Understanding objects*, one of the suite of British galleries. This exhibition was on Level 4 of the museum, which

---

16   Baxandall 1991: 39.

Figure 6.7   V&A British galleries, Room 123. Northern section (left): *Queen Victoria* displays. Southern section (right): *Understanding objects*, with the computer interactive on curatorial registration marks
Source: © F. Monti/Trustees of the Victoria & Albert Museum.

received fewer visitors than the lower levels of these galleries.[17] The gallery could be accessed from galleries 122 and 125c, which lay to each side of it (Figure 6.8).

Room 123 was conceptually and spatially divided into two parts by a large, centrally positioned display unit. The northern section illustrated aspects of the long reign of Queen Victoria, through a traditional object–label interpretative scheme (Figure 6.7, left). There was a showcase with objects, historical footage and two centrally placed free-standing showcases with striking exhibits. Public toilets and stairs were also accessed from this space.

The southern portion of Room 123 employed a variety of interactive media to encourage visitors to look closely at objects and to find out what can be learnt from handling and observing them, an approach used in several places in the British galleries (Figure 6.7, right). Here visitors could examine a chest of drawers; learn from interaction with lift-the-flap labels the curatorial techniques of object analysis; look for clues that would reveal a chair to be a fake; detect traces of conservation treatments on porcelain with the aid of ultraviolet illumination; and use an interactive screen to learn about trademarks. A large central display unit, exploring the theme of collecting, physically separated the two sections (Figure 6.8). We observed that the two areas promoted very distinct behaviours due to their content and means of interpretation. In the Victorian displays, visitors predominantly looked at objects and read labels, while in the *Understanding objects* area, hands-on activities were more general and the objects less striking.

6.4.1   Analysis of Visitor Movement Patterns

Flow count to measure movement types   This exercise was conducted from 1.00 to 2.00 pm during a weekday. Both the museum and the gallery were busy at the

17   McManus 2003.

time. During the hour, 133 people walked in and out of Room 123. Of these, 64 (48 per cent) engaged in at least a minimum level of interaction with the displays and 69 (52 per cent) passed rapidly through the space using the shortest route, some to access the toilets or to take the lift.

Tracking visitor movements   Twenty visitors were tracked. Sixteen (80 per cent) explored either the northern or the southern section of the gallery, indicating that the room was perceived and used as two separate spaces. This split was probably due to a centrally positioned showcase which effectively divided, in visual, spatial and subject-matter terms, the southern *Understanding objects* section from the displays about Queen Victoria.

Static snapshots   The placement of 37 individuals was tracked in this exercise. The prominent model of the Albert Memorial and the centrepiece commemorating the Golden Jubilee were popular among visitors. The film footage from the funeral of Queen Victoria (in the case opposite the eastern door) was another focal point. Among those who visited the *Understanding objects* section, the *Protecting new designs* display was popular. The attraction of these centrally displayed and eye-catching objects demonstrated the attraction of visually pleasing exhibits and the influence of a prominent location within the gallery.

6.4.2   Structured Observation of Visitor Behaviour

The sample for the structured observation using the gallery observation sheet was a total of 40 visitors. Of these, 26 were female (65 per cent) and 14 were male (35 per cent). Apart for the 70–79 age group, visitors from all adult age ranges were represented in the sample, with most visitors aged between 50 and 59.

The time spent in the gallery varied: half the visitors looked at exhibits for two to six minutes, while half spent from seven to 11 minutes, a considerable time for a gallery in a popular museum. Visitors who spent longer in the room were those who explored both sections of the gallery. Shorter viewings were recorded in relation to eye-catching objects or exhibits in the visitor's path, which suggested that prominent and visual objects successfully draw the viewer's attention, but do not necessarily hold it for long.

6.4.3   The V&A *Understanding Objects* Gallery: What We Observed

Exhibit layout and visitor movement   In this gallery overall, two viewing patterns were prevalent among the 40 visitors observed, depending on the point of entry (Figure 6.8). Visitors coming from Room 122 tended to focus on the gallery section at their right. Other studies have found that 'if all other factors are equal, people will

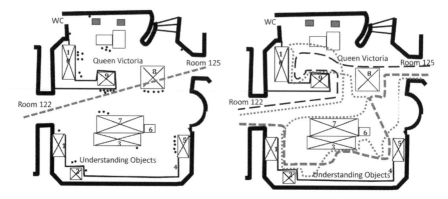

1 *Examining objects* flip-books **2** Antique armchair with labels **3** Examine a chest of drawers **4** Computer interactive & handling collection on registration marks **5** *Protecting New Design* display **6** UV box to show repairs on ceramics **7** *Antique Collecting* display **8** Model of the Albert memorial **9** Gold centrepiece **10** *Queen Victoria Celebrations* display with video

Figure 6.8   **V&A British galleries, Room 123: layout and space syntax. Left: the dotted line indicates the conceptual and spatial sub-division of the gallery; the static snapshot of visitors is represented by black dots. Right: recurrent movement patterns**

Source: © F. Monti/S. Keene.

turn to the right'. However, Bitgood points out that the design of the space is a key factor in determining whether or not turning right occurs.[18] Others, entering from Room 125c, were attracted by the space immediately visible (as in the British Museum *Enlightenment* gallery), a trend this time reinforced by the presence of the video within the *Queen Victoria Celebrations* display (Figure 6.8). This was on the main line of sight for the flow from Room 125c. A minority of visitors (four out of the 20 tracked) explored both sections of the gallery irrespective of their point of access.

What sort of interaction?   Three dominant interaction patterns emerged among visitors: traditional object and label viewing (10 out of 40), hands-on interaction with some of the interpretative media (20) and object-label exploration with additional viewing of the video footage of Queen Victoria (a further 10).

About half of the visitors used mainly sight to engage with the gallery content: close object inspection, reading labels and looking at photographs, pictures and historical film footage. The other visitors used their physical and tactile senses, exploring the gallery's hands-on activities and interactions.

---

18   Bitgood 1995; 2006: 466; Dean 1994: 51; Melton 1935.

It was noted that visitors younger than 40 were more inclined towards hands-on interaction and new communication media (such as touch-screens, hands-on displays and lift-up labels). Older individuals were more likely to use the traditional display formats. This finding may be attributed to the subjects of the two areas; the Victorian topic may be more interesting to mature visitors, while the theme of the *Understanding objects* section may have greater universal appeal. Or younger visitors may have felt the need to increase their understanding, while older people had already sufficient knowledge of the subjects or may have regarded the practical activities as trivial.

Those who engaged in explorative and physical activities spent longer in the exhibition space. Hands-on interaction, as opposed to a visual viewing style, seems to correlate with a closer inspection of the objects on display, or at any rate it is more time-consuming. Interview surveys would help to clarify this.

Degrees of interaction   Visitors' interactions with both displays and interactive media were analysed as:

- visual – a passing glance;
- explorative – an action to find out what something is;
- discovery – an interaction which results in a discovery of something about the object;
- immersive – a deeper engagement, during which the visitor starts making links between objects and concepts explored.

Overall, 32 uses of exhibits were observed (Figure 6.9), varying according to the characteristics of the visitor and the nature of the exhibit. Discovery and immersive interactions were noted in relation to the chest of drawers, the lift-the-flap labels and the footage of Queen Victoria. In line with the observations of other researchers, these findings suggest that:

- visitors are attracted to familiar objects;[19]
- people favour a simple intuitive and ergonomic design that conveys possible actions, and that is in close proximity to the exhibit;[20]
- people enjoy taking an active role in the meaning-making process;[21]
- curiosity plays an important part in our choices of what information to attend to;[22]
- moving images and videos are a medium people respond to positively, perhaps because they are a familiar aspect of our lives.[23]

---

19 Csikszentmihalyi and Hermanson 1995: 37; Hood 1993: 718.
20 McManus 2003: 4–5; Morris Hargreaves McIntyre 2003: 12.
21 Morris Hargreaves McIntyre 2003: 2.
22 Csikszentmihalyi and Hermanson 1995: 36.
23 McManus 2003: 6.

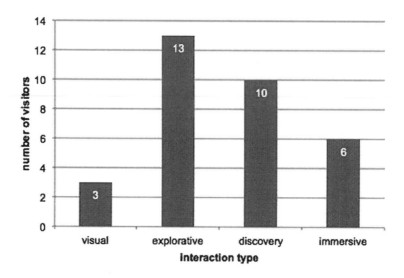

**Figure 6.9   V&A British galleries, Room 123: number of visitors using
the interactive exhibits, observed in the *Understanding objects*
section**

Source: © F. Monti/S. Keene.

Only one visitor out of the 40 observed used the *Protecting new designs*
computer interactive. Visitor research in other British galleries rooms indicates
a satisfactory rate of use of interactives.[24] Possible reasons for the low use of
this interactive include a lack of guidance on the relationship of the screen to
the adjacent objects; the design of the screen, which does not readily convey its
use and purpose; and its obscure site within the gallery. Or perhaps its subject
matter (copyright and patenting) is not very appealing. Additionally, the sample
for this exercise was of adult visitors; younger audiences or social visitors may
have found it more interesting. No-one compared the interactive with the objects
it related to in the nearby showcase.

In contrast, the chest of drawers exhibit was popular with visitors, who seemed
to enjoy this type of activity, especially when with friends or relatives. The
familiarity of the object doubtless adds to its appeal. This exhibit could be
identified as an example of the constructivist approach to learning, where the
viewer creates personal knowledge from the exhibit and the process itself is a
constructivist act.[25]

24   Morris Hargreaves McIntyre 2003: 5.
25   Hein 1995, 1998.

Figure 6.10   The *Music room* in the Horniman Museum: vista from the gallery entrance

Source: © S. Keene, courtesy of the Trustees of the Horniman Museum.

6.5   THE *MUSIC ROOM* IN THE HORNIMAN MUSEUM

Our third gallery was the Horniman Museum *Music room* (Figure 6.10). This South London museum has important ethnography and natural history collections and galleries,[26] and an outstanding collection of musical instruments. The *Music room* is in a new part of the museum and displays some 1,600 instruments from around the world. As described by Vitmayer, this gallery 'draws on the rich diversity of the collection's musical instruments, and the music of the people who made them'.[27] Ironically, to some poignantly, musical instruments in displays are as silent as any, but the Horniman has found ways of enabling them to be heard.

The gallery is articulated in three sections: *Rhythms of life*, *Ideal sound* and *Listen to order* (Figure 6.12). Three sound benches, where samples of music can be listened to, are situated in front of an impressive wall showcase with an array of musical instruments arranged according to how they produce sound (*Listen to order*, Figure 6.11). This area was the focus of the investigation.

---

26   Horniman Museum website: www.horniman.ac.uk [accessed 16 July 2012].
27   Birley 2002: 3.

Figure 6.11   The *Music room* in the Horniman Museum: the three sound benches. The *Listen to order* display is on the right, along the whole length of the wall

Source: S. Keene, courtesy of the Trustees of the British Museum.

BOX 6.1   THE SOUND BENCHES IN THE HORNIMAN MUSEUM MUSIC ROOM

The sound benches are an exceptionally enjoyable interactive design that is immediately understood by every visitor, young or old (Figure 6.11). Each is white, with a bench long enough for one or more users to sit on. Only one person can operate the display, although more than one can listen. The 'screen' is projected from above. Using a large easy-to-handle scroll wheel, one can scroll along a sequence of musical instruments corresponding to the array of displayed instruments in front of the bench. Using large intuitive buttons, one can select a musical instrument and hear music played from it, or one like it, through headphones or speakers embedded in the table – music can often be heard in the gallery. Often this is in the context of a field recording made in the original source country, or of a band or musical group. While one listens, more information is displayed about the instrument or musicians. The benches are not an add-on interactive, but are an integral part of the display.

6.5.1   Analysis of Visitor Movement Patterns

Flow count to measure movement types   As this gallery is a self-contained space off a central atrium, it was assumed that those entering the exhibition would do so as a deliberate choice. Indeed, preliminary observation confirmed that almost

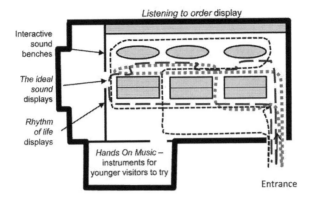

Figure 6.12 **The *Music room* in the Horniman Museum: plan showing the three display sections: *Listen to order*, *Ideal sound*, *Rhythms of life* and the sound benches, with examples of the three observed movement patterns**

Source: © S. Keene, courtesy of the Trustees of the British Museum.

all the visitors to the *Music room* spent at least two minutes with the exhibition. As such, it was not necessary to count those viewing the displays versus those walking through, as everyone engaged significantly with the exhibits.

Tracking visitors' movements   Over a two-hour period, 18 people were tracked. Fifteen out of 18 visitors followed the viewing pattern suggested by the exhibition layout, commencing their visit with the *Rhythms of life*, moving on to *Ideal sound* and then looking at the *Listening to order* showcase (Figure 6.12). Three out of 18 people went straight to the sound benches after entering the gallery. This may demonstrate a previous acquaintance with the sound benches, curiosity about them, a personal preference for interactive activities or simply a wish to sit down while viewing the display in front of the benches – only visitor interviews would ascertain this.

Static snapshots of visitor placing   For this study, 54 visitors were observed. Although the three sound benches were not immediately visible when entering the room, their popularity clearly emerged. At any time, each of the three sound benches was occupied by at least one person. The viewer can either use the desk as a multimedia catalogue, with information on the objects in the display in front of them, or otherwise explore the images, music and text independently from the showcase. The videos complementing the *Rhythms of life* display also attracted and held visitors. In a similar fashion to the observations in Gallery 123 at the V&A (6.4.1), their placing just opposite the entrance was a very effective way to draw the visitor into the intended entry point of the displays.

6.5.2   Structured Observation of Visitor Behaviour

Overall, 25 visitors were assessed for this observation exercise, 11 of them female and 14 male. Across the age ranges, there was an almost equal distribution, with the largest group (eight out of the 25 visitors) aged 50–59.

6.5.3   The *Horniman* Music Room: What We Observed

Exhibit layout and visitor movement   This gallery is self-contained and more compact with a less complex layout than the other two galleries. It is easier for the visitor to see what is on offer when they enter through the door from the atrium. As such, nearly all followed the curators' intended viewing plan, with the exception of the three individualls who headed straight for the sound benches.

Time in the gallery   Judged by the time visitors spent in it, it was evident that the gallery promoted longer visits. The minimum time visitors spent (four to five minutes) was high in comparison to the previous studies. As observed above, it was assumed that most visitors intended specifically to visit it, while the other galleries are on main circulation routes. The duration of visits varied considerably, from four to 93 minutes. Six out of 25 visitors spent 10 or 11 minutes with the displays. Impressively long viewings of 30–31 minutes (three out of five visitors) to a maximum of 93 minutes (one person) were also recorded. If we look collectively at visitors who spent more than 20 minutes in the gallery (10 out of 25), the average visit time was 39 minutes. These long visits can be read as an indication of a high incidence of a specialist audience within the sample, but alternatively the data can suggest a successful exhibition design. Further evaluation would need to be carried out in order to understand this better.

What sort of interactions?   Variations in behaviour were detected between weekday and weekend samples. Different environmental conditions led to particular uses of the gallery and of the sound benches. During the week, when numerous school groups animated the exhibition and the sound benches were bustling with excited children, a lower incidence of single adults was detected. On Sunday morning, however, single adults were observed undertaking thorough viewings of the exhibition.

Diverse gallery conditions also influenced the rate of recurrence and type of interaction with the sound benches recorded among adult visitors (Figure 6.13). Although, overall, 64 per cent of the sample interacted with the sound benches, a comparison of weekday and weekend behaviours indicated greater use among Sunday adults (75 per cent of this sample), when the gallery was quiet, against the 59 per cent recorded among weekday visitors. The intensity of the engagement also differed similarly. Sunday visitors developed either a discovery (50 per cent) or immersive (50 per cent) engagement, while weekday visitors showed a distribution across the different interaction ranges, with a prevalence of explorative engagements (four out of eight occurrences) (Figure 6.13). These results suggest a correlation

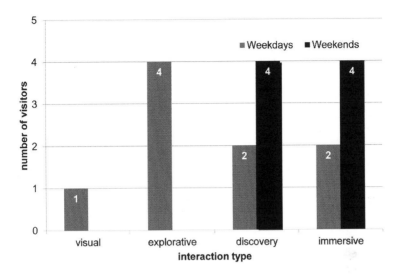

Figure 6.13   The *Music room* in the Horniman Museum: sound benches:
visitor interactions on weekdays and weekends (n=15)
Source: © F. Monti/S. Keene.

between environmental circumstances and depth of interaction among adult visitors, a finding supported in the study of *Egyptian death and afterlife: mummies* at the British Museum (below, Chapter 8). Busy and noisy gallery conditions deterred single adults from using the interactive benches, and even when they did engage with them, it was less intensively than at weekends.

Degrees of interaction   Despite the lengthy visits to the gallery overall, visitors did not always completely view the object-dense *Listen to order* showcase. This may have been due to the classificatory display, to a degree of visual monotony or to its specialist content. Also, there are other competing exhibits in this area, such as the sound benches and the visually captivating *Ideal sound* wall case display of glittering instruments (Figures 6.10 and 6.11).

Our observations at the Horniman Museum highlighted the importance of easy-to-use interactives designed to draw and hold a variety of users for extended times and to promote interest in the objects on display. They also suggested that object-based displays (as opposed to displays centred on ideas), presented in a visually appealing way, have a strong attracting, holding and communicating power for visitors.[28] Our observations suggested that offering several sensory dimensions (sound, vision and touch) in exhibitions can be an effective strategy.

---

28   Bitgood 2000: 2.

6.6   APPLYING THE CONCEPTS: WHAT WE LEARNED

Using the key concepts (space syntax, design idioms, beauty and usability, flow, object biographies and learning models and styles) as tools to evaluate and assess these three very different galleries assured us that they can be applied in practice. We found that they gave us considerable understanding of why visitors were behaving in certain ways and some of the reasons why they reacted as they did to the various exhibitions and exhibits: to the gallery layout and space, types of exhibit and interactives and hence curatorial intentions and design decisions.

However, the potential of the concepts is not yet fully realised; a more complete understanding of people's emotional and cognitive responses and the reasons behind the behaviours we observed could be gained by interviewing visitors as well as observing them. This particularly emerged in relation to flow, usability and learning models. Although some obvious physical indications of the outcomes of visitors' interaction with objects can be gathered from visual analysis, interesting aspects of the process of flow, usability and learning takes place only in people's minds.

This is further discussed in the following chapter, where the concepts are used as the basis for comparing the three galleries.

CHAPTER 7

CONCEPTS AND COMPARISONS:
THE THREE GALLERIES

In Chapter 6 we presented our experience of using our selected concepts as tools to analyse three famous galleries: the British Museum's *Enlightenment* gallery; the V&A's *Understanding objects* gallery, part of the suite of British galleries; and the Horniman Museum's *Music room*. In this chapter, we combine the data from the assessments and evaluation and use them in a comparative analysis of the three exhibitions. This enables a further critical consideration of the advantages and shortcomings of employing the concepts as evaluation parameters.

The research programme and research method for this stage of the research are described in Chapter 6. Concept checksheets, with scores for the degree of correlation with each concept, were used in this assessment (see the introduction to Part 1 above and see Appendix 2 for the concept checksheets). The data from the investigation are available online at www.ucl.ac.uk/silent-objects.

Below we compare the three galleries within the framework of the key concepts.

7.1   FROM ARCHITECTURE: SPACE SYNTAX

Some of the investigative procedures from space syntax theory were employed to assist us in understanding how space affects the visitor–object interaction (above, 2.3):[1]

- assessment of the characteristics of the exhibition space;
- tracking visitors' movements; and
- snapshot recordings of visitors' static placing in relation to spatial features.

The analysis diagrams for the galleries – movement tracking and visitor placement snapshots – are shown in Chapter 6 under the different galleries.

Criteria for the use and configuration of space can also be used to supplement this graphic analysis, in a similar way to the other concept criteria (Appendix 2).

---

1   Hillier and Tzortzi 2006: 282.

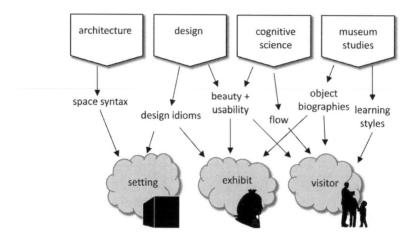

Figure 7.1   Theory, concepts and the elements of the visitor experience
Source: © F. Monti/S. Keene.

The criteria we used are those set out in 2.4 above, where the use of space syntax analysis is discussed:

- Can the spaces in the gallery be seen from the entrance(s) (vista)?
- Are all spaces integrated or are there obscure areas?
- If there is an intended path around the exhibits, is this clear? Do visitors follow it?
- Are there large prominent exhibits that dominate attention or do visitors view most of the exhibits?

Space syntax analysis even without computerised analysis did suggest the extent to which different gallery layouts influenced visitors' movement and directed them towards or away from objects in an exhibition context. In line with the results of other syntactic studies of space in museums,[2] we found that in each of the three exhibitions the configuration of space defined, to a different extent, how people moved through it. This enabled us to compare the layout of the three venues for their strengths and weaknesses. In each, key features could be identified that shaped patterns of movement.

The layout of the *Music room* in the Horniman Museum had been very effectively designed; there is a clear view of the whole gallery from the entrance and visitors generally followed the viewing paths intended by the curators (Figure 6.12). Here, the layout of the displays in the room space maximised the impact of objects; all of the spaces created around the showcases are integrated.

---

2   E.g. Choi 1999; Hillier and Tzortzi 2005; Psarra and Grajewski 2002.

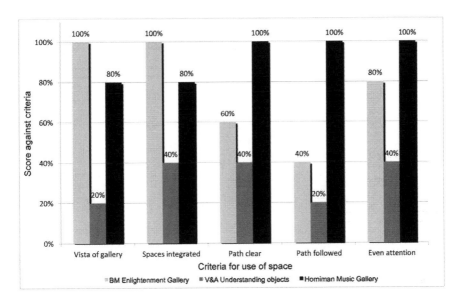

Figure 7.2   The three galleries assessed against criteria for the use of space. For scoring, see concept checksheets (per cent of maximum score)

Source: © F. Monti/S. Keene.

In contrast with the integrated spaces in the *Music room*, in the *Understanding objects* gallery (V&A), visitors perceived and explored the room as two separate sections (Figure 6.8). The positioning of a large showcase, *Antique collecting*, along the gallery's long axis confers a dual personality on the space. In particular, the southern part of the gallery is outside the axial line of sight at the eastern entrance, and consequently it is not seen by viewers entering from that direction. The colour theming in the two sections of this gallery suggests that such a spatial dichotomy was intentional, and indeed the two sections address very different subject matters. However, we observed that this configuration led to unbalanced patterns of exploration. Visitors tended to dwell longer in the integrated northern section and around eye-catching objects in prominent central positions.

In the *Enlightenment* gallery (British Museum) a different situation was observed (Figure 6.4). There is an outstanding vista of this gallery from the entrance, but visitors tend to move along the long axis of the room in a clockwise or anticlockwise direction, rather than viewing the exhibition by the seven themed sub-divisions.[3] In this gallery, the shape of the space, the lines of sight and the natural tendency

---

3   Since our observations in 2004, a large stand with an orientation panel has been installed in front of the main entrance from the Great Court. Visitors now have to choose to turn either sharply left or right on entering, and this has probably altered viewing paths.

of visitors to move in an orderly way along the perimeters of a room were stronger than the design and architectural elements that attempted to suggest a different viewing mode. The observations in both these two galleries suggested that vista is a determining factor in visitor movement patterns within a space.

7.2   FROM DESIGN: DESIGN IDIOMS

Analysis based on the main design idioms that feature in exhibition design, using concept checksheets, was used to gauge the physical qualities of the three venues (see above, Chapter 3, and Appendix 2):

- colour;
- lighting;
- text;
- use of space or juxtaposition of objects.

We focused our attention on the design and presentational elements of exhibits in relation to visitors' reactions to them. Our concern was first the broad design strategy and subsequently the individual elements of displays. We were able to identify which individual exhibits attracted and held visitors' attention for the longest time, and then to move on to understand some of the reasons for this.

7.2.1   Design Idiom: Colour

To different degrees, colour was employed in all three galleries to improve visitor encounters with objects. In the British Museum *Enlightenment* gallery, colour was used to evoke the atmosphere of the room and to enhance features of the objects on show: it was not utilised to highlight the different sections of the exhibition or to pick out recurring messages. A similar use of colour was observed in the *Music room* in the Horniman Museum. Conversely, in the V&A *Understanding objects* gallery, different colours were employed to emphasise sections of the exhibition, to evoke certain feelings, to accentuate object features and to convey messages, with the intention of facilitating viewing and narrative delivery.

7.2.2   Design Idiom: Lighting

Lighting can be used to define exhibition spaces and to highlight the texture, characteristics and quality of an object. Earlier visitor studies in the V&A British galleries recommended that if gallery lighting were improved, it would increase visitor satisfaction rates.[4] Our study found that the *Understanding objects* gallery was well lit in design terms. There, light was used to accentuate exhibits'

---

4   McManus 2003: 5.

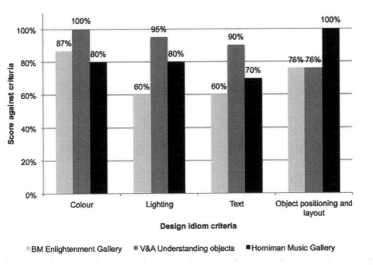

Figure 7.3   The three galleries assessed against criteria for the use of design idioms – colour, lighting, text and object layout. For scoring, see concept checksheets (per cent of maximum score)
Source: © F. Monti/S. Keene.

characteristics, while still respecting their conservation requirements. Equally successful was the *Music room* in the Horniman Museum, although there was no additional lighting for dark areas. In the *Enlightenment* gallery, this idiom was instrumental in re-creating the atmosphere of the past; the natural light filtering through the high windows complemented the achievements of the artificial illumination system. This finding illustrates how the intensity and direction of daylight within a gallery can be controlled effectively to create different effects in an exhibition and to catch the eye of the viewer.[5] However, despite this attention to lighting design, objects in the *Enlightenment* gallery were occasionally not fully visible, their characteristics were not enhanced and no additional lighting was provided to facilitate viewing. Perhaps this is inevitable given the design strategy.

7.2.3   Design Idiom: Text

Exhibition text needs to be readable, visible and designed to enrich the visitor's experience. In this respect, the *Understanding objects* gallery offered well-designed texts, with an adequate register (grammar and style) and without using specialist terminology. The information was also imaginatively put across by using visual images, yet even so, the key messages of the exhibition could have been clearer. In the Horniman *Music room* the exhibition concepts were effectively delivered.

5   E.g. Belcher 1991: 127.

The graphics of the text panels and labels were clear and sharp, but occasionally the length of the text and the use of specialist terms may have been an obstacle to comprehension. The different sections and themes within the *Enlightenment* gallery were presented on elegant black panels with text written in golden characters. Although this practice is not condemned in the literature,[6] a more striking contrast between background and text would be more legible, without compromising the stylish visual effect. The text was too long at times, but the limited use of jargon was remarkable considering the subject matter. However, the key messages of the exhibition could have been communicated more unequivocally.

7.2.4   Design Idiom: Object Placement and Juxtapositions

Objects can be juxtaposed to bring out some of the cultural context of exhibits. Overall, this design idiom appeared to have been effectively implemented in all three venues; objects were successfully combined to assist visitors to create narratives. At the V&A *Understanding objects* gallery in particular, artefacts were meticulously displayed to enhance their key characteristics. However, a different positioning of striking and large exhibits (such as the centrally placed model of the Albert Memorial) could have improved this gallery's circulation patterns, as we found in using space syntax analysis. In the British Museum *Enlightenment* gallery, smaller objects, or objects with inscriptions, were occasionally not fully visible. An upright position would render their key characteristics clear to all. The *Music room* in the Horniman Museum, where objects were just as dense as in the *Enlightenment* gallery, was an example of good practice in its use of space and display strategies: the exhibits were visible, shown at optimum angles and key artefacts were placed in prominent positions to assist in the delivery of messages.

7.3   FROM COGNITIVE SCIENCE: BEAUTY AND USABILITY

A design that combines aesthetic appeal and functionality is the most likely to engender rewarding experiences among its users.[7] The criteria we found to analyse these elusive gallery qualities are shown in the concept checksheets (Appendix 2). We also used structured observations of visitors' behaviour. This exercise facilitated a valuable overall understanding of the display strategy in relation to aesthetic appeal and usability.

Despite the difficulty of creating exhibits which are simultaneously functional and pleasing to the eye, the evaluation indicated that each of the three exhibitions had a distinctive and visually attractive design capable of engaging visitors with objects, in different ways and to different degrees. Was their success with visitors partly to

---

6   Serrell 1996.
7   Norman 2002: 42.

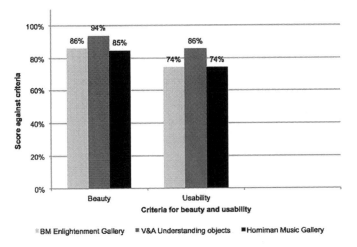

Figure 7.4   The three galleries assessed against criteria for beauty and usability. For scoring, see concept checksheets (per cent of maximum score)

Source: © F. Monti/S. Keene.

be ascribed to their capacity to trigger an emotional response to their appearance? Does this reaction in turn affect how visitors think and elaborate information?[8]

This could explain why individuals, notwithstanding evident occasional frustration towards some display elements, spend a considerable amount of time interacting with them. In the example of the wall presses in the *Enlightenment* gallery in the British Museum, it may be that the overall atmosphere and the visual qualities of the gallery affected their cognitive processes and their attitude towards the displays. On the other hand, the reverential attitude that was observed could be a response to the 'temple of culture' feel of this grand space at the heart of a highly respected institution. A follow-up evaluation commissioned by the British Museum indicated that the gallery 'creates a powerful impression with the majority of visitors, irrespective of their level of knowledge about the subject matter' even if 'the purpose of presenting the collection as it would have been in the nineteenth century is lost on most visitors'.[9]

Visitors appreciate exhibits where the intuitive design makes them easy and practical to use. This was demonstrated by the high success rate (in terms of number and duration of interactions) of the sound benches in the *Music room* in the Horniman Museum and by the chest of drawers in the *Understanding objects*

8   Norman 2004.
9   British Museum 2005.

gallery in the V&A. Conversely, when usability considerations are subordinated to visual impact, such as with the wall presses in the *Enlightenment* gallery, this is more challenging and individuals have to find personal ways of interacting with the displays. Despite some visitors' frustration with the lack of interpretation in the wall cabinets (expressed to the volunteers at the *Hands on* desk and in the comments book), many people were observed contemplating the displays for their general aesthetic impact (beauty): looking at the wall cases from a distance, scanning lower and upper portions and taking photographs, rather than focusing on objects as corollaries to the themes in the floor cases as the curators had intended (usability).[10]

From a visitor-focused perspective, any interaction with the exhibition environment is a positive outcome, even when it is not as intended by the museum. But, if the museum prefers to avoid its planned message being distorted, a degree of guidance is advisable when unusual interpretation or low-usability design is employed. Following our research exercise, the British Museum prepared information sheets that guided visitors in viewing the wall presses and offered information on the objects they contained, without compromising the visual appearance of the room. These were a good example of a symbiotic marriage of usability and beauty.

7.4   FROM COGNITIVE SCIENCE: FLOW

The state of flow is a personal condition, characterised by focused concentration, complete immersion in the experience or activity and a distorted sense of time, within which self-awareness is temporary lost.[11] Flow theory was selected for its potential to explore and identify display solutions to persuade the visitor to investigate an object (Stage 3 in the visitor–object interaction model).

In this evaluation, the flow-inducing character of the exhibitions was measured against the principles that characterise experiences likely to promote flow states:

- communicate clear goals;
- match activities to the level of skills of visitors;
- promote a high level of focus in the visitor as their response to the degree of demand of the activity.[12]

This exercise enabled a correspondence to be traced between flow-type experiences and duration of interaction. The principal observations are discussed below.

---

10   Sloan 2004: 6.
11   Csikszentmihalyi 1988.
12   Csikszentmihalyi 1997.

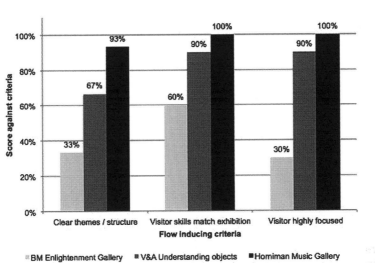

Figure 7.5   The three galleries: scores against criteria for their potential to induce flow. For scoring, see concept checksheets (per cent of maximum score)

Source: © F. Monti/S. Keene.

The data suggested that, of the three venues, the displays in the *Music room* in the Horniman Museum were the most likely to promote a flow state (Figure 7.5). We noted that a guide to the gallery was placed on the wall next to the entrance (however, research elsewhere suggests that although visitors like to have panels available, they actually take little notice of them.[13] Although direction and feedback on the use of the sound benches was not provided, their simple and effective design made them a highly intuitive and enjoyable experience. They appealed to a very wide range of visitor groups, from schoolchildren to pensioners. Visitors can, according to their knowledge, skills and motivation, truly use this interpretative medium for a better appreciation of the displays, although the association between the sound benches and the long wall of displayed musical instruments visible in front of them could be more strongly indicated. It was noted that when the gallery was busy, conditions made it difficult to reach a state of total absorption in the activity and interaction times were shorter.

The V&A *Understanding objects* gallery included a range of different activities, thus catering for a wide audience. Goals were clearly stated for the majority of interactive exhibits. Feedback regarding the duration and nature of interactions was offered for users. An exception was observed for the computer interactive *Date a design*, which was unsuccessful with visitors. According to our analysis, it

---

13   Slack, Francis and Edwards 2011: 157.

would have been more usable and popular with a clear explanation of its purpose, a user-friendly interface and a close association with the objects it interpreted. Such a distance between interpretative device and object is one of the common pitfalls of interactive-rich galleries.[14] Proximity to the eye-catching and user-friendly chest of drawers was another reason for the neglect of the computer interactive (see Figure 6.8, above, for the layout of this gallery). In the competition for visitors' attention, the weaker element is often overlooked.[15] The design of the space was successful in creating a number of secluded corners where individuals who venture away from the main visit path could spend significant undisturbed time with the exhibits if those were of interest to them.

The assessment of the *Enlightenment* gallery indicated that some of the necessary prerequisites for flow engagement were missing. The sparse conceptual and topographical guidance could make viewing the gallery seem an overwhelming task, perceived as beyond one's skills. The homogeneous label and object display approach could, at times, result in a lapse in concentration. Occasional overcrowding and noise hindered deep interaction. As a result, the overall flow inducing properties of the gallery were lower than in the two other venues (a 42 per cent score against the maximum). These results, however, contrast with the finding that the *Enlightenment* gallery was a place capable of enabling contemplative experience (7.3). Such an inconsistency indicates a possible limitation of an evaluation method exclusively focused on measuring flow potential; such an isolated approach would not be advisable because it would fail to detect other satisfactory and meaningful types of experience, which are not quantifiable in terms of the four flow parameters.

7.5   LEARNING STYLES

Education, or learning, models apply to the provider: the manner in which an instructive experience is provided (or, at least, offered). In museum literature they are usually understood as didactic, behaviourist, discovery and constructivist.[16] Personal learning styles, in contrast, apply to the individual: how each prefers to learn. The style may be analytical, common sense, experiential or imaginative. We analysed learning models and corresponding learning styles in each of the three galleries, with particular reference to efficacy in setting the conditions for an enriching interaction with objects. Each exhibition was assessed using the concept checksheets, where the criteria are listed (Appendix 2).

Assessed against the criteria for learning modes and styles listed in the concept checksheets (see also above, Table 5.3), the *Understanding objects* gallery in the

---

14   Morris Hargreaves McIntyre 2003: 13.
15   Bitgood 2000: 34.
16   Hein 1995.

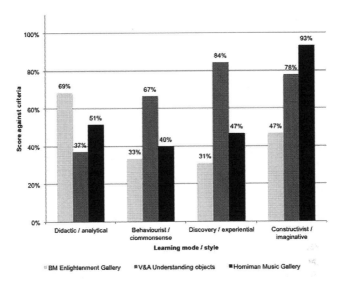

Figure 7.6   The three galleries: scores against criteria for education modes and learning styles. For scoring, see concept checksheets (per cent of maximum score)

Source: © F. Monti/S. Keene.

V&A and the *Music room* in the Horniman Museum both scored highly (78 and 93 per cent respectively) against the characteristics of the constructivist model: there was substantial identification with Hein's paradigm.[17] The V&A *Understanding objects* gallery was even more closely identified with the discovery learning style/experiential learning due to the mostly successful interactives included. However, the *Understanding objects* gallery also rated highly against the behaviourist and discovery models, consistent with other indications that it was suited to a wide range of visitors. A high score against more than one learning style is symptomatic of a lively and open exhibition approach, of promotion of hands-on interaction with the exhibits and of an evident wish to make visitors a participatory element of the space.

Although at first sight we assumed that the *Enlightenment* gallery in the British Museum followed the traditional didactic model, the results of our analysis suggested otherwise. The gallery did not score highly against any learning model, the didactic model being slightly dominant, arising from the object labels provided in the horizontal cases. The presence of the *Hands on* desk and the Rosetta Stone facsimile conferred on the space some of the connotations of the constructivist model, but with a score of 47 per cent, this identification was not as strong as in the other two galleries. The reason for the weak identification with any learning

---

17   Hein 1995, 1998.

model was the comparative lack of interpretative information on the objects in the gallery or on the organising principles behind the arrangement of the cases and their contents. However, this does not mean that the gallery was unsuccessful with visitors: not every individual has educational motives for a museum visit.

The *Enlightenment* gallery would be the one that offered the most productive experience to analytical learners. This was the one that promoted individual contemplation and would be particularly appealing to those visitors who assimilate by thinking and observing, and favour interpretation that offers facts and sequential ideas. Overall, the analytical style does not encourage social interaction among visitors in groups. However, when the *Hands on* desk in this gallery was available, it offered scope for other types of learning style, particularly experiential and imaginative (discovery and constructivist exhibit styles). This is an example of how the educational model of a gallery or exhibition can be broadened to appeal to a wider range of visitors.

The findings for the V&A *Understanding objects* gallery testify to the museum's desire to provide for all learning styles; due to the provision of interactive exhibits, this gallery would be slightly preferred by experiential learners (100 per cent, with high scores against the other learning styles).

Common-sense learners might prefer the *Music room* in the Horniman Museum. By using the sound benches and other interactives, they would be able to test out personal theories on an individual level.

Visitors who prefer to acquire knowledge imaginatively would also like the *Understanding objects* gallery, but would enjoy the *Music room* as well. They prefer feeling and watching, listening and sharing ideas, and favour interpretation that encourages social interaction, along with a search for personal meaning.

7.6   THE KEY CONCEPTS: A CRITICAL LOOK

All of the concepts were useful in understanding visitors' interaction with galleries and objects. However, we noted some reservations and pointers to the even more effective application of them.

7.6.1   Space Syntax

Space syntax, applied in the practical form that we used, using gallery diagrams to record the main visitor paths and static snapshots to record where visitors congregated, was a very effective way of analysing the effects of gallery layout on visitor behaviour.

7.6.2   Design Idioms

Design idioms were also effective, especially in analysing the reasons for visitors' engagement with particular exhibits. We found that the effects of colour, lighting, text and object placement and juxtaposition could be assessed using our detailed checksheets.

7.6.3   Beauty and Usability

We assessed these concepts through the checksheets and also by structured observation of visitor behaviour (Appendices 1 and 2). Although these concepts are elusive, we felt confident that we had assessed these effects by this means.

7.6.4   Flow

Flow states keep the visitor with an object for a longer period. For example, the prolonged and intense visits recorded in the *Music room* (above, 6.5.3) correlated with the high flow potential measured in the gallery. However, not all lengthy interactions are synonymous with this condition; extensive viewing of individual exhibits may be due to other factors, such as a visitor's personal recollections and interests. In addition, different intensities of flow, as measured by observation of behaviour and duration of interaction, were observed to correlate with the number of flow conditions met by the exhibit. These findings are significant as they suggest that if the exhibits are conceived with the four flow-defining principles in mind, they may promote longer and deeper visitor interactions with the objects.

However, we consider that the assessment of flow state was only partially satisfactory. Our method comprised observations of visitor behaviour (Appendix 1) and an assessment of the gallery against predetermined criteria (Appendix 2). Visitor observations allowed inferences to be drawn on the ability of the displays to promote flow by observing the length and characteristics of the interaction, but they did not clarify what was happening in people's minds. It is true that observations of the apparent allocation of attention or direction of gaze (by tracking movement patterns within the gallery, counting the number and measuring the duration of stops at exhibits) are, according to Csikszentmihalyi, the father of flow theories,[18] valid for identifying flow. Observation techniques similar to ours have in the past been claimed to identify visitor attention patterns.[19]

Despite this, we felt that to be certain on the occurrence of flow states, there needed to be direct evidence on the nature of visitors' responses. For example, visitor engagement with displays could be explored using personal narrative essays. This

---

18   Csikszentmihalyi 1978.
19   E.g. Harvey et al. 1998: 605.

method was employed by Filep to assess the dimensions of flow as contributing to visitor engagement and satisfaction.[20]

7.6.5   Learning Modes and Styles

We found a similar problem with assessing the learning potential of the galleries. Observed visitor behaviour, together with the identification of the predominant educational stance of the exhibition, gave an indication of visitor responses to different display approaches. It was difficult, however, to measure the actual impact on the visitor of a specific educational stance or to assess its effect on their appreciation of objects without interviewing visitors directly.

A different issue with learning evaluation also emerged. In the course of the evaluation, it became evident that the concept of educational models did not allow for other equally rewarding types of interaction. Although under the impetus of funding agencies much energy is devoted to sourcing, measuring and encouraging learning outcomes in museum visits,[21] learning is not the sole objective of visitors when they enter museums. Rather, research indicates that social, intellectual, emotional and spiritual reasons are also important drivers.[22] People can enjoy the visual contemplation of objects or spaces, as observed in the *Enlightenment* gallery (7.3), or establish emotional bonds with objects which transcend the desire to learn. It was thus decided that, since the objective was to identify the kind of object encounter which placed the visitor in the position to choose what they wanted to see, it was important to be aware of non-learning experiences as well as establishing the educational stance.

7.7   EVALUATION METHODS: VISITOR INTERVIEWS

It was at times difficult to ascertain the causes of a visitor's specific reaction to displays and interactives from observation alone; for example, the long interactions recorded at the *Music room*'s sound benches. Were they the result of a true appreciation of the information offered, or of visitors' difficulties in understanding the way the desk worked, or of experimentation with the interactive, or were people simply resting at the benches and admiring the display in front of them while listening to relaxing music?

Sometimes this could be clarified during the checksheet assessments or by practical tests of the space. Although the variety of evaluation methods provided many insights into visitor behaviour, interviews with visitors (as undertaken in

---

20   Filep 2008.

21   E.g. Bellamy and Oppenheim 2009.

22   Morris Hargreaves McIntyre 2005b: 8.

the chapters that follow) are needed to supplement the results of observations and gallery assessment.

Direct communication with visitors would enable a deeper understanding of people's emotional and cognitive states and the ways in which external factors affect them. Specifically, reports of concentration levels, perception of intellectual challenge, ability to understand the interpretation and a sense of being able to use the exhibition according to personal preferences would be valuable indicators of flow experiences.

Direct accounts from visitors would be useful to validate observations. However, they have significant disadvantages. They are expensive to undertake, difficult to analyse and intrusive to visitors, who have come to enjoy the museum. Interviews can also be misleading due to the 'halo effect', when respondents are reluctant to criticise because of their regard towards the institution and their desire to please the interviewer.[23]

We found that our observations of visitors and assessments of the galleries against criteria drawn from our five key concepts (space syntax, design idiom, beauty and usability, flow and learning styles) generated a wealth of data and deep understanding of the exhibitions and their visitors even without using these additional tools.

7.8   THE CONCEPTS AS TOOLS: THE VISITOR–OBJECT INTERACTION

This exercise demonstrated that the five concepts selected are effective tools to use to assess visitors' relationships with various aspects of galleries and exhibits. They can also be applied to address the core elements of the visitor–object interaction (visitor, object, setting) that are at the heart of this enquiry: how to make silent, unattractive objects of interest to visitors (Figure 7.7).

In particular, notions of space syntax and elements of design raised the possibility of using spatial and design characteristics to improve and facilitate visitors' encounters with inconspicuous objects (Stage 1). Ways to make people aware of the potential richness of objects (Stage 2) were derived from the assessment of the venues in terms of design idiom, and by analysing the beauty and usability character of the galleries. Design elements and the flow-generating potential of an exhibition presented clues on how to encourage object investigations (Stages 2 and 3). Finally, an assessment of the learning models behind specific exhibition solutions allowed reflection on and identification of the different communication

---

23   Orna-Ornstein 2001: 12.

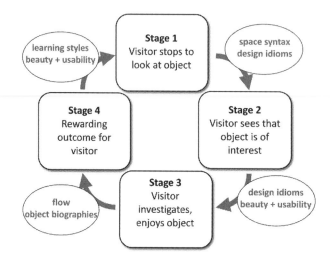

Figure 7.7   The stages in visitor interaction with exhibits and the associated concepts
Source: © F. Monti/S. Keene.

stances which place the visitor in a position to have a rewarding encounter with an object, whatever its appearance (Stage 4).

These case studies also suggested that the potential of some concepts (that is, flow, beauty and usability and learning models) would be better realised by using a variety of evaluation tools. For a comprehensive understanding of visitors' emotions and cognitive reactions to specific objects and exhibition systems, observations and gallery audits need to be complemented by direct communication with visitors.

On a conceptual level, the exercise promoted a reflection on the partial inadequacy of learning models as a meaningful tool for measuring the outcomes of museum visits. Besides the educational benefits of encounters with objects, it is necessary to consider reactions to objects that unfold in association with, or independently from, learning processes and that cannot be quantified in educational terms. Museum objects engender emotional responses, trigger memories, stimulate social interactions among individuals and are the subject of wonder and aesthetic contemplation.[24] These models need to be considered when investigating the visitor–object dimension, as they represent ways to empower museum goers by placing them in the position to decide what they wish to concentrate on during a visit and the depth and extent of the interaction.

---

24   Spalding 2002.

7.9   SIGNIFICANT FACTORS IN DISPLAYING OBJECTS

This case study confirmed that meaningful criteria can be derived from general concepts and then applied to assess display and exhibition settings. It suggested a number of factors that appear to be key to effective solutions to the display of inconspicuous objects. This informed the design of the experiments at the Petrie and Horniman Museums (Chapters 10 and 11) when the concept of object biographies is also applied.

These observations suggest that the following factors particularly influence visitor behaviour and interaction with displays:

- *Line of sight and strong display elements*
  - People pay attention to what is in their path, unless a strong visual element elsewhere diverts their gaze, something that is suggested by tracking exercises and analysis of visitor placings.
- *Strategic placing and effective exhibit design*
  - Effective design and strategic positioning can draw the attention of visitors to specific objects. The high level of visitor interest in the centrally placed exhibits, such as the model of the Albert Memorial in the *Understanding objects* gallery at the V&A, and the popularity of the neatly and effectively arranged exhibits within the *Protecting new designs* display in the same gallery evidenced this.
- *Moving images*
  - Videos and moving images can have a powerful attracting power on visitors, as noticed with the footage of Queen Victoria in the V&A *Understanding objects* gallery and in the *Music room* in the Horniman Museum.
- *Colour*
  - Striking colours are commanding visitor magnets, as seen, for example, in the choice of objects viewed at the British Museum.
- *Sound*
  - Sound enhances visual perception,[25] as demonstrated particularly by the sound benches at the Horniman Museum.
- *Graphic display of information*
  - Information presented visually, rather than as text,[26] effectively attracted and hold visitor attention, as with the sound benches at the Horniman Museum.
- *Personal involvement*
  - Visitors welcome interpretative guidance and yet they also appreciate a degree of freedom of choice which stimulates their sense of personal

---

25   Driver and Spence 2000.
26   Robertson 2002.

discovery and wonder. This was found in the reactions gathered with the *Hands on* desk in the *Enlightenment* gallery and the sound benches at the Horniman Museum.

- *Object-centred display*
  - Exhibits which centre on objects have been found to be more communicative than those which focused on abstract ideas.[27] Such displays in the three venues engendered a closer and deeper inspection of the objects and were consistent with longer visits.
  - This finding supports other studies which have found benefits in object-centred displays, as compared to idea-centred displays. In these, objects are tangible elements of a discourse and the museum is the 'vessel for the bundle of relationships enacted through each of the thousand specimens on display and in store'.[28]
- *Multi-sensory and displays using varied media*
  - Displays employing a variety of interpretation media and artefact-based activities promoted long interactions across a wide range of audiences, offering a variety of different types of engagement and learning style. This was observed in the *Hands on* desk in the *Enlightenment* gallery, the *Understanding objects* space within Room 123 at the V&A and the visual and audio experience offered by the sound benches at the Horniman Museum.

We tested these conclusions in the design of a number of experimental exhibits, which we will report in Chapters 10 and 11.

---

27   Jordanova 1989: 23 and 40; Peart 1984; Spalding 2002: 9.
28   Alberti 2005: 261.

CHAPTER 8

MUMMIES, OBJECTS, VISITORS AND STORIES AT THE BRITISH MUSEUM

In this chapter the practical exploration into the modes of visitor interaction with objects from Egyptian collections is taken further. The mechanisms of object selection and encounters and the extent to which people create narratives from sequences of viewed exhibits were investigated in Room 63, *Egyptian death and afterlife: mummies* at the British Museum. In this gallery there is an extreme contrast between spectacular objects and inconspicuous, silent ones. One of the older permanent galleries in the museum, it was opened in 1999. It is particularly interesting to compare the studies of this gallery with that of the *Tomb-chapel of Nebamun* gallery, which opened 10 years later in 2009 (Chapter 12).

Investigating the gallery was as much a further trial of the key concepts as an analysis of the gallery. We used space syntax diagrams (Figures 8.4 and 8.5), observation of visitor interaction (Appendix 3) and assessment of the exhibition using concept sheets, but this time supplemented with semi-structured interviews with visitors (Appendix 4 – interview questions; Appendix 5 – interview responses).

8.1 *EGYPTIAN DEATH AND AFTERLIFE: MUMMIES* (ROOM 63)

Room 63 at the British Museum is one of two adjacent Egyptian funerary rooms (Figure 8.1) colloquially known as 'the mummy galleries' that instantly arrest visitors' attention with a dazzling array of spectacular objects (Figures 8.6 and 8.7). Dedicated to the display of the British Museum's world-famous collection representing ancient Egyptian funerary customs, 41 per cent of visitors cite ancient Egypt (which will include the ground-floor galleries and the Rosetta Stone) as the main reason for their visit to the British Museum.[1]

The gallery is on the upper floor of the museum, and hence some effort is required to reach it. It is aligned on the east-west axis on which six adjacent corridor rooms trace, through their opulent displays, the development of ancient Egyptian culture.

---

1   Morris Hargreaves McIntyre 2011.

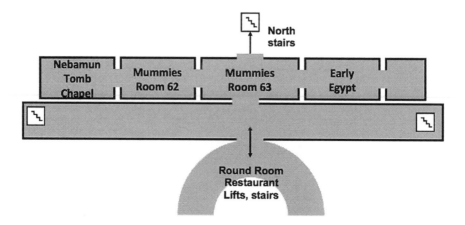

Figure 8.1   *Egyptian death and afterlife: mummies* (Room 63): location
within the British Museum upper floor
Source: © F. Monti/S. Keene.

The gallery can be accessed from four symmetrical entry points, two leading out
of this suite of galleries and two linking to the other ancient Egyptian galleries.
The displays in the 16 showcases, wall-mounted or tall and free-standing, do
not impose a specific viewing route, although the arrangement creates a central
corridor (Figure 8.2). The glass displays on either side of this corridor chart the
chronological development of funerary practices (explained in panels at the west
and east ends), while the wall cases offer a more detailed exploration of some of
the associated themes, such as mummification procedures and funerary equipment.

Although each display could be looked at individually, the careful viewer who spent
some time in the gallery would be able to understand the conceptual organisation
of the cabinets. From every access point the visitor has an impression of the whole
exhibition, but only closer inspection will reveal the content of showcases which
are off the main central route.

8.2   THE EVALUATION PROGRAMME

This study was designed to address primarily the question inherent in Stage 4 of
the visitor–object interaction model: how to set the conditions for a rewarding
object encounter.

The objectives were:

- to find out if visitors make connections between objects;
- (if they do) to better understand the mechanisms behind such connections;

Figure 8.2 **View of *Egyptian death and afterlife: mummies* (Room 63), central pathway**

Source: © Trustees of the British Museum.

- to understand the stories visitors create;
- to identify which objects best enabled visitors to make such links and the reasons for their success.

8.2.1 The Research

The evaluation took place in November 2005. Visitor interactions were observed and recorded for an hour (266 visitors) in order to note movement and viewing patterns. In the static snapshot of visitor placements, 168 visitors were observed. A total of 30 visitors were interviewed (interview questions can be found in Appendix 4 and the responses can be found in Appendix 5).

8.3 OBSERVATION OF VISITOR INTERACTION

A range of degrees of interaction with the displays was observed (Figure 8.3). Over a third of visitors (96 out of 266) walked slowly down the central corridor of the gallery, glancing at the objects in the showcases on either side: the objects adjacent to this pathway were thus the most viewed. A further third showed at least a minimum degree of interaction with objects.[2] A small minority of visitors (10) engaged relatively deeply with the exhibition, methodically viewing most of the

---

2 Minimum interaction was defined as spending 30–60 seconds viewing and demonstrating interest in at least one object.

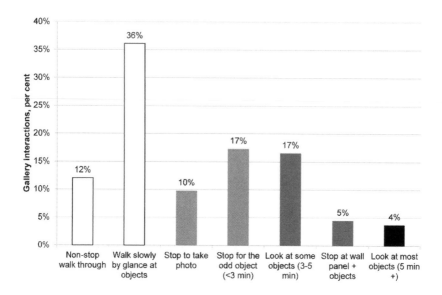

Figure 8.3   *Egyptian death and afterlife: mummies* **(Room 63): observed visitor interactions with the exhibits. Darker shading indicates longer interaction (n=266; the chart shows per cents of interactions)**

Source: © F. Monti/S. Keene.

objects, reading text and checking the information by looking at the objects again. For a similar number, wall-text panels were the focus of attention; objects were only briefly glanced at to supplement their reading. In contrast, 32 people passed through Room 63 without paying any attention to the content of the space.

User level and noise varied. When school groups were present, adults visiting the gallery on their own tended to spend less time in the room; in the afternoon or when the gallery was less busy, visitors looked at the exhibits for longer. Hence, the observation of visitor interaction was undertaken in the afternoon, when the target audience of this study (the single visitor) was more likely to be present.

8.4   VISITORS AND THE USE OF SPACE

Visitors passing through the shortest route from north to south spent less time in the gallery than those walking east to west. The tendency to enter and exit a space by the shortest possible route was also observed by McManus in a traffic pattern mapping of the V&A's British galleries.[3] However, the north-south entrances connect the general

---

3   McManus 2003: 26.

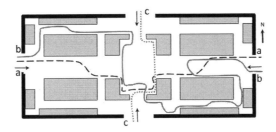

Figure 8.4 *Egyptian death and afterlife: mummies* **(Room 63): typical routes taken by visitors viewing the gallery**

Source: © F. Monti/S. Keene.

museum spaces of the north stairs and the Great Court, whereas the east-west axis is on the line of the whole suite of Egyptian galleries 61–65, so it is likely that people entering from the shorter axis were simply taking this route from one area to another.

No repeated viewing sequence was noticed. People started by looking at what they saw when they entered the space, and moved on from object to object, possibly influenced by proximity, the visual characteristics of objects, motives for their visit and their personal interests (Figures 8.4 and 8.5).

Figure 8.5 *Egyptian death and afterlife: mummies* **(Room 63): static snapshot of visitor placings**

Source: © F. Monti/S. Keene.

The static snapshot did record some exhibits as more popular (Figure 8.5). The display of skulls, like others showing human remains, was one (Figure 8.8). The *Burials at Deir el-Bahri: the priests of Amun* showcase was very successful at attracting visitors' attention, as it was on the central pathway, but less so at retaining it (Figure 8.6). The initial attraction may be ascribed to the high visual impact of the showcase, with seven imposing and striking painted wooden coffins displayed upright, as well as some smaller artefacts (i.e. two shabti[4] boxes, remains

---

4 A shabti is a small figure about 10–12 cm high, made from ceramic or stone, which represents a servant for the departed in the afterlife. They were often included in a burial in large numbers.

Figure 8.6   *Egyptian death and afterlife: mummies* **(Room 63): on the main path through the gallery, visitors often walk past cases like this one, however spectacular:** *Burials at Deir el-Bahri: the priests of Amun*

Source: © S. Keene, courtesy of the Trustees of the British Museum.

of floral garlands and a dozen shabtis). The custom of displaying coffins upright is a fictional representation drawn, consciously or unconsciously, from popular culture – traditional mummy films tend to portray them in such a position.[5] This adds to the initial visual attraction for the viewer. But once attention was gained, the text interpretation did not seem to hold it for long (14 object labels ranging from 20 to 109 words, and one 205-word text-panel with a black and white plan of a tomb). Perhaps this amount of text was perceived as too much of an effort to read. Furthermore, when viewed from close by, as they have to be, the tall wooden coffins and mummy-boards from Deir el-Bahri perhaps overwhelmed the visitor due to their size and towering appearance.

---

5   MacDonald 2003: 90.

8.5 INTERVIEWS WITH VISITORS

Thirty people were interviewed for the purpose of this study. Open questions were asked that did not prompt for any particular reply (for questions and response data, see Appendices 4 and 5 respectively). Nearly two-thirds of the interviewees were female. The sample was fairly evenly distributed across the age ranges, with rather more visitors between the ages of 25 and 34; none were under 18 or above 75. Nineteen out of 30 interviewees were visiting the museum on their own, while eight were with a partner or friend who was not present during the interview.

The sample was not representative of people with a keen interest in ancient Egypt: only two had visited the country, one for scuba diving and only one for its heritage.

8.5.1 Visitor Satisfaction with the Gallery

Table 8.1   **Interview Q1: what are your impressions of the gallery you just looked at? (Number of responses; interviewees could make more than one remark)**

Positive responses	Positively impressed	10
	Enjoyed the displays and interpretation	7
	Informative	4
	Wonderful objects	4
	Stunned by the good preservation of objects and mummies	3
	It highlights the importance of visual arts in the past	1
	Makes me want to read more on the subject	1
	Total positive responses	30
Critical responses	Crammed; difficult to follow the conceptual layout	4
	Too much written interpretation	2
	Would like to see objects in their original context	2
	Too crowded when busy	2
	Total critical responses	10
Other remarks	Sceptical about the display of human remains	3
	Critical about repatriation issues	2
All responses		55
Number of interviewees		30

More than two-thirds of the respondents said they were satisfied with Room 63, which they describe as 'a very impressive exhibition; atmospheric' and 'a wonderful and amazing gallery'. Conversely, 11 visitors were critical of the exhibition; in particular, the display of human remains or issues of repatriation and de-contextualisation of the objects were questioned by some. Four declared themselves disappointed because the object-space ratio did not feel adequate, and two explained how the crowdedness of the space constituted an obstacle to the appreciation of the collections. They were:

- overwhelmed by the amount of objects;
- couldn't understand the conceptual layout and organisation of the display cabinets; and
- because there was too much to take in.

8.5.2   What Interested Visitors the Most?

Asked 'Which things did you find most interesting? Why?', 51 different objects from the displays were mentioned; all the respondents could provide at least one example from Room 63. Four examples were from other galleries.[6]

In the context of Room 63, most interviewees expressed their interest in *mummies*, which were regarded as the focal point of the exhibition. The evaluation suggested that visitors use the term in a general sense to mean mummified human remains and anthropoid coffins. For example, the coffins from Deir el-Bahri in Case 13 were often called *mummies*. This perception is fostered by the interpretation of mummies by means of labels, information panels, diagrams and the results of CAT scans, thus drawing a lot of attention to this material and contributing to its iconic status. In displaying these collections, museums commonly take one of two approaches: this scientific one, or a more spiritual one where a suggestive surrounding is created to recall the mysticisms of the original funerary context, as for example at the Allard Pierson Museum in Amsterdam, where a basalt coffin in the centre of the display area can be touched by visitors.[7] Together, these practices feed into our perception of mummies as both dead and alive. This fascination with the *living dead* emerged strongly from the research commissioned to inform developments at the Petrie Museum of Egyptian Archaeology.[8]

It was common for people who expressed their preference for *mummies* to precede the word with 'of course', 'obviously', 'for sure' and 'definitely'. This may indicate that they genuinely found this type of object of absorbing interest, but on the other hand they may have presumed that we expected this reply or it may indicate a lack

---

6   It was found early in the interviewing process that the term 'gallery' was confusing to visitors. Particular care was taken to ensure that the respondents were clear that the Room 63 exhibition was the subject of the conversation.

7   MacDonald 2003: 89.

8   Fisher 2000; MacDonald 2003: 89.

of confidence in the uncertain environment of the museum as a social space; a sign of trying not to sound too inexpert, even when pursuing new information.

The wall panels *Wrapping the body* and *Preserving the body* ranked high among visitor preferences as tools for their appreciation of the objects on show. However, both observations and visitor accounts showed that at times the two wall panels were treated as exhibits in their own right and could make objects redundant or place them in a subordinated position. The gallery was for some a book with three-dimensional illustrations, as in the words of a visitor:

> *I loved to read about the process of mummification and wrapping of the body. The illustrations added to the written explanation, and, if I really wanted to understand more, I could look at the objects to find examples of what I read.*

Tomb models were another favourite. People explained that their appeal lay in their ability to offer visual snapshots of everyday life and therefore to make viewers feel 'closer to the people of the past'. This highlights the importance of figurative depictions, particularly in a society where images – from television, computers, advertising and cinema – are the leading medium of communication. The three-dimensional information provided by the tomb models is analogous to the televisual inputs to which we are accustomed.

People can be transported to stories of ancient lives through observing objects and, on a more abstract level, to the broader concepts reflected in the displays. For example, although *mummies* were a favourite choice for many, some visitors referred to concepts derived from the viewing of death-related exhibits, such as 'how scientists used mummies to understand about the lives of the people' or 'the reconstruction of the possible life and death of a young woman'. Visitors seem capable of both admiring the physicality of objects and of deriving stories about them through examining physical details. Often, however, they need interpretative help from the museum to see the concepts behind the objects. We will see later how the stories created are seldom the product of personal thought, but rather of the repetition of concepts expressed in wall panels and labels. And the presence of both artefacts and concepts among responses may, in part, be a reflection of the way the questions were posed. Although the line of questioning at first led people to talk about 'the things which they found the most and least interesting' (Appendix 5), the question that followed invited them to recall concepts, feelings and emotions elicited by the gallery.

8.5.3   Feelings, Emotions and Silent Objects

In six instances, beauty was the explicit reason for a preference. A woman, for example, explained her attraction for the coffins of Henutmehyt as follows: 'I aesthetically loved the contrast between the gold and the black of the wig'

Table 8.2   Interview Q4: if you think of the objects in the gallery, do any images, ideas or feelings come to mind?

	No.
Issues related to death and the display of human remains	8
Parallels between ancient Egyptians' lives and ours	7
Achievements in terms of craftsmanship and artistry	3
Triggers sense of the past	2
Mankind's futile expenditure on funerary practices and provision for immortality	2
Not really	2
Colonialism and repatriation	2
It is nothing new and it does not provoke any fresh feelings	1
Cult and care for the dead (in many different forms) has always existed	1
Each object evokes different feelings and creates different images	1
Everything is so old here (US interviewee)	1
It reinforces the stereotype of Egypt as a place of wonders and mysteries	1
Pictorial details on wooden coffins made me think of their natural environment	1
Beauty of objects from so long ago	1
It made me consider how much human beings can learn about the past	1
Symbolism found in all the small details	1
One wonders if the depiction in museums reflects reality or if it is all speculation	1
Total responses	36
Number of interviewees	30

(Figure 8.7). Visual characteristics, such as size, fine detail, colourfulness, elaborate decorative patterns and enigmatic symbolism were also quoted as reasons for a choice of favourite objects. By the same token, objects which were 'too small; too many; too plain; too dull-looking; common' and of 'easy manufacture' appeared among the things that visitors liked least (10 out of 36; Appendix 5). This dismissal of lesser things can be explained in terms of the *general value principle*: visitors (usually unconsciously) calculate the ratio between the benefits and the costs of attending to an object.[9] If the effort in terms of time, difficulty of understanding and detour from the main path is perceived to be high in relation to the gain, the visitor will not attend to the exhibit. These results highlight the importance of visual appearance in these visitors' selection mechanisms. Nevertheless, if objects coincide with visitors' personal interests, other factors may overcome the visual.

---

9   Bitgood 2006: 464.

Figure 8.7   *Egyptian death and afterlife: mummies* **(Room 63): the gleaming gold and black coffins of Henutmehyt – a visual feast**
Source: © S. Keene, courtesy of the Trustees of the British Museum.

The survey found bad news for silent objects: clear evidence that visitors base their assumptions on the importance and worth of objects from the past on visually driven values and consumerism (see Appendix 5 for responses). When seeking the causes for people's indifference towards 'small objects, objects of daily use and, in particular, shabtis' (Figures 1.1 and 8.9), we saw prejudices that are deeply rooted in our society's cultural framework:

> – *I looked at them in the past, but today I was in for a sensory interaction.*
> – *I know they are important, but there is not a big story behind them.*
> – *It takes too long to understand them; manufacture is not so good ... anybody could have made them.*

One person, however, demonstrated awareness of biased viewing mechanisms, explaining that 'some things are less fabulous looking than others, but I know that if they are exhibited here, they must be important even if they don't look much'. The testimony above highlights the position of authority that museums hold in the eyes of visitors and that some will ignore it in pursuit of their own interests.

Novelty is another factor in selection and viewing mechanisms. Objects that are numerous are considered more common and therefore less worthy of attention, and replication of similar objects in close proximity can make for a tedious show, as a visitor commented in relation to shabtis: 'There are really too many of them. They are small, and they all look the same.' Even an abundance of striking objects such as coffins can have a negative effect:

> *I was very interested [in mummies and other funerary objects] at first, but now that I see so many of them in museums, I really don't look at them anymore. And they are on television all the time too.*

8.5.4   The Voice of the Museum: Narratives and Associations

When talking about shabtis and coffins, visitors also mentioned that not being able to read the inscriptions limited their appreciation of the objects. This finding supports the result from the Petrie Museum booklet experiment (below, 10.4.4), where the contextualising and evocative properties of translations for inscribed artefacts from ancient Egypt emerged strongly.

Table 8.3   Interview Q5: did you find out anything new about ancient Egypt?

	No.
Not really; I already knew a lot	6
Yes, a lot, but can't think of anything in particular	6
Details about mummification process	6
It was a very complex and advanced society	4
Reminded of the links between Egypt and Africa	3
Shabtis, although small and dull-looking, have interesting stories	2
Regardless of class, all people treated the dead with respect and care	2
Overall it tells us nothing new; I gained some information about specific pieces	1
Not today, I came for a sensory immersion	1
Objects as illustrations to pieces of knowledge which I collected through the years	1
Complex cult of the dead – the dead were not really dead for them	1
Mummies are so well preserved, they have hair, teeth, etc.	1
I didn't realise Egyptian history comprises so many periods	1
Soul-houses that were placed in tombs of the less well-off to substitute material things	1
A lot can be learned about people from human remains (e.g. teeth: diet)	1
Total responses	37
Number of interviewees	30

Interview questions 4 and 5 (Tables 8.2 and 8.3) were designed to show how the displays affected visitors on an emotional as well as cognitive level, and to understand what stories or associations they made from objects. We wanted to establish whether visitors constructed narratives by linking objects in different showcases, but our evidence suggested that unless links between exhibits are suggested by text interpretation, individuals have difficulty in making links across exhibits. Each display – objects, written interpretation and illustrative material – was perceived and treated as a separate entity, and the stories that people leave with are often those suggested by the museum in wall panels and labels and by juxtaposing objects. For example, many interviewees cited mummification and wrapping procedures, as detailed in those two wall panels. Similarly, the text explanation of the importance of looking at human remains as a means to learn more about the people from the past also captured people's imagination (Case 14).

Visitors tended to accept the interpretation offered by the Museum in an uncritical manner. Possibly due to the aura of authority surrounding this great institution, most people did not take a critical stance, although some raised issues of displaying human remains and repatriation of objects. Perhaps the interviewees had insufficient self-assurance and knowledge of the subject to take an antagonistic position to the narratives presented by the Museum. Also, even if respondents had original or dissenting thoughts, they may have not felt it proper to share them in the context of the interview, as they might fear that their views were wrong or that it would be inappropriate to challenge the expertise of the museum world which, in their eyes, the researcher represented.

Some connections between objects were noted. For example, one visitor recalled that it was satisfying to look at the tomb models and recognise things which they saw on display elsewhere in the museum. Another noted that:

> *The Egyptians must have found inspiration for the pictorial representation of their language from the natural world around them, and their daily life ... I have seen those birds and plants in tomb frescos, and some of the pots among objects of daily life.*

A woman enthusiastically explained that looking at the displays in Room 63 made her realise that the ancient Egyptians were a relatively egalitarian society, as provisions for the dead were available in different forms for all, regardless of their wealth or class. Others reflected on the similarities between a culture who existed so long ago and ours.

8.5.5   Ethics and Morals: Repatriation and Human Remains

Two ethical and moral dilemmas central to museum display policies also emerged: human remains and repatriation. Five people expressed discomfort they experienced when seeing human remains in showcases. One visitor, still clearly disturbed from the experience, poignantly recalled her feelings on first seeing the human remains in Room 63:

> *It made me feel funny: these are real people! Once I started thinking like this, I could not look at them anymore, and I felt the urge to leave the room. This cannot be right.*

Cameron and Kelly discuss public reactions to an exhibition in Australia, *Death – the last taboo*, and found that if treated in a serious and factual way, even though explicit and detailed, this subject was welcomed in a public exhibition as helping to dispel myths and fears.[10]

Two individuals commented, on repatriation, that they were very surprised by the amount of displaced heritage on show in the galleries and in the museum in general. One visitor said: 'It made me realise how much the British have stolen from other cultures; I wonder how do Egyptians feel when they see their things here.' It is interesting to observe that visitors share some of the major theoretical debates of modern museology. Whatever position individual institutions choose to take, it is important that this is done with respect for the sensibilities to its audiences and that visitors are informed, both in the galleries and at the information desk, about the rationale behind specific display policies.

The links people make and the considerations they reach are informed by their cultural milieu and life circumstances. Some subjects, however, such as death are universal yet very personal, and transcend cultural and temporal barriers. This could be one of the reasons behind the fascination people feel for the ancient Egyptians, for whom funerary customs played such a pivotal role. Their remains manifest a material culture which, to our eyes, is mysterious, scary and fascinating at the same time. By looking at *mummies*, people are reminded of their mortality and can partake in the story on show in the museum. A man from Switzerland touchingly recalled how seeing how much the ancient Egyptians cared for their dead reminded him of his experience with his deceased mother:

> *Until recently, death was something that we would not want to see ... But today, in Switzerland, we are going back to an approach more similar to the one of ancient times. You can keep the dead at home, and people come and mourn him/her with you. When my mother died, I helped to wash her body, to get her dressed, and I even applied her make-up. It was a way to say goodbye to her.*

---

10   Kelly 2010: 202–7.

Figure 8.8   *Egyptian death and afterlife: mummies* **(Room 63): visitors studying the skulls display. Many text panels and labels can be seen**
Source: © S. Keene, courtesy of the Trustees of the British Museum.

The same visitor went on to explain how his faith, Christianity, through the dogma of resurrection helped him to make sense of the ancient Egyptians' elaborate funerary customs and beliefs of life beyond death:

> *My faith helps me to see how somebody who believes in an Afterlife, and in the ancient Egyptian's case an Afterlife where you are both matter and spirit, the body needs to be preserved intact.*

However, these reservations appeared only to be held by a minority of visitors, as some of the most popular cases were those that displayed human remains. For example, the neighbouring Room 64, *Early Egypt*, also contains a case with a human body preserved through natural desiccation which is the most popular exhibit in this gallery.

Visitors generally appeared to be satisfied with the style and amount of text in the wall panels, group labels and object labels, but there were critical comments that 'there is too much to read', that 'the amount of text takes the attention away from the objects' and that it was 'difficult to understand a clear connection between objects and labels'.

Illustrations, images and graphic representation of information play an important role in the narrative and are of great benefit to visitors' understanding of concepts: some of the stories people left with were informed by visual aids (see 8.6).

8.6   ASSESSMENT OF *EGYPTIAN DEATH AND AFTERLIFE: MUMMIES* (ROOM 63) AGAINST KEY CONCEPTS

The following analysis of the exhibition is derived from the concepts of design idioms, beauty and usability, flow and learning styles.

8.6.1   Space Syntax

The findings from space syntax analysis are summarised below:

- Room 63 has the feel of a corridor-like-space, with four points of access, located on the east-west long axis in the middle of the Upper Egyptian galleries.
- All the elements of the gallery are visible from each of the four points of access.
- All the spaces created by the displays are integrated within the room.
- The layout of the displays does not suggest any viewing pattern. Most people move along the long central axis of the gallery and spend more time with exhibits which line the path. This is the shortest route between the entrance and exit, as previously observed in other studies.[11]
- When not following the central axis route, visitors move around the space in a free-flow manner. Their viewing choices are mainly determined by circumstantial factors (i.e. busy and available showcases; points of entry), serendipitous encounters with objects, and personal taste.
- When the gallery is not busy, there is enough space between the showcases to enjoy their content. However, when many visitors are present, the exhibition feels oppressive and overcrowded.

8.6.2   Design Idioms

We will now turn our attention to the individual design elements: colour, lighting, text and use of space. In Room 63, *colour* is predominantly employed as a means of enhancing objects rather than of differentiating specific themes or messages. The red floor covering in some of the cases is striking and effective in attracting the eye to sombre-coloured objects in some cases (Figures 8.6 and 8.7).

---

11   Dean 1994: 51.

Lighting consists of traditional spotlights directed at key features of individual displays. Light levels are quite low, contributing to the aura of mystery. Lighting is employed neither to define exhibition space nor to highlight specific object features. No additional solutions are in place for particularly dark spots. The view of objects is at times obstructed by reflections on the case glass. However, on a sunny day, natural light filters through the room from the glass skylight, bathing the space in a golden glow.

Text panels and object labels are present in great numbers in this gallery. As recorded on an internal audit, there are 54 text panels and 312 labels accompanying the 539 objects.[12] The language used mainly avoids specialist terminology, and the length of object labels and introductory panels complies with the standards advised in museum literature (above, 3.2.4).[13]

Despite this, the high ratio of labels to objects and the formal and didactic style did not enhance the information process. Literature indicates that visitors are more likely to read where text:

- consists of short passages;[14]
- is carefully placed;[15]
- asks provocative questions, as long as this does not feel patronising to the reader.[16]

Research on the effects of using questions in label titles as attractors and motivators and on visitors' recall and learning of the label content indicates that effective exhibition text needs first to attract attention and then to establish a communication link with the reader if it is to lead to comprehension.[17] Labels which are brief, clear and entertaining are easy to understand and remember. A study by Bitgood, Dukes and Abbey found that people were much more likely to read shorter labels than longer ones, and that the length of the text had more effect than did interest in the content on how much of the text was read.[18]

The displays and text reviewed here would not be current practice in the British Museum; it is valuable to set a benchmark for this type of exhibition in the context of visitors' current expectations. The British Museum is increasingly

---

12   O'Hara 2004: 2–3.
13   E.g. Serrell 1996: 167.
14   Bitgood and Patterson 1993; Borun and Miller 1980.
15   Bitgood, Benefield and Patterson 1989.
16   Hirshi and Screven 1990; Litwak 1996.
17   Litwak 1996a: 9; Slack, Francis and Edwards 2011.
18   Bitgood, Dukes and Abbey 2006: 5.

using 'gateway objects' to introduce gallery themes, which appear to be a more immediate and appealing way to communicate to visitors.[19]

Naturally, visitors are not expected to attend to the whole text. Reading for comprehension, a trend particularly common among social visitors, does not require attention to be paid to an entire label. Partial reading of labels is not necessarily a negative indication. It may signify that the label has failed in its communicative purpose, but it may alternatively be that the visitor is familiar with the topic and therefore requires only a short scan of the text to confirm their previous understanding.[20]

The panels in general provided a combination of text, illustrations and photographs related to the subject discussed, although in a formal interpretation and text style. The graphic design of the written material did not accomplish a clear hierarchy of information through introductory boards, thematic panels, group labels and object labels. As a result, it was at times difficult to grasp the conceptual layout of the exhibition, and the association between objects and ideas was not always obvious.

The observed lack of integration between objects and written interpretation suggests that curators, designers and interpreters, despite their expertise and proficient contribution, perhaps did not collaborate closely throughout the duration of the project.

Visual and aesthetic concerns and parameters characteristic of our culture were central to the arrangement and juxtaposition of objects. Most of the displays were eye-pleasing and attractive, although they did not venture into original or thought-provoking associations. Artefacts were grouped on the basis of archaeological provenance, theme or chronological period. As a result, some displays were more effective than others in delivering key messages to visitors. This treatment contributed to the gulf between visually attractive and inconspicuous objects.

8.6.3   Beauty and Usability

Room 63 was potentially a visual feast, with its abundance of eye-pleasing and wonderful objects. However, due to the proximity of large objects and showcases combined with the usually crowded conditions and high noise levels, the gallery did not come across as a harmonious space. Furthermore, the profusion of objects and text panels, often not closely associated, could be perceived as visual clutter that nullified the attracting and holding powers of individual exhibits. Topographical and conceptual guidance was available in the form of wall panels, but the

---

19   Slack, Francis and Edwards 2011.
20   McManus 1989: 184.

visitor who wandered around from case to case employing impromptu selection mechanisms could fail to notice this, especially at particularly busy times. The written interpretation, although verbose and not always adjacent to the related objects, seemed to capture visitors' attention with its richness in illustrations, photographs and the choice of subject. The register of the text is didactic, but generally appropriate to the gallery audience. In conclusion, although neither the general aesthetic qualities nor the usability of the gallery are very high, they are in balance.

8.6.4 Flow

The flow-inducing ability of Room 63 was measured against the four principles fundamental to flow states. The displays were audited on their ability to communicate clear goals, to provide unequivocal feedback, to offer activities matched to the skills of visitors and to promote a high degree of concentration in the visitor as a response to the adequate challenge posed by the activity.[21]

Table 8.4 **Flow-inducing characteristics of Room 63 style (see Appendix 2)**

Characteristics	Score
Clear set of goals	6/10
Unequivocal feedback	5/10
Challenge of activity matches visitor's skills	12/20
Visitor completely focused on activity	3/10
Potential to induce flow	26/50
	52%

Table 8.4 gives an indication of how the gallery rated against the flow principles. It shows that Room 63 is not particularly likely to induce a flow-like state as many of the necessary requirements are missing. The main obstacles have been identified as the high levels of crowdedness and noise which can hinder deeper and prolonged interaction with the displays; the large amount of text; the didactic approach which may become monotonous after a while; the lack of interactivity; and ambiguous topographical and conceptual guidance. This can lead to frustration in the viewer, especially families with children.[22]

---

21   Csikszentmihalyi 1997.
22   Morris Hargreaves McIntyre 2011.

8.7   PERSONAL LEARNING STYLES AND OBJECT BIOGRAPHIES

The gallery was assessed against the four personal learning styles (which are closely related to educational models) categorised by, for instance, Kolb, Honey and Mumford and Serrell (above, 5.4).[23]

Table 8.5   Room 63 analysed according to learning style (see Appendix 2, Concept checksheets)

Learning style	Score	%
Analytical	17/25	68%
Imaginative	12/35	34%
Experiential	9/35	26%
Common sense	7/35	20%

The analysis summarised in Table 8.5 indicated that the gallery followed a didactic model that those who prefer an analytical learning style would find congenial. An absolute identification with such a paradigm was, however, not found, as the gallery did not impose the rigid linear viewing mode characteristic of traditional didactic displays, and nor did it present a progression of topics starting from simple to complex. Few of the characteristics of the behaviourist and discovery models that appeal to common-sense and experiential learners were detected in Room 63. Some of the elements of the constructivist paradigm (imaginative learners) were observed to some degree. For example, the layout of the displays allowed visitors to choose personal viewing patterns and the subject of the gallery facilitated connections with familiar concepts and objects.

Room 63 was both object- and interpretation-rich, yet because of the intellectual overload imposed by the amount of written interpretation and the object-dense displays, the exhibits were generally under-interpretive (above, 5.5).[24] At the same time, the profusion of objects and their visually driven presentation were characteristic of the misinterpretive model, which leads to sensory over-stimulation coupled with an intellectual deficit. As a result of this combination of elements, the viewer was at times overwhelmed by the excess of text and objects, thus losing sight of the exhibition's messages.

We were particularly interested in investigating whether people constructed narratives and stories from exhibition components or accepted those offered by the museum

---

23   Honey and Mumford 1982; Kolb 1984; Serrell 1996: 51.
24   Wittlin 1971: 145.

without question or elaboration. We found evidence that visitors only occasionally elaborated concepts from what they saw to form stories about the material remains on show. Although some visitors made connections between objects across displays, links were often the direct product of the interpretation provided. The stories people derived from objects were the product of *exhibit* (the physical characteristics of the displays – e.g. juxtaposition of objects, design characteristics and lines of interpretation), *setting* (level of noise and crowdedness) and *visitor-related* factors (such as socio-cultural background, life circumstances and reasons for the visit). However, the gallery and its contents were capable of touching the visitor on a deep and personal level, as revealed by the experiences recalled in terms of images, feelings and cultural analogies.

8.8   CONCLUSIONS

Room 63 is a spectacular gallery in traditional British Museum style, enjoyed by a high proportion of visitors to the museum. The key concept framework enabled an analysis of the visitor encounter from several perspectives, by examining the spatial syntax, the object characteristics and their presentation, the viewer's emotional, aesthetic, affective and cognitive reactions to the exhibits, and their interplay with the surrounding environment.

Two-thirds of the visitors whom we interviewed were pleased with the gallery as they found it, but a substantial proportion found problems. These can be attributed in part to the rise in the number of visitors to the British Museum over the 11 years since the gallery was constructed. However, we found a number of elements that, if avoided during the gallery project, we thought could have led to longer visitor engagement and greater satisfaction. The displays in Room 63 hinted at a partial disconnection between the creative forces involved – designers, curators and interpreters. It may be that, in tune with the museum policies and procedures of the time, these highly skilled professionals worked in a specialist-based compartmentised approach.

Since its creation in 1999, a specialist interpretation team has been established (2005) and gallery projects now take a different form. Also, the number of visitors to the British Museum has increased by 10 per cent since this gallery was planned (and in some years more), so that it is often more crowded than when it was planned in 1999.[25]

There was a particular issue with engagement with silent objects in this gallery. Not only were inconspicuous objects ignored, some (such as the displays of shabtis) were positively disliked and objected to: when asked what they found less interesting in the gallery, inconspicuous objects were those named. This, we concluded, could be at least partly explained by the findings from our analysis.

---

25   British Museum, various years: *Annual Report and Accounts.*

Figure 8.9 *Egyptian death and afterlife: mummies* (Room 63): there are at least three displays of shabtis in Room 63 in different showcases – important to ancient Egyptian burial practice, but too many for visitors? Would shorter texts help?

Source: © S. Keene, courtesy of the Trustees of the British Museum.

PART 3

BEYOND THE VISUAL

The next three chapters further explore and test the tools we developed from the concepts. These are now applied in a series of case studies in order ot evaluate and also to develop exhibits that engaged senses beyond the purely visual.

We analysed a different type of visitor experience, using the sense of touch and personal interaction: the *Hands on* desks at the British Museum. The results are reported in Chapter 9.

We also applied our key concepts to set up experimental exhibits in the Petrie and Horniman Museums, using audio labels, a handing box and graphic and colour interpretation. These were designed to test our findings on the factors we had found to significantly affect visitor–object interaction.

The display factors we tested were:

- line of sight and strategic placing;
- strong display elements and effective exhibit design;
- colour;
- sound;
- graphic display of information and moving images;
- personal involvement;
- object-centred display.

Some of these exhibits used audio labels to add sound to an exhibit; touch, in a handling box; active involvement and choice, in an explanatory booklet; and a choice of a range of interpretations for one exhibit.

To evaluate them, we used the observation sheet (Appendix 1) and concept checksheets (Appendix 2), as well as questionnaire-based interviews with visitors (Appendices 7–10). As such, we were able to obtain a depth of information about visitors' reception of these exhibits.

The investigations are described and discussed in Chapter 10, while in Chapter 11 we reflect further on the findings and conclusions from these experimental exhibits, especially within the framework of the visitor–object interaction model.

Data for these studies are available on the website, www.ucl.ac.uk/silent-objects.

CHAPTER 9

HANDS ON THE PAST AT THE BRITISH MUSEUM

Touch is the sense least employed in exhibiting museum objects. This is due to concerns about security and the conservation of collections, as well as a lack of established practice outside education services, where handling collections have been used for a considerable time.[1] The first British Museum *Hands on* desk was introduced in the *HBSC Money* gallery in 2001. It was soon very popular and at the time of the evaluation reported here (2004), there were *Hands on* desks in six of the galleries in the Museum. Since then, the value of touching and handling museum objects has been more fully recognised.[2]

As an interesting and different approach to visitors' interaction with objects, there have been a number of evaluations and investigations of this visitor experience. The first was commissioned from Francesca Monti by the British Museum and her 2004 report is the source for this chapter.[3] This was also the first exercise in the *Silent objects* research project; it delivered interesting and useful results. The British Museum subsequently introduced improvements and refinements, and fully consolidated the *Hands on* sessions as a highly popular museum programme that has recently been enjoyed by its millionth visitor.[4] In this chapter we revisit Monti's results using the lens of the concept-derived approach.

Results from a later report by Morris Hargreaves McIntyre are compared to ours.[5] Ten years after its introduction in the British Museum, the history and development of the *Hands on* programme has been reflected on and more fully described by Frost.[6]

The *Hands on* programme at the British Museum offers visitors the chance to pick up and handle objects similar to those in the collections but mostly specially purchased, with a few specially made replicas.[7] Many of the objects are

---

1   Durbin 1990, 1996.
2   Chatterjee 2008; Chatterjee and Noble 2009; Pye 2007.
3   Monti 2004.
4   Frost 2011: 26–7.
5   Morris Hargreaves McIntyre 2008.
6   Frost 2011.
7   Frost 2011: 27.

inconspicuous ones that may well have been silent objects had they been viewed in a glass case. In 2004, as now, *Hands on* sessions were available to visitors for specified times each day. Members of the British Museum's volunteer team were specially trained to provide the sessions, which were a chance for visitors to discuss and ask about objects as well as to closely inspect them.

9.1   AIMS AND OBJECTIVES

The aim in this chapter is to examine and analyse the findings from Monti's evaluation in 2004 as a case study on facilitating the connection of the visitor with silent objects, using the key concepts that we have developed.

The objectives in the original investigation were:

- to gather statistical and qualitative factual information which will inform the British Museum as to future policies on the *Hands on* programme;
- to provide research information on the effectiveness of this form of object interpretation in visitors' understanding of the information context of objects;
- to provide research information on visitors' views on the importance of coming into physical contact with 'real objects'.

A wealth of information and insights were gained into people's engagement with objects in this direct fashion and of the advantages and issues found, which contributes to our investigation into silent objects.

9.2   THE *HANDS ON* DESKS: ABOUT THE INSTALLATIONS

Each *Hands on* desk was staffed for specific periods by one of the British Museum volunteers. Users could discuss the objects, if they wished, with the volunteer, who was trained and knowledgeable about the objects on the desk. Most of the items were specially purchased although genuine and similar to those in the collections, while some were accurate replicas or reconstructions.

The evaluation programme reported in this chapter focused on the six object-handling activities available at the British Museum during the months of February and March 2004. These were:

- five different *numismatic-related sessions* – Room 68 – *HSBC Money* gallery;
- *Ancient Greece, money and pottery* – Room 72 – *AG Leventis* gallery of Cypriot antiquities;

- *Chinese money* – Room 33 – *Hotung* gallery – China, South Asia and Southeast Asia;
- the *Enlightenment* gallery: *discovering the world in the 18th century*;
- *Astrolabes and scientific instruments* – the Reading Room;
- *Buried treasure: finding our past – Hotung 2* – temporary exhibition gallery.

9.2.1　The Volunteers

The British Museum has a thorough training programme for all its volunteers. For the *Hands on* desks, the volunteers were trained at three different levels: about the objects and safe handling procedures from the curatorial and conservation staff; advice on how best to deal with the public in order to promote engagement and learning from the Education Department; and on safety measures and other technicalities and procedures in relation to the Museum as a public place.[8]

Volunteers had various reasons for assisting at the desks:

- to inspire people;
- to entertain;
- to feel that they were actively part of the Museum environment;
- to communicate to people that *often in museums the little objects constitute history*, rather than only the more grandiose and iconic exhibits doing so;
- to convey a sense of reverence for the objects and to inform visitors not solely regarding the technicalities of specific objects, but on their importance within a larger scheme;
- to educate people on how to best deal with objects;
- to offer good experiences that will make visitors more inclined towards future visits;
- to teach people that all objects can be interesting and have fascinating stories to tell us if we are capable of decoding them;
- to equip visitors with a set of transferable skills that will allow them to better appreciate similar objects on display.

The volunteers derived great satisfaction from facilitating handling at the desks and a sense of achievement when they saw visitors' faces light up while holding an object. One of their greatest pleasures was to see a user coming back to the desk with other family members or friends to share their experience.

9.2.2　The Objects

Volunteers could select for each shift a number of artefacts they would like to work with for the day. Volunteers had noticed that people seemed to prefer curious-

---

8　Frost 2011: 31.

Figure 9.1   The *Hands on* desk in the Roman Britain gallery with some shiny gold replica objects, small coins and various other objects (see Box 9.1)

Source: © S. Keene, courtesy of the Trustees of the British Museum.

looking objects, objects which conveyed a sense of their antiquity, artefacts they were familiar with and ones which they found visually attractive.

The volunteers were in general very positive about the *Hands on* desks. Their only concerns were:

- in crowded circumstances, the safety of the objects and visitor supervision;
- the need for more suitable object-handling desks: some desks needed to be larger due to their popularity;
- the need for better signage and orientation in the Museum to guide people to the object-handling activities.

9.2.3 The Desks

Most of the desks were specially designed to blend in with the gallery rather than standing out as a piece of new equipment.

Some issues were noted: one desk was too small and one was too high, so that the volunteer had to stand in order to communicate with visitors, while one was too low, so that adults could not easily handle the objects. Most of the desks have since been re-designed specifically to resolve these issues.[9]

9.3   RESEARCH METHODS

Five different methods were used to investigate and evaluate the desks:

- 'mystery shoppers';
- a group interview with volunteers;
- quantitative evaluation of gallery visitors versus users of *Hands on*;
- observations of *Hands on* activities;
- user survey: questionnaire interviews with users.

9.3.1   Mystery Shoppers

Mystery shopping has been used in market research since the 1940s and earlier to assess quality of service or compliance with regulations, or to gather other information about products or services. Mystery shoppers are anonymous to the organisation under investigation. They perform specific tasks and then provide detailed reports or feedback about their experiences. A mystery shopper survey is designed like any other: to gather data and information on specific questions.[10]

Six paid mystery shopper volunteers carried out this research: four recruited from UCL postgraduate students, one person external to the university environment, and the principal researcher. They were provided with briefing notes prepared by the evaluator on the objectives, scope and logistics of their exercise. Each mystery shopper tested all six *Hands on* desks in the British Museum, making their visits as spontaneous as possible and addressing specific issues related to the user experience. At the end of their sessions, they reported back by interview with the principal researcher.

---

9   Frost 2011.

10   For commercial mystery shopper surveys, there is a trade organisation (the Mystery Shopping Providers Association – Europe and other countries: http://www.mspa-eu.org/en) that has produced standards and a code of ethics for mystery shopping, as this method is by its nature deceptive and could be misused.

9.3.2   Group Interview with Volunteers

A group of five British Museum volunteers who were regularly involved with the *Hands on* desks were interviewed for 45 minutes. There were also many informal discussions with the volunteers during the evaluation.

9.3.3   Quantitative Evaluation of Gallery Visitors versus Users of *Hands on*

The objective here was to count the number of visitors using the *Hands on* desks around the Museum and compare it to the number of gallery users. The data were collected by location and time, differentiating between weekdays and weekends. In the Reading Room a visitor count was carried out concurrently with the user count.

The British Museum volunteers, under the supervision of the manager of the volunteers, undertook this study themselves. For each desk, two separate one-hour periods were selected, typical of a quiet time (11.30–12.30) and of a busy time (13.30–14.30) in the Museum. For the purposes of this exercise, a volunteer would stand next to the *Hands on* desk and keep count of the number of users.

User numbers were also noted by the evaluator during the two-hour observation exercise at each of the six desks (9.4.2).

9.3.4   Investigation: Observation of Hands on Activities

The objective of this investigation was to gain an understanding of the dynamics of the user interaction with the *Hands on* sessions, including:

- time spent at the desk;
- number of objects examined;
- level of interaction with the volunteer and the objects;
- initial behaviour after leaving the desk.

The evaluator spent two one-hour periods at each desk observing the *Hands on* activities. One hour was representative of a busy time and one of a quiet time. Weekends were monitored separately, for the *Buried treasure* exhibition and the *Enlightenment* gallery, in order to assess whether different trends developed at those times.

9.3.5   Investigation: Questionnaire Interviews with Users

The interviews had four main objectives:

- to collect the opinions of those visitors who took part in the object handling, general comments on their experiences and suggestions for future developments;
- to explore the user–facilitator relationship, in particular the role that the visitor would like the facilitator to take;
- to assess to what extent this service links to other museum activities, such as other object-handling sessions, related displays, and temporary and permanent exhibitions;
- to explore specific issues in relation to the objects available at handling sessions, for example, to investigate which object types most often attracted visitors' attention and why.

Interview responses were compared to the results of observing users' behaviour at the desks.

Following a preliminary observation to assess user numbers, each of the six *Hands on* desks was observed for a period of two to three hours, aiming to collect on average 10 questionnaire interviews per desk. This was achieved, making a sample of 60 visitors in all. A short pilot survey was carried out, during which it was found that replies were quite consistent, so a larger sample was not necessary.

Users were interviewed at the end of their object-handling session. The interviewer, strategically placed to also observe the object-handling activities, asked the first user leaving the desk whether they would be willing to take part in the survey. At completion, the interviewer would approach the next user leaving the desk. Interviewees were not subject to any other selection criteria.

9.4   THE *HANDS ON* DESKS: WHAT WE OBSERVED

The *Hands on* sessions were inspirational activities enjoyed by all categories of visitor. Their format allowed for a multi-level interaction with the objects, regardless of the visitor's age, nationality, language spoken, prior knowledge of the subject, socio-cultural environment of origins or level of education.

9.4.1   Orientation and Signage

The mystery shoppers were instructed to take a *Hands on* leaflet from the Information Desk in order to guide their visit from one handling desk to another. However, it soon became apparent that the information on the leaflets was not accurate (shortly afterwards, the leaflets were withdrawn from circulation while an updated version was prepared, and they are now shown on the public map of the galleries and on the museum's website). The mystery shoppers eventually found their ways around the object-handling desks by using their briefing notes.

BOX 9.1   *HANDS ON* THE PAST IN ROMAN BRITAIN

Walking through the Roman Britain gallery, I noticed the desk first. As I went up to it, a large silver platter caught my eye, and on closer inspection a number of silver coins, a circular bronze item with swirling Celtic decoration, a photograph of two ponies pulling a small vehicle, and a ribbed gold beaker with an accompanying piece of metal with embossed decoration.

I asked if the silver platter was genuine. The volunteer explained that it was not but that it was an exact replica of one displayed nearby – even to the weight. I felt that that was reasonable, although I didn't feel quite as inclined to investigate the object once I knew it was a replica. The bronze circular object was a terret and the engaging photograph showed the sort of equipage it would have been used with. 'When Julius Caesar invaded he was met by Boadicca with 6,000 British chariots like this one.' The gold cup was also a replica, of the Rillaton cup also to be seen nearby. This cup had been found in Cornwall in 1837. Gifted to the then king, it was now on loan to the Museum since the death of King George V, who had used it as a shaving cup.

These lively stories certainly inspired me to take a greater interest in the gallery displays.

Navigation around the museum galleries proved to be difficult for non-habitual visitors to the British Museum and the scarcity of signage at some desks during the mystery shoppers' visits added to the confusion.

This was also the experience of visitors: 92 per cent of those interviewed had come across the desks by chance whilst visiting the galleries. Three users had been recommended to come to the desk by a volunteer from another *Hands on* session and four were looking for a desk in a specific gallery; these people said that they did not have problems in finding the desks (however, as we shall see below, sometimes people are reluctant to report problems in interviews even when they have been observed to have difficulty).

9.4.2   Visitors and their Use of the Desks

Visitor behaviour   The handling sessions attracted a wide range of museum audiences. Generally, the desks seemed to be more frequented by visitors whose mother tongue was English, although non-native speakers with an adequate level of English also figured regularly. Expectations that certain objects and related handling sessions would appeal to specific visitor profiles (for example, ancient Greek money and pottery to schoolchildren, and Chinese money to tourists from the Far East) were not borne out: myriad permutations of visitor behaviour and object preference were observed at all six desks.

On average, about 10 visitors an hour engaged with the *Hands on* desks. There was no noticeable difference between busy and quiet times in the Museum, although the desks tended to be busier at the weekend.

The number of visitors using the desk was not necessarily related to the number of visitors in the gallery: the crucial factor was the presence of other users at the desk. The *horror vacui*, or *empty desk syndrome*, was the biggest deterrent. Volunteers were sometimes able to encourage users by starting a conversation as they walked nearby. Conversely, visitors were attracted and reassured by the presence of other people at the desk, and in turn began interacting with the objects and the volunteer. When a user completed their session and left the desk, the new arrival took centre stage. More passers-by were in turn attracted by the desk activities, and the cycle continued. This observation was checked against the quantitative data gathered during the visitor versus user count (9.3.3).

The visitors and the objects   Visitors were generally very satisfied with the selection of objects available for handling and said that they would welcome an expansion of the programme to the collections of other departments. The survey showed that 72 per cent of users touched or examined in detail at least at five objects during their sessions. It was observed that visitors first chose to look at:

- 'curious-looking artefacts' (26 per cent);
- objects that immediately convey their antiquity (24 per cent);
- objects with aesthetic appeal (22 per cent);
- types of objects in relation to a personal interest (21 per cent).

Volunteers informed us anecdotally that a *nocturnal*, a *wooden pig* from Papua New Guinea, and *Chinese jades* rated high among visitors' favourite objects. Intact ceramic items were popular, but pottery shards were not very appealing.

With little exception, people from all nationalities, of all ages and from all walks of life enquired about the age of an object and verified that it was not a facsimile. The age of an object and the fact that it was an original seemed to be important to many, and was a common denominator across different visitor profiles. Knowing how old something was and that the object really existed x years ago seemed to give people a sense of time and made their session at the desk special.

There was no standard behaviour at the desk: some users were more tactile; some asked a lot of questions; some were keen listeners; some were too nervous of the objects to touch them; some could not put them down again; some were respectful of the objects, while some were less so; some just wanted to share their knowledge with everyone at the desk; some treated the *Hands on* desk as an information point; and some were just people who wanted to talk to someone.

9.5   ANALYSING THE EXPERIENCE USING THE KEY CONCEPTS

The evidence gathered from observations and visitor interviews is now discussed within the framework of the key concepts: space syntax, design idioms, beauty and usability, flow state and personal learning styles (Figure 9.2). Many changes and adjustments have been made to the desks, signage and timing since that time, some of them in response to these findings from 2004.[11] For interview questions, see Appendix 6; for the data, see www.ucl.ac.uk/silent-objects.

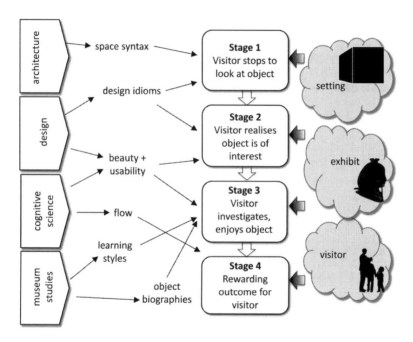

Figure 9.2   **The relationship between theory and key concepts, and the stages of the visitor–object interaction**

Source: © F. Monti/S. Keene.

9.5.1   Space Syntax (Architectural Theory)

We found that users were not visiting some of the *Hands on* desks even though the desk was in their line of sight or on the path they were following, for example, as they entered the gallery. We employ the concept of design idioms (9.5.2) to help explain this.

---

11   Frost 2011.

Users' behaviour after a *Hands on* experience was affected by the location of the desk in relation to the space syntax of the gallery. If the desk was near the gallery entrance or exit, visitors tended to leave the gallery, but if it was in the middle of the room, they were more likely to further explore the exhibits after their object-handling session. We observed this equally among visitors who encountered the *Hands on* desk on their way into the gallery and those on their way out. The *HSBC Money* gallery and the *AG Leventis* room were examples of this situation.

Where the desk was centrally positioned in the gallery, as in the *Enlightenment* gallery or the *Buried treasure* temporary exhibition, some visitors were observed to follow their *Hands on* session with an indepth exploration of the gallery displays (Morris Hargreaves McIntyre found a stronger tendency to stay in the gallery in their later study – possibly some desks had been re-positioned).[12]

9.5.2   Design Idioms (Colour, Light, Information and Text, Object Arrangement)

Few of the object-handling desks immediately attracted the attention of those walking by, even those in a prominent position. The overlooked desks were those where the design and appearance blended in with the gallery itself.

For example, the *Hands on* desk in the China gallery was opposite the main door, yet it was not instantly obvious to the visitor entering the room. This could be attributed to its modest size or to its style. Both the desk and the two chairs, although aesthetically attractive and in harmony with the oriental theme of the gallery, tended to merge with the surrounding ambience.

Two exceptions were the spacious desk in the Reading Room, where brass astronomical instruments placed on the burgundy cloth were a magnet for the visitor's eye, and the desk in the *Buried treasure* temporary exhibition, where a brightly coloured semi-circular handling area was very visible. This desk was especially popular.

According to the users' survey, a quarter of users were not clear on what the function of the desk was when they first approached it. At the time of this evaluation, not all the object-handling desks consistently displayed a signboard and even when the *Hands on* session was advertised by means of a sign next to the desk, 56 per cent of the survey's respondents had not noticed the signboard at all. However, other research at the British Museum indicates that text panels and signs attract little attention from visitors, so this may not help.[13]

---

12   Morris Hargreaves McIntyre 2008: 39.
13   Slack, Francis and Edwards 2011: 154.

Overall, the need for better signage was strongly suggested in all the five evaluation exercises. Visitors would have liked to have clear visible signs at each desk to clarify the exact nature of the service, and the days and times during which the activity took place. The volunteers, too, would have welcomed a clearer signage system, as they would be spared from constantly explaining the function of the desk and not be mistaken for information desks.

9.5.3   Beauty and Usability (Interaction Design)

All the desks should be comfortable for the volunteer to use. The ergonomic ratio between table and chair should allow all the volunteers, regardless of their size or stature, to be sitting comfortably on the chair without disappearing behind the desk (such as in the *Enlightenment* gallery) or being perched over the objects (such as at the *Chinese money* desk in the *Hotung* gallery). In the *Enlightenment* gallery, the design style of the desk appeared to have taken priority over usability issues. The handling desk was an exhibit per se, but its formal appearance could be a deterrent to some visitors. Due to the ergonomics of the desk in relation to the chair, the volunteer was often obliged to stand to avoid disappearing behind it.

Some desks, especially the *Chinese money* desk in the *Hotung* gallery and that in the *Cypriot antiquities* gallery, would have benefited from being larger to allow the safe handling of objects.

9.5.4   Flow (Cognitive Psychology)

During times of peak user numbers, crowding was identified as a problem:

- it made the volunteer/s feel anxious for the objects and overburdened with work;
- it created potential hazard situations for the objects;
- it was a deterrent to users.

We observed that, not unexpectedly, visitors spent a shorter amount of time at a desk during busy, crowded periods. Mental immersion in an experience is unlikely in such conditions, and possibly also less so when interacting with others.

9.5.5   Learning Styles (Learning Theory and Museum Studies)

The visitors who handled objects could be broadly characterised as those who took an active role in the session, and others who let the volunteer and circumstantial events take the lead.

Active, entrepreneurial users rarely allowed external factors to influence their *Hands on* experience, either in duration or number of handled objects. According to their personal interests, they either spent just a couple of minutes at the desk, enquiring about one or two objects they were particularly captivated by, or engaged in a long session. We surmised that their preferred learning styles were common sense and experiential. Users from the other group were more acquiescent and often interacted with all or most of the objects available, spending an average of five to eight minutes at the desk, perhaps preferring analytical or imaginative learning styles.

It emerged from the user survey that having a professionally trained volunteer *to tell them about the objects* rated equally with *being able to establish a tactile interaction* with the collections (both at 26 per cent). This is a particular feature of the British Museum's *Hands on* programme that is unlike comparable interactive exhibits in other museums.

Successful strategies for non-English speakers were observed: interaction could be established by means other than language, objects could be employed to substitute for words and gestures and signs could convey basic explanations. Some volunteers confirmed that this was a particularly rewarding experience for them, which required a high degree of patience and empathy with the visitor.

9.6   THE VISITOR–OBJECT INTERACTION

Results can also be examined using the visitor–object interaction model (Figure 1.4).

9.6.1   Stage 1: The Visitor Stops to Look at an Object

Space syntax and design idioms are the relevant concepts at this stage.

Visitors' intimate *Hands on* encounters with objects depended first on their stopping at a desk. At the time of this research exercise, visitors very seldom deliberately sought out the *Hands on* desks: 92 per cent of those interviewed had come across a desk by chance (90 per cent in Morris Hargreaves McIntyre's evaluation). This depended in turn largely on the space syntax of the gallery and hence the path they took through it, and on the design idioms attracting their attention; as we have seen (9.5.1), both of these concepts could have been more effectively employed. However, British Museum visitors, if they are targeting their visit at a particular gallery or object at all, are unlikely to be specifically looking for a facility such as this.[14]

When a visitor did approach a desk, this could either be unprompted or else be solicited by the volunteer. Few individuals confidently walked up to an empty desk: these were usually people who were already familiar with this type of service

---

14   Slack, Francis and Edwards 2011: 155, 157.

Figure 9.3   The *Hands on* desk in the *Enlightenment* gallery with a variety of objects from a prehistoric flint axe to a shiny Egyptian statuette centre front – a good visitor attractant

Source: © S. Keene, courtesy of the Trustees of the British Museum.

or those who were generally very self-confident. Reluctance to approach the desks may have been related to a lack of clarity about their function.

If the desk was already bustling with activity, it was easier for the visitor to approach unnoticed and watch while deciding whether to participate or to continue with their gallery visit. Curiosity played an important role here.

In an empty desk scenario, the volunteer's behaviour was crucial in attracting users: standing holding an object, greeting and smiling at those clearly curious about the desk or inviting visitors to look at an object were all successful ways to entice those walking by. (However, it is recognised that not everyone is comfortable with these more proactive techniques and it would not be advisable to adopt them wholesale.) As a good example, on the day of the evaluation, the volunteer in the *HBSC Money* gallery was successfully attracting people's attention to the desk by means of a Pegasus coin, using the opening line: 'Would you like to hold a *x* years old coin?'

Even once they had found or come across a desk, 78 per cent of users were not aware of the existence of *Hands on* desks in other galleries. Among those who already knew about other handling stations, only two were correctly informed on the full extent of the *Hands on* programme. Most respondents claimed to have walked by 'similar looking desks' while visiting the galleries and only retrospectively realised what these were.

9.6.2   Stage 2: The Visitor Becomes Aware that the Object is Interesting

Three typical situations have been identified here:

- the visitor's attention is drawn to an object and they will quiz the volunteer about its age or authenticity;
- the volunteer takes a leading role, initiating a session by presenting the visitor with interesting information in relation to a specific object;
- a visitor approaches a desk with an exhibit-related question, which can be answered employing a similar object available at the desk. Further interaction with the objects will often follow from the initial explanation.

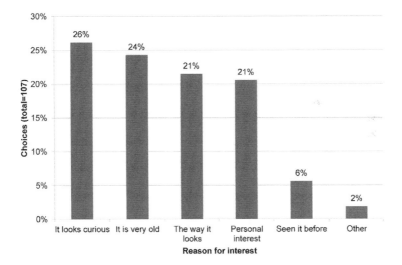

Figure 9.4   *Hands on* – interview Q13: what makes an object interesting to you? (multiple choice, per cent of selections. N interviewees=60; n responses=107)

Source: © F. Monti/S. Keene.

Respondents ascribed the reasons for their object preferences principally to *wanting to know what a curious-looking object is* (26 per cent) and to the fact that *an object looks very old* (26 per cent) (Figure 9.4). A total of 21 per cent of preferences were because of *personal interest* in that object type. No-one said that the aesthetic appearance of an object interested them.

In fact, however, we observed that it was most often the aesthetically attractive or striking objects that first drew visitors' attention. For example precious, shiny or glittery objects, or ones that were beautifully crafted and well proportioned, such as a Kaori shell, a gold necklace or some Chinese jades, were popular first choices. Possibly this mechanism operates unconsciously: although people cite strictly rational reasons for their initial preference, visual attributes are in fact the stronger attraction. This intriguing aspect of visitor–object interaction would merit further investigation. British Museum research into developing *gateway objects*, which symbolise the theme of an exhibition more accessibly than does a text panel, has provided similar findings on the qualities of an object that attract visitors.[15]

When asked 'Can you remember which object on the desk *first* attracted your attention?', visitors mostly volunteered coins, jades, jewellery and objects of precious metal, and when asked 'What other type of object would you like to handle at the desk?', visually attractive and precious things scored highly (for instance, jewellery, textiles and decorative tiles) in addition to 'Old books and manuscripts', 'Objects related to well-known historical events', 'Mummies' and objects clearly related to the theme of the gallery (Appendix 9, Questionnaire Q14, and see website for data: www.ucl.ac.uk/silent-objects).

Other reasons for attraction were related to the volunteer's performance and style of delivery. In particular, using a certain quality of an object to attract passers-by, for example, an association with well-known historical characters or events, made it more appealing to the visitor.

9.6.3   Stage 3: The Visitor Investigates and Learns about the Object

Respondents mostly remembered the correct item when asked which object first drew their attention (83 per cent), and indeed they often enthusiastically started to list all the other objects they encountered. Their answers almost always tallied with the evaluator's observation of their activities prior to the interview, also confirmed by the volunteer at the desk. This indicates visitors' active cognitive engagement in the object-handling activities.

9.6.4   Stage 4: The Visitor Has Had a Rewarding Experience

Would they repeat the experience?   The best test of a satisfactory experience will be if the visitor wishes to repeat it. Nearly half (43 per cent) of users had prior

---

15   Slack, Francis and Edwards 2011: 156.

experience of handling museum objects. Six visitors had interacted with another *Hands on* desk in the past and one individual had already experienced all the other *Hands on* desks in the Museum. A total of 75 per cent of visitors said they were either very likely or likely to visit another *Hands on* desk on the same day. However, 13 per cent of these added that they would not go out of their way looking for one. In contrast, in the temporary *Buried treasure* exhibition, four out of 10 visitors declared themselves less likely to participate in other handling activities in the Museum that day, probably because the exhibition itself was the specific reason for their visit.

Of respondents, 83 per cent were either very likely (56 per cent) or likely (27 per cent) to engage in other handling sessions during future visits to the Museum – a higher proportion than those who would do this again on the same day. This positive response is even more significant considering that the majority of negative replies came from visitors from overseas, who could not be certain of future visits to the British Museum. Interview responses suggested that people regarded two object-handling sessions per visit as a reasonable number.

When visitors had had prior experience of handling museum objects, this was very limited: most examples related to science or natural history collections, or to handling models or facsimiles (the British Museum has now introduced other tactile exhibits in some galleries).[16] The uniqueness of the objects made available at the *Hands on* desks was a pleasant surprise to the majority of interviewees – which supports the tactics of the proactive volunteers who actively solicited visitors to their *Hands on* desk.

Most favoured aspects   Asked 'What was your favourite aspect of this experience?' (Figure 9.5), *touching the objects* rated highly (26 per cent). However, this was to be expected, as this was the key aspect of the *Hands on* experience. Perhaps more significantly, the same degree of preference was expressed for *having somebody to tell me about the objects*.

It is interesting to juxtapose these two different aspects of the experience. While *touching the objects* actively engaged the user in a novel way, *being told about the objects* was very much in line with the traditional museum paradigm of visitors learning from an authority figure – a curator, a blue-badge guide, an audio guide, a label or a volunteer at the *Hands on* desk. Nearly as many choices were for the more interactive occupation of *asking questions whilst holding the objects,* and a fifth for being able to look at details of them.

Many respondents selected more than one favourite aspect, suggesting that multiple factors contributed to a positive experience.

---

16   Frost, personal communication 2011.

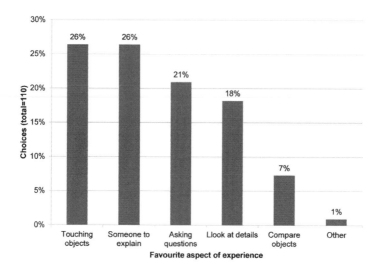

Figure 9.5   *Hands on* – interview Q15: what was your favourite aspect
of this experience? (multiple choice, per cent of selections. N
interviewees = 60; n responses = 110)

Source: © F. Monti/S. Keene.

9.7   CONCLUSIONS

We can now see what these findings mean for the wider elements of the visitor
experience: environment, exhibit and visitor.

A number of variables contributed to the success of object handling for an
individual visitor. These variables were related to the style of delivery of the
volunteer, the selection of objects available for handling in relation to the personal
knowledge and interests of the user, the conditions at the desk during the session
and the overall museum environment at the time of the visit. Although some of
these elements could be controlled and altered to improve the service, others
transcended the competencies and powers of volunteers and *Hands on* organisers
alike.

9.7.1   Environment

The visitor–object interaction (Stage 1) is most importantly mediated by aspects
of the environment, such as the space syntax of the gallery, and by design idioms
including those that attract people. We have identified above the less than optimal
space syntax and design idiom issues regarding the *Hands on* desks (9.5.2). These
could be easily rectified (and indeed were some time ago).

There were also environment problems when a gallery or desk was crowded, but in a sense these were problems of success. One way to address this would be to concentrate *Hands on* sessions at times when the particular gallery is not expected to be crowded.

9.7.2 Exhibit

Hands on sessions allowed visitors to establish a connection with the types of artefacts that they might otherwise have overlooked, or only partially appreciated, in a traditional display setting. They were also a source of much satisfaction among the British Museum volunteers who facilitated the object-handling sessions (9.2.1).

There was general satisfaction with the range of objects offered at the different desks. Arranging for the volunteers themselves to select objects for the desks meant that they could make use of their experience of visitor preferences, but also to offer objects that had interesting connections and histories.

Some of the desks needed to be larger to allow for safe and relaxed handling of objects and for visitors to gather round them, and measures such as limits to the number of objects available at any one time have since been introduced.

9.7.3 Visitor

Object handling is a bridging activity between the museum and its audiences, capable of transcending the barriers of age, class, gender, nationality and, occasionally, language.

We concluded that visitors genuinely appreciated this service: the intention to visit another desk, or having visited one already, was strong evidence of this. The *Hands on* desks were a distinctive variation on the general museum visit experience, invoking as they did the senses of touch and of voice communication, as well as generating social interaction.[17] Morris Hargreaves McIntyre found that 96 per cent of visitors said that 'the desks increased the quality of their visit'.[18]

Interview respondents were generally either satisfied with the *Hands on* service or reluctant to come up with negative comments about it: 62 per cent of users maintained that they found no faults in it (Figure 9.6). It is difficult to know whether this is evidence of genuine satisfaction or of the *halo effect* – the wish to please the interviewer and a reluctance to criticise.[19] Although the evaluator subtly tried to solicit constructive criticism, it was evident that users felt uncomfortable with this.

---

17   Frost 2011: 31.
18   Morris Hargreaves McIntyre 2008: 43.
19   Orna-Ornstein 2001: 12.

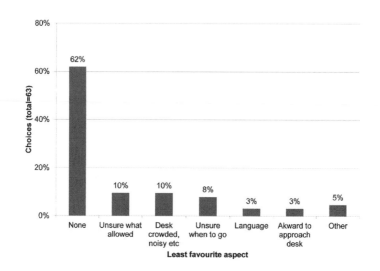

Figure 9.6   *Hands on* – interview Q16: what was your least favourite aspect
of this experience, if any? (Multiple choice, per cent of selections.
N interviewees = 60; n responses = 63)

Source: © F. Monti/S. Keene.

Within the paying *Buried treasure* temporary exhibition, users of the *Hands on* desk were less reluctant to criticise. This behaviour may indicate that when people pay for a service, their expectations raise and they feel that criticism is legitimate. Problems at this desk were crowded conditions at the desk and lack of signage. Two respondents also commented about the presence of facsimiles, claiming that 'handling reproductions is not as exciting and informative as handling original archaeological finds'. (Morris Hargreaves McIntyre found that some people were not concerned that they were handling replicas, but a few found them less engaging.)[20]

A quarter of those who commented on the service were extremely satisfied with the *Hands on* desks as they were. However, users themselves recommended better orientation from the Information Desk, clear visible signage at the desks and the provision of maps indicating the whereabouts of the *Hands on* desks within the Museum.

This study suggested that the greatest strength of the *Hands on* programme lay in its flexible format, its ability to reach across many visitor levels and its adaptability to the individual needs of users. Unlike gallery displays, which are inevitably forced to conform to certain presentation and interpretation criteria with a specific audience in mind, the *Hands on* desks intrinsically possessed a chameleon-like quality which

---

20   Morris Hargreaves McIntyre 2008: 37.

allowed a perceptive and enthusiastic volunteer to tailor each session according to the perceived preferences of the users. In so doing, object handling became informative while entertaining, and above all capable of firing visitors' imagination with objects. Such a programme can be used to enable galleries such as the *Enlightenment* gallery, which are predominantly analytical, to appeal to a wider range of audiences.

Symbolically, this programme represented a great gesture of confidence in the public, and users and volunteers alike felt privileged to be entrusted with objects from the past.

9.8   KEY RECOMMENDATIONS

The investigation and analysis enabled us to make some key recommendations to the British Museum on how they might improve the *Hands on* desk experience and increase the number of visitors using it. Our recommendations (which have since been addressed by the Museum) were:

- provide more effective promotion for the *Hands on* desks, possibly through leaflets, since when visitors do find them, they are much enjoyed;
- provide each desk with a clearly visible sign, with particular attention to the size and the colour scheme employed in its design;
- the *Enlightenment* gallery's lack of signage needed to be addressed. A satisfactory compromise between aesthetics and usability could be achieved in consultation with the design department, without having to deprive this historic gallery of its visual charm;
- aim to have at least one visitor per desk at all times: this is crucial to increasing usage. This would address the *empty desk syndrome* (9.4.2), according to which it is easier for visitors to approach a busy desk;
- to increase usage among non-English speakers, it was suggested that interaction between volunteer and user be established by means other than language: objects and visual aids could be utilised to substitute language and basic explanations could be delivered by means of signs.

9.9   COMPARISON WITH OTHER FINDINGS

Morris Hargreaves McIntyre's 2008 exercise was on a larger scale and had a different focus. (In fact, part of its brief was to check Monti's results: some of her recommendations had been implemented in the interim years, but their conclusions and recommendations in general concurred with hers.) Visitors did not spend long at a desk; *Hands on* experiences are very much enjoyed, and so it would benefit visitors to be facilitated in going to more than one desk; most of those using the desk had come across it incidentally; signage could still be improved.[21]

---

21   Morris Hargreaves McIntyre 2008: 44–7.

CHAPTER 10

EXPERIMENTS WITH SOUND, COLOUR AND INTERACTION

Exhibits that use a variety of media beyond the visual can especially engage visitors. This was demonstrated in the results of our comparative evaluation of concepts (Chapter 7) as well as in other research findings.[1] From these, we selected factors that we expected to be particularly relevant to the display of silent objects and set up a number of test exhibits of Egyptian antiquities in the Petrie Museum, UCL and the *African worlds* gallery in the Horniman Museum.

These test exhibits were designed to assess the impact of offering visitors the chance to use sound and touch as well as sight in interacting with objects. This time the focus was specifically on our primary concern, inconspicuous objects that the visitor was likely to overlook. Unlike the study of the *Hands on* desks at the British Museum (Chapter 9), these exhibits were to be encountered by visitors in the normal way and were not mediated or facilitated by staff.

In this chapter we describe the test displays and observations, while in Chapter 11 we analyse and discuss the results and report our conclusions.

10.1 RESEARCH OBJECTIVES

The experimental exhibits were set up to address specific interpretation strategies:

- with one single object – an ancient Egyptian ostracon (writing tablet);
- with a whole display of related objects, geology and stone in ancient Egypt, in the Petrie Museum;
- the same interpretation of similar objects in two different museums – ancient Egyptian headrests – in the Petrie and Horniman Museums.

The experiments' relevance to the visitor–object interaction model are shown in Table 10.1. Some ideas, such as *visual information* or *focus on obj*ect, were tested

---

1   E.g. Driver and Spence 2000; Robertson 2002.

in more than one experiment. This replication was part of a triangulation strategy aimed at ensuring that the results were not specific to one situation.

10.2   THE SETTINGS FOR THE EXPERIMENTS

10.2.1   The Petrie Museum of Egyptian Archaeology

The Petrie Museum is part of University College London. The collection includes about 80,000 objects. Though there are some spectacular items such as the Fayum portraits, the collection mainly comprises artefacts of daily use and humble appearance, exhibited in two main galleries. The visitor experience here differs from that with Egyptology collections in larger venues. Compared to the British Museum, the Petrie galleries are small, with object-rich displays designed for a primary audience of those with a specific interest in Egyptian antiquities. In the Petrie Museum there are no human and colossal-size statues and coffins. As a result, this museum feels like an archaeology collection of everyday objects, in contrast to the Egyptian exhibitions at the British Museum, which are usually perceived as eye-catching and mystifying displays of objects of art. :

> *[Inconspicuous and silent objects] are included in the displays because of their scientific importance. In a way [the objects at the Petrie Museum] are all problematic because of their scientific importance and invisibility. One may argue that all archaeology is problematic because you don't have consent by definition. Nevertheless [all the objects on display at the Petrie Museum] are potentially stimuli to knowledge because all the information is available online. The most problematic issue is human remains; whatever you do with them you are not going to do the right thing. However, human remains are important because they make people remember that ancient Egyptians were human beings, and stories can be told in relation to their context. Ultimately, people should decide what they think is important.[2]*

10.2.2   The Horniman Museum's African Worlds Gallery

The *African worlds* gallery was larger and more spacious than the Petrie Museum, with displays including many large and dramatic objects that communicated the diversity and creativity of the whole African continent. It brought together artefacts which defy cultural and temporal boundaries, explained through the testimonies of elders, maskers, drummers, diviners, exiles, curators and anthropologists. The ancient Egyptian headrest selected for this study was exhibited among other headrests and thrones (Figure 10.9). This venue was chosen to provide results that could be compared with those from the Petrie Museum experiment, and to establish

---

2   Interview with Stephen Quirke, Curator, the Petrie Museum.

Table 10.1   Experiments: by venue, object, interpretative method, ideas tested and relevance to the visitor–object interaction model

	Booklet	Geology display	Audio labels
Venue	*Petrie Museum*	*Petrie Museum*	*Petrie Museum* *Horniman Museum*
Object	Hieratic ostracon	Collection of rock samples	Two wooden headrests
Medium	Visual: small booklet with six colour-coded pages, with two layers of information.	Mixed media: object labels and wall panel with visual information; video of quarries; handling box	Audio: FeONIC™ audio solutions employed to create an audio label
Method	The booklet placed on a small table next to the display of the ostracon so that people could pick it up and look at it	A new display of stone interpreted through graphic labels and graphic panels; an object-handling box; and a video	Audio information about the headrest delivered through FeONIC™ movement activated device attached to the showcase*
Factors tested	Personal involvement Visual information Colour coded and attractive Touch Object-centred Layered information	Graphic information Object-centred Video Multi-sensory Layout of objects	Strategic placing Line of sight Object-centred Sound enhances visual perception Multi-sensory
Questions addressed	Stage 1: stops and looks Stage 2: awareness of interest Stage 4: rewarding outcome	Stage 1: stops and looks Stage 4: rewarding outcome	Stage 1: stops and looks Stage 2: awareness of interest Stage 3: investigates object

Note: *We are very grateful to FeONIC Technology for lending and setting up these test displays, using their Whispering Window devices: http://www.feonic.com.

the impact on visitors of the same interpretation technique for very similar objects in different museum settings.

10.3   THE RESEARCH

The research project was conducted in 2004–2005. The interpretation methods tested consisted of:

- in the Petrie Museum: a colour-coded, multi-layered booklet for an ostracon with hieratic inscriptions (Figures 10.1 and 10.2);
- in the Petrie Museum: a mixed media geology display: object labels, a wall panel with graphic information display, a video of ancient Egyptian quarries and an object-handling box (Figure 10.5);
- in the Petrie Museum: an audio label for a wooden headrest;
- in the Horniman Museum: a very similar audio label for a similar wooden headrest (for both of these, see Box 10.3 and Figures 10.7, 10.8 and 10.9).

In a further stage, visitors were asked to try all three of the exhibits in the Petrie Museum in order to compare their preferences and reactions to these different display techniques.

10.4   BOOKLET FOR THE HIERATIC OSTRACON

The ostracon is a piece of limestone about 25 cm square, with a hieratic inscription written in black and red ink. It is 3,250 years old, recording the gifts that women brought to a feast (Figure 10.1). This study was conducted in the Petrie Museum Pottery Gallery. A small booklet with seven tabbed pages, each a different colour, was made, presenting information about the object. Drawing on our findings from investigating the British Museum *Hands on* desks (and subsequently also found by Slack, Francis and Edwards),[3] we chose to present the information that was almost universally sought by users. Separate sheets in the booklet asked:

- where is it from?;
- how old is it?;
- what is it made of?;
- how was it made?;
- what writing system is it?;
- what does it say?;
- what does it tell us about its time?

---

3   Slack, Francis and Edwards 2011: 161.

On each page a flip-up tab could uncover additional information. The booklet was placed on a small table next to the showcase containing the ostracon with a sign that linked it to the object and invited visitors to pick it up and scan through its pages (Figure 10.2).

Figure 10.1   The ostracon exhibit in the Petrie Museum. Above: the gallery arrangement; below: the ostracon display (in the second showcase from the front).

Source: © Petrie Museum of Egyptian Archaelogy, University College London 8617+1.

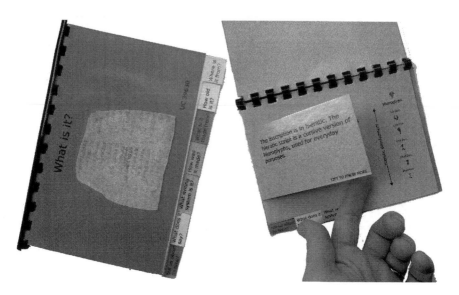

**Figure 10.2   The ostracon exhibit in the Petrie Museum: the red
interpretative booklet with indexed pages and lift-up flaps**
Source: © F. Monti/S. Keene.

10.4.1 The research

This exhibit was designed to test hypotheses on the potential of several display
techniques:

- that the use of colour that stands out from the setting will attract visitors
  to stop and investigate;
- that visitors engage with graphically presented information and
  information that is layered so that they can select as they wish;
- that active involvement and the use of touch engages visitors;
- that visitors will become more engaged with an exhibit where display is
  centred on the object.

The evaluation consisted of unstructured and structured (timed and counted)
observations of visitor behaviour, counts of degrees of interaction with the
display and questionnaire interviews with users.

Two three-hour periods with 23 visitors in total were observed. Visitors were
aged between 18 and 65, and were almost all scholars or students with a keen
interest in these collections.

10.4.2 Unstructured Observation of Visitors

Of the 23 visitors observed, eight ignored both the showcase and the booklet and nine paid attention to both; others looked at one or the other. Visitors who paid attention to the booklet seemed to be influenced by the normal museum code of behaviour: even though the label explicitly invited them to pick it up, they often hesitated, so as to make sure that it was really permitted. Visitors easily related the booklet to the object in front of it.

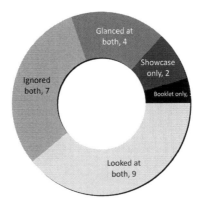

Figure 10.3 **The ostracon exhibit in the Petrie Museum: what visitors did (from observations, numbers of visitors: n=23)**
Source: © F. Monti/S. Keene.

10.4.3 Structured (Timed and Counted) Observation of Visitor Behaviour

Visitors who looked at both the ostracon and the booklet spent between 30 seconds and five minutes with the exhibit. Several read the information page by page and lifted the flip covers to find out more. Five individuals appeared to be deeply absorbed in the booklet.

The page with the translation of the ostracon's text engaged users for the longest and prompted them to look at the object (although the length of the text and small font size also determined the time spent reading).

10.4.4 Interviews

A further 15 people were interviewed after being observed to have looked at the ostracon in its standard display without the booklet, and again after looking at it with the booklet (see Appendix 7).

BOX 10.1   THE TEXT OF THE OSTRACON LABEL

Deir el-Medina   UC39630

Hieratic limestone sherd inscribed in ink with a list of
the gifts that women brought to a feast.

**Table 10.2   The ostracon exhibit in the Petrie Museum: visitors' opinions on
the display with and without the booklet (Questions, Appendix 7)**

Exhibit viewed without the booklet	Exhibit viewed with the booklet
People were generally satisfied with the amount of information from the standard label	14/15 users looked systematically at the booklet page by page
four people: label 'very clear and concise', one: 'very attractive and informative'	10/15 users were satisfied with amount of information (plus three wanted more, two less)
Respondents noted their knowledge about the item was 'poor' or 'very poor'	Some specially liked the colour coded pages
Various suggestions on practical ways to improve the ostracon's display	Preferences for content:
	7/15 users – the translation of text
	3/15 users – socio-historical information, writing system
	No-one was interested in the material or date

All replies to qualitative statements scored positively (Table 10.2 and Appendix 7, Q7), particularly those on using illustrations to convey information; allowing visitors to choose what they wanted to know; the compelling qualities of flip-windows; and that the booklet made them look at an object that they would have otherwise missed. We noticed the 'halo effect' in one eager-to-please visitor's response, a common problem in audience survey interviews.[4] The researcher distanced herself from the museum as far as possible, explaining that the interviewing process was part of independent research the outcomes of which greatly relied on people's genuine opinions.

10.4.5   The Ostracon Experiment: What We Observed

Half of the visitors who passed the exhibit stopped to find out about the colourful thing on the table and then went through its pages while examining the ostracon in the showcase. Even those who did not seem particularly absorbed could hardly

---

4   Orna-Ornstein 2001: 12.

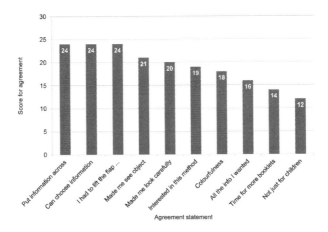

Figure 10.4 **The ostracon exhibit in the Petrie Museum. The ostracon booklet: scores for visitors' level of agreement with statements. The score is calculated as 2 x a strongly agree or disagree count, 1 x agree or disagree (n=28). For detailed data, see www.ucl.ac.uk/silent-objects**

Source: © F. Monti/S. Keene.

resist glancing or looking at the ostracon in detail. This behaviour indicates the attraction of bright colours, an appeal to innate human curiosity, and is also suggestive of the authority of museums. Viewers automatically assumed, as they reported when interviewed (Chapter 11), that the special treatment of the ostracon was an indication of some special status and that it would be worth their while to spend time with the object.

Visitors described the text translation as enabling them to connect directly with the object and with the people in the past whose lives were recorded in the inscription:

- It offers a glimpse into the role of women in society.
- It let me see the real meaning of the object.
- It brings to life the everyday living conditions of the Ancient Egyptians, the unfamiliar hieratic writing is made meaningful.
- It contextualises the piece.

Visitors suggested a number of improvements to the booklet, including improving the readability, modifying the bright colours, which were felt to be childlike, adding more illustrations, a graphical representation of information and a larger font size. The need for a large and clear font for labels is often found in visitor studies.[5]

---

5   Creative Research 2002: 9.

Two respondents praised the booklet for its effectiveness, but reservations were expressed on introducing similar booklets for more than a handful of selected objects, as repetition would nullify the impact.

10.5 GEOLOGY DISPLAY IN THE PETRIE MUSEUM

This experiment focused on a group of 36 stone objects. The new display comprised a wall case with the objects, two wall panels, a handling box with sample of rocks, a video of ancient Egyptian quarries and a stone trail for younger visitors.

Object display: 17 examples of worked stone next to unworked specimens of rock. The specimens illustrated how the material can change after crafting and how the same type of stone can look different due to variations in colour and texture. Object labels subtly departed from the Museum's standard format, using a large font, colour-coded information and an example of the use of the type of stone (Box 10.2 and Figure 10.5).

Wall panels: a large map of Egypt showing the location of relevant quarries, and a succinct introduction to the display with evocative photographs of Egyptian quarry sites and a map of possible provenance sites.

Handling box: visitors were invited to pick up the objects by means of a label next to the box. Because of health and safety considerations, the box could not be next to the geology display; instead, it was positioned on a location visible from the front desk.

Video: of Egyptian quarries, approximately three minutes in duration, placed adjacent to the handling box. It featured evocative images of Egypt with atmospheric background music to recall the original context of the objects and to highlight the importance of researching and preserving the ancient quarry sites. It use a non-linear narrative structure to accommodate casual viewing.

BOX 10.2 THE TEXT OF A NEW STYLE OBJECT LABEL USED IN THE GEOLOGY DISPLAY

13. Siltstone	Wadi Hammamat

No unworked specimen; worked: **41369**
Used for palettes during the Predynastic; later also for small vessels and statuary, stelae and sarcophagi.

**Figure 10.5   Petrie Museum: the geology display of rock specimens, with text
panel including a map of Egypt**

Source: © Petrie Museum of Egyptian Archaeology, University College London 8617+2.

10.5.1   The Research

The layout was designed to investigate the attracting power of the various exhibit
components and visitors' consequent absorption of information (Table 10.1). The
particular display techniques tested were:

- graphic information;
- layout of objects;
- touch and handling;
- video;
- object-centred display; and
- the use of multiple display elements.

10.5.2   Prior Evaluation

Before setting up the display, a preliminary survey of 37 visitors was carried out.
This determined that there was most interest in the type and provenance of the
stone.

Table 10.3   Questionnaire Q1: could you tell me what are your overall impressions of the geology display? (N=28; responses n=34)

General comments	Excellent; very good; very interesting; informative; fine
	Objects look boring/not interested in these objects
Design	Too much to read on one panel (uses of stone); I enjoyed the panel about uses of stone
Effective object-space ratio	Hard to see, particularly label on the top shelf; too much to see in a small area
	Video and handling box should be with the cabinet
Interpretation strategy	Panel with map puts objects into context; good to learn stories behind the objects
Multi-sensory and mixed media	Touching things greatly adds to the experience; better than looking at objects; multimodal display draws attention on the subject of stone (even if not so exciting); the use of different media gives you a better understanding of the objects
	The mesmerising music and video images lead you towards the display
	It relates the objects to other displays
	I never usually look at this stuff, but I enjoyed video and photographs

Due to the location of the display case, it was not possible to undertake any covert observational studies. The assessment thus consisted of a semi-structured questionnaire.

10.5.3   Interviews

Over a period of two weeks, 28 people agreed to be interviewed for the survey. Genders were evenly represented; most respondents were knowledgeable and interested in aspects of Egyptology. None were particularly interested in geology (Questions, Appendix 8; data are available at www.ucl.ac.uk/silent-objects).

Objects of daily life were the main interest of 10 out of 28 respondents; funerary customs were the main interest of five. Writings (five out of 28) were of particular interest among younger visitors and Friends of the Petrie Museum.

As soon as visitors were invited to inspect the geology display, it became obvious that they did not make the connection between the wall displays, the video and the handling box. As such, the video and handling box were pointed out, and interviewees were

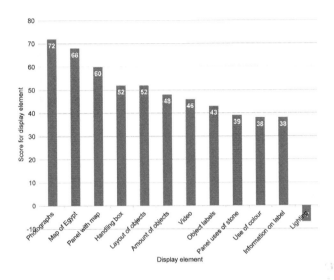

Figure 10.6   Petrie Museum geology display. Survey, Q3: how do you rate the following elements of the display? (N=28; for calculation of scores, see data, www.ucl.ac.uk/silent-objects)

Source: © F. Monti/S. Keene.

asked to comment about their experiences with the geology display in its entirety. Even so, only a third of visitors interacted with all the components of the display.

10.5.4   The Geology Exhibit: What We Observed

Visitors were asked 'Could you tell me what are your overall impressions of the geology display?' (Questionnaire Q1, Appendix 8). Seven out of 34 comments were very positive: 'excellent; very good; very interesting; informative' and even 'fantastic'. Nine visitors commented on the multi-sensory approach 'The use of different media gives you a better understanding of the objects'; 'I never usually look at this stuff but I enjoyed the video and photographs'.

Visitors were asked to recall the order in which they looked at the elements of the exhibit in order to identify which had the strongest attraction. Besides a slight prevalence of the 'objects – panel with map – uses of stone' viewing sequence (seven out of 28), no specific trend emerged. Visitors with a long-standing interest, studying for a qualification in Egyptology or archaeology, or with a prior knowledge of the collections were more apt to prefer an object-centred approach. Perhaps those with an understanding of the subject are less reliant on interpretation and are confident to look at the objects before seeking clarification. Conversely, this result may reflect a visitor's propensity for an analytical learning style.

Graphic information   Visually striking elements of the display were generally the most liked: the photographs of Egyptian quarries and the map of Egypt were regarded as very good by 19 and 16 out of 28 viewers respectively. There was a very strong consensus on the usefulness of the map and on its ability to provide information comprehensively and clearly. Photographs were also regarded as a successful way to convey difficult narratives, to the extent that 15 out of 28 visitors would welcome more (online data from Q3; see www.ucl.ac.uk/silent-objects). These results underline the success of a visually based communicative strategy.

The video   Despite our previous findings on the attraction of video with the V&A *Understanding objects* gallery (above, 6.4.3), the video footage of quarries was the least popular exhibit: it was only viewed by half the visitors (even so, nearly all visitors felt able to give it a rating, perhaps from a cursory glance. We noticed in general that people are confident to remark on things they may not have properly observed).

Its low attraction cannot be ascribed only to its distance from the object display, as the handling box next to it attracted 86 per cent of respondents. Visitors suggested as reasons the placement of the screen on a tall cabinet, the size of the screen and a lack of indication of its presence, i.e. low usability. The need for close proximity and a clear bond between object and interpretation was also found in studies of the British galleries at the V&A and in tests of new display techniques at the British Museum.[6] Even so, four visitors selected the video as of particular interest (Q3; see data at www.ucl.ac.uk/silent-objects).

What was of interest?   When asked which elements were of particular interest, however, preferences were somewhat different: six out of 28 choices were for the objects, an equal number for the map and five for the handling box. The video, despite its low usability, was mentioned by four respondents.

10.5.5 Geology Display: Conclusions

The mixed media approach was positively received (Table 10.3); this is in line with previous visitor studies, such as the summative evaluation of the V&A's British galleries[7] and the study of the *HSBC money* gallery in the British Museum,[8] as well as our own study reported in Chapters 6 and 7, especially of the V&A *Understanding objects* gallery. In particular, tactile and visual clues facilitate visitors' encounters with inconspicuous objects.

---

6   McManus 2003: 10; Morris Hargraves McIntyre 2003: 10; Slack, Francis and Edwards 2011: 163.

7   Creative Research 2002: 11.

8   Orna-Ornstein 2001: 20.

In a further question, visitors were asked which elements of the exhibit they had looked at. Additional remarks that were volunteered enabled us to interpret these viewings in terms of personal learning style. Those who stated that they preferred the visual dimension were drawn to the video, photographs and the map of Egypt; tactile and experiential learners particularly enjoyed the handling box, while analytical individuals favoured the facts and sequential ideas of the object labels and the wall panel about uses of stone.

In all, from this mixed media installation, we concluded (from the video placement) that usability is very important; that (from the handling box) touch and handling are popular with the majority of visitors; that (from the variety of display elements) it is very worthwhile to address a range of learning styles; that objects, no matter how apparently silent, are still the most attractive part of a display for many people and that to make the most of a display, the different elements must be clearly connected and in close proximity. Finally, we learned that attractive and stimulating interpretation can make even the least prepossessing of objects interesting to visitors and that using a range of media is appreciated:

> *If visitors were to leave the Petrie Museum with one thing, I would like their knowledge of Ancient Egypt to be challenged; that they understood how huge the time of Ancient Egypt history is; and that Ancient Egypt is not just about mummies and pyramids.*[9]

10.6   WHISPERING HEADRESTS AT THE PETRIE MUSEUM AND THE HORNIMAN MUSEUM

An ancient Egyptian wooden headrest from the Petrie Museum and one in the *African worlds* gallery at the Horniman Museum were interpreted by means of an audio label triggered by visitors' movement (Figures 10.7–10.9). The talking label was created using FeONIC Technology's device, which transformed the glass surface of the vitrine into an audio speaker. This technology is called Whispering Windows because it creates a quite personal and intimate experience.[10]

10.6.1 Questions and Aims

The experiments were designed to test the hypotheses, derived from the key concepts, that:

- visitors will stop to investigate an audio label in a museum context and search out the object that the label relates to (Stage 1);

---

9   Interview with D. Challis, Audience Development Officer, Petrie Museum, 2005.
10   Feonic: http://www.feonic.com.

Figure 10.7   Petrie and Horniman Museums: audio label exhibits: whispering headrests in the Petrie (left) and Horniman (right) Museums

Source: © Petrie Museum of Egyptian Archaeology, University College London 8617+2/ F. Monti/Trustees of the Horniman Museum.

- visitors will become aware that the object represents a gateway to interesting cultural information (Stage 2);
- visitors will wish to learn about this information (Stage 3).

The investigation was conducted using two similar objects and audio clips, but in very different galleries: the Petrie Museum and the Horniman Museum *African worlds* gallery (Figure 10.9). In this way we aimed to identify the issues relating to the audio label independently from those arising from the setting.

A first-person narrative style was chosen for the whispering labels. This employed the concept of object biographies[11] and was designed to offer visitors different ways into the histories of the headrests. Aspects of the lives of two objects, from their creation to their arrival and display at the museum, were narrated to the visitor (Box 10.3).

A poetical and autobiographical tone was used to suggest the multiple lives and identities of the ancient artefacts: objects of daily use and magical items in Ancient Egypt, archaeological specimens and museum exhibits. Narrated by a RADA-trained actor, the audio clips were slightly controversial in both style and content in

---

11   Alberti 2005; Kopytoff 1986.

BOX 10.3   THE TEXTS FOR THE WHISPERING HEADREST AUDIO LABELS

Petrie Museum headrest	Horniman Museum Headrest
Please ... look at me.	Please ... look at me.
I am the wooden headrest in the tall showcase, next to the alabaster and gold jar.	I am the wooden headrest from ancient Egypt next to many more headrests and stools from other parts of Africa. I am exhibit number one in the centre of the display.
I am not gold, but I have stories to bring you from 4,000 years ago, from when I was made ...	I am not gold but I have stories to tell you from 4,000 years ago, from when I was made ...
I was brought out of Egypt a century ago by a foreigner who came looking for knowledge of the people who made me.	I was taken from Egypt a century ago by a foreigner who came looking for knowledge of the people who made me.
They carved me, fine hard wood, into the desert hare that they saw running at the edge of their fields.	I was carved out of three pieces of wood for people to rest their heads on me.
In their sleep, I lifted their weary heads from the hard ground and guarded them from nightmares, from the monsters of the dark.	In their sleep I lifted their weary heads from the hard ground and guarded them from nightmares, and the fearsome monsters of the dark.
In the Afterlife, too, I protected them. Those resting on me should fear no danger on their eternal journeys.	In the Afterlife, too, I accompanied them. Those resting on me should fear no danger on their eternal journeys.
I am the sleeper's companion. I am the dream-maker, the guardian against evil.	I am the sleeper's friend. I am the dream-maker, the guardian against evil.

order to offer visitors a chance to critically consider issues related to the practices of museology and archaeology.

10.6.2   Setting up the Experiments

In the Petrie Museum, the small gallery was normally fairly quiet; no significant variations were found between weekend and weekday visitor behaviour. The audio-labelled object was installed in a showcase on a route followed by many of the visitors (Figure 11.2). Initial observation there suggested that the installation

**Figure 10.8   Petrie Museum: the whispering headrest: carved out of wood,
shaped like a desert hare**

Source: © Petrie Museum of Egyptian Archaeology, University College London 8617+2.

needed some adjustment: the relationship between object and label needed to be stronger; it had to be easy to quickly identify the relevant object; and the range of the movement sensor that triggered the audio had to be limited to the area immediately adjacent to the object. A large label with an audio icon was introduced; the object was moved to a prominent position near it; and the sensor was set to detect movement a metre from the object.

The intention was to replicate the experiment in the Horniman Museum *African worlds* gallery, but due to local circumstances it had to be varied somewhat. Visitor conditions in the Horniman varied greatly depending on the day of the week and the time of day, so relatively quiet times were chosen for observation when visitor numbers were comparable to those in the Petrie Museum. The showcase containing the exhibit was in a segregated location not on the visitors' normal route (see Chapter 2 and Figure 2.2) and the display included a number of large objects that could be viewed from a distance (Figure 10.9, image to right). As such, many visitors did not approach closely enough to start the audio and examine the object. At the Petrie Museum, an explanatory label and panel could be added, but the Horniman's design and display policies required the standard labelling format to be adhered to. Although an explanatory panel was placed nearby, it was not noticeable enough to make the object–audio connection obvious, especially since the Horniman headrest was in a showcase which included other headrests and prominent items such as thrones.[12]

---

12   The importance of object–interpretation proximity has also been found by Slack,

Figure 10.9   The Horniman Museum *African worlds* **gallery from the main entrance (left). This was a gallery with a complex layout including a raised central walkway. The headrest case (right) was on the right of the far end of the raised section**

Source: © S. Keene, courtesy of the Trustees of the British Museum.

10.6.3   Investigation Methods

The audio labels were assessed by means of:

- unstructured observations, simply to observe how a number of visitors interacted with the audio-labelled objects over a set period of time;
- structured observations (timed and counted) to record the number and extent of interactions with the audio label on and off during a set period of time; and
- interviews with users using a questionnaire as the basis for brief discussions (see Appendix 9 for the questionnaire; for the response data, see www.ucl. ac.uk/silent-objects).

In the Petrie Museum, all three of these assessments could be made, but in the Horniman Museum, it was not possible to conduct the structured observations due to the out-of-the-way location of the installation. Here, a sample of visitors were requested to seek out the audio-labelled object and to be interviewed afterwards.

Observations and interviews: the Petrie Museum   Over three two-hour weekday periods and one three-hour weekend period, 28 visitors were observed.

Interviews were conducted with a further 26 individuals, plus four who completed the interview questionnaire voluntarily. Of these, 20 were people with a high level of knowledge about the subject, 25 were women and there was a spread of ages.

Francis and Edwards 2011: 161.

*Observations and interviews: the Horniman Museum **African worlds** gallery*   A total of 25 visitors were observed in their initial interactions with the installation.

Following this, a further 15 visitors viewing the *African worlds* gallery were invited to test the audio display and subsequently to be interviewed about it. They were mainly single individuals between 25 and 35 years old; compared to the Petrie Museum audience, the Horniman audience in this evaluation was more informal, from different ethnic backgrounds, and visiting the museum out of personal interest towards the themes and objects on display or as a leisure pursuit rather than for study or professional interest.

10.6.4   Initial Observations: No Audio Compared to Audio Active

In both galleries, visitors were observed over three-hour periods. For half of the time, the audio was off; for the other half, it was active. It was striking that in the Petrie Museum, when the audio label was active, by far the majority of visitors stopped to investigate, while when it was off, very few did. The difference was not so great in the Horniman Museum due to the location of the object (Figure 10.10).

10.6.5   Dynamics of the Interactions: Identifying the Object

The second part of the observation in the Petrie Museum focused on the dynamics of the interactions of the 28 visitors who were observed. Fourteen out of the 28 identified the headrest as soon as the audio voice prompted them to do so, but those who did not take in the introductory line 'please look at me, I am the wooden headrest in the tall showcase, next to the alabaster and gold jar' struggled to find the object. However, in the subsequent interviews, none of the Petrie visitors said they had been unable to locate the object, possibly wishing to please the interviewer or to avoid being thought unobservant (the halo effect, referred to previously, 10.4.4) (Table 10.4).

In the Horniman Museum, 15 visitors viewing the *African worlds* gallery tested the audio exhibit. Because of the gallery characteristics outlined above, these visitors were invited to test the display rather than being observed covertly. Even so, eight out of the 15 found it difficult to locate the relevant headrest and two found it very difficult or did not find it. This indicated the low usability of the display and that it was easy to confuse the headrest with other exhibits within the showcase.

10.6.6   Initial Reactions to the Audio Labels

Of the 28 visitors covertly observed in the Petrie Museum, 25 began to interact as they triggered the audio in walking past, while three were attracted to the display by overhearing the audio playing. People often displayed more than one initial

Table 10.4   How easy it was to find the headrest (from observations and interviews)

Petrie observations	Petrie from interviews	Responses	Horniman from interviews
12	15	Very easy	2
6	9	Easy	3
3	6	Difficult	8
7	0	Very difficult/not at all	2
28	**30**	**Total responses**	**15**

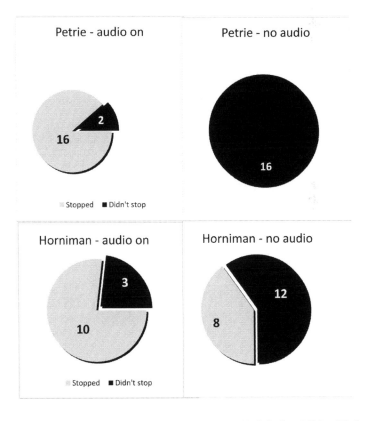

Figure 10.10 Petrie and Horniman Museums: audio label exhibits. Visitor actions when passing the exhibit with audio on versus audio off (from observations, number of visitors)

Source: © F. Monti/S. Keene.

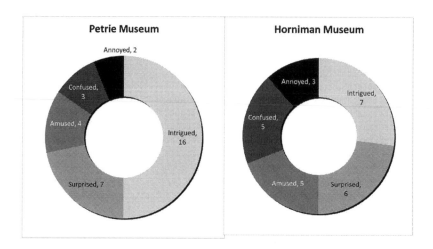

Figure 10.11 Petrie and Horniman Museums: audio label exhibits. Interview Q2: what were your initial reactions when the talking label started to play? (From interviews, number of responses, some multiple)
Source: © F. Monti/S. Keene.

reaction. Body language, facial expressions and comments overheard suggested that most common reactions were curiosity (over half those observed) and appreciation. One visitor displayed annoyance (Figure 10.11).

In the Horniman Museum, similar observations were made: of the 15 people observed, seven reacted with curiosity and six with surprise.

These reactions were further investigated in the visitor interviews in both museums.

In both museums, most visitors were curious and interested, surprised or amused. A few were confused, mainly because of usability factors – they could not locate the relevant headrest or make the link between the audio label and the object – and a few were annoyed for various reasons (for data, see www.ucl.ac.uk/silent-objects).

10.6.7 What Visitors Did While Listening

In both museums, most visitors read the object label as well as listening (Figure 10.12). Most visitors appeared to search for written information shortly after the audio label started, so this may indicate that they wanted some general explanation about the installation.

From observations, the Petrie Museum visitors spent on average about 71 seconds with the display. Some listened to only the first part of the audio clip and spent

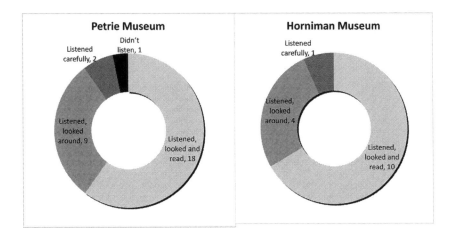

Figure 10.12 Petrie and Horniman Museums: audio label exhibits. What visitors did while listening to the whispering labels (from observations, number of actions)

Source: © F. Monti/S. Keene.

about 30 seconds at the exhibit; over half of them stayed for the entire audio clip of 72 seconds; three visitors stayed longer, about two minutes.

Reasons for not listening to the whole recording included:

- It was too long.
- [I] didn't realise it was playing for me.
- It was not loud enough.
- There was too much background noise because of the drilling.
- It was already playing and it was difficult to make sense of it.
- The information is not to the point and requires too much thinking.

Seventeen out of the 28 Petrie Museum visitors observed were deeply absorbed in their interaction with the display to the point of becoming oblivious of the surrounding environment (a flow state), despite a loud drilling noise during one observation session. In two instances, this state was also noticed for those who did not find the headrest but who nevertheless listened to the audio clip with complete attention. Fifteen out of 28 visitors appeared at ease during their interaction, while four appeared uncomfortable due to the heat and noisy building works outside. A correlation between these data and the results on the depth of engagement suggested, unsurprisingly, that environmental factors and usability are important to a flow state.

In the Horniman *African worlds* gallery, 14 out of 15 visitors listened to the whole recording (as they were asked to do).

10.6.8 The Nature of the Audio Label

Each label was about 70 seconds in duration. The majority of the Petrie respondents (24 out of 30) thought the length of the audio clip was about right, while three people thought it should be shorter and three longer. Similarly in the Horniman, 11 out of 15 respondents thought that the amount of information was about right.

To create an object-centred interpretation and an immersive experience, a first-person narrative was chosen for the audio-clip scripts (Box 10.3). This style was positively received in both venues: in the Petrie Museum, 12 out of 30 participants thought it evocative, while five out of 30 thought it absorbing; in the Horniman Museum, five out of 15 visitors found it evocative and the same number informative. Fewer of the Horniman visitors found it absorbing, probably due to poor sound quality and perhaps because they knew they were being observed.

10.6.9 Information Provided and Absorbed

When asked 'Do you think you have a good idea of what the object is after having listened to the talking label?' (Appendix 9, Interview Q6), in the Petrie Museum, 27 out of 30 visitors said they had a good or very good understanding of the object; in the Horniman Museum, all 15 agreed with this. When asked whether listening to the audio clip improved their understanding of the object, 20 out of 30 interviewees in the Petrie Museum declared they had a good idea, and seven believed they had a very good idea of what the exhibit was after having heard the whispering label. The responses in the Horniman *African worlds* gallery would have been influenced by the investigation strategy there, because people had been invited to look at the display and were expecting to be interviewed about it.

To cross-check the responses, interviewees were asked to briefly describe the headrest in their own words. Replies were clustered according to four themes: audio-derived information, aesthetic judgement, physical description and personal response. In both venues, half of the descriptions reflected information received from the audio label; the Horniman audience, despite expecting questions, did not evidence greater attention to it (Table 10.5).

10.6.10 Likes and Dislikes

Taking the museums together, nearly 70 per cent of comments were appreciative: they had made the visitor look closely at an object they might otherwise have missed and stimulated curiosity about that and similar objects. Others found it had brought the object to life for them and that it had pleasantly varied the pace of the museum visit.

Table 10.5   Interview Q7: how would you describe the object in your own words?

In the Petrie Museum	In the Horniman Museum
Audio-derived information (15) Ancient wooden headrest; wooden headrest shaped as a hare; to protect and rest the head	*Audio-derived information (11)* Wooden headrest from ancient Egypt; a stand for your head to protect it; wooden headrest from 4,000 years ago; headrest from Africa
Aesthetic judgement (8) Beautifully carved piece of wood; elegant and fluid design; dull looking yet historically tantalising; Bauhaus	*Aesthetic judgement (11)* Fairly plain and dull-looking headrest
Physical attributes (3) Unusual shaped headrest; sinuous and tactile form; mysterious and curious	*Physical attributes (1)* Semicircle on a stick
Personal response (4) I thought it was Horus; combination of artistry and practicality	*Personal response (2)* Unusual to sleep on it; funerary; piece of esoteric culture
Total reactions 30	Total reactions 25

The question on what they least liked about the installation (Figure 10.14) and their suggestions for improvement elicited the following comments and suggestions:

- Sound too obtrusive.
- Display should be clearer as to its function [three out of 30].
- Adjust the volume according to surrounding noise levels.
- Improve the sound quality [the Horniman].
- Make the sound–object relationship clearer.
- Adjust sensor to detect only visitors very near the showcase.
- Should allow people to switch it on and off.

Visitors were asked if they would have liked to know even more about the headrest. There was no very clear pattern, but in both museums some wanted conventional label content, such as date, provenance and manufacture, as well as questions of interest to them personally. In support of the value of multi-sensory experiences, two individuals mentioned that they would like to touch the object to learn more about it from a tactile inspection.

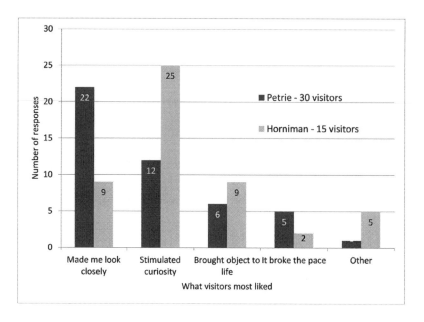

Figure 10.13 Petrie and Horniman Museums: audio label exhibits. Interview Q11: what did you most like about the talking label? (Multiple-choice question, number of remarks)

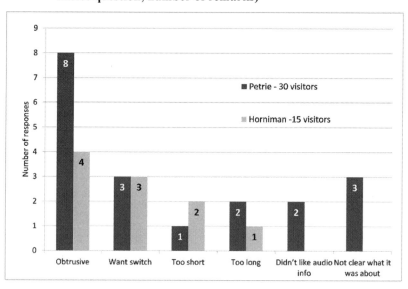

Figure 10.14 Petrie and Horniman Museums: audio label exhibits. Interview Q12: what did you least like about the talking label? (Multiple-choice question, number of remarks)

Source: © F. Monti/S. Keene.

10.6.11 The Audio Labels: What We Concluded

Table 10.6   Summary of findings on the whispering headrests

Petrie Museum	Horniman Museum
Location	
Few noticed the item from afar and walked towards it; most found it as they walked past or had heard the audio playing	Segregated location and objects competing visually made the installation hard to identify
Initial reactions	
Most, curiosity and interest; then, surprise; with a few people confused, amused or annoyed by the repetitive audio that they could overhear	
Identifying the relevant object	
18 found it very easily or easily; 10 had difficulty. In interviews none said they had had difficulty	8 out of 15 participants found it difficult to identify the headrest, 2 very difficult, even though they had approached the display with a general indication of what to expect
Length of audio	
24 of 30 people thought the length about right; 3 felt it should be shorter and 3 longer	
First person narrative style	
Evocative, informative or absorbing: Petrie, 26 out of 28: Horniman, 10 out of 15	
Aspects most appreciated	
The whispering label's ability to make them look closely at an object which they may otherwise have missed (22 out of 46 multiple-choice replies); 12 that it had stimulated their curiosity about the headrest and similar objects	9 out of 25 visitors said the display offered an opportunity to look closely at an object that they may otherwise have ignored; 25 that it stimulated curiosity; others, that it brought the object to life
Wanted to know anything else	
14 of 30 did: most were interested in the provenance, date and details of manufacture	8 of 15: yes. Most commonly date and provenance. Two individuals mentioned that they would like to learn more about the object by touching it
Least liked/suggestions	
Make sound less obtrusive (8 out of 30) and clearer as to its function (3 out of 30). A switch was suggested to allow visitors to control the audio,and volume adjustment	Make sound less obtrusive (4 of 15); improve sound quality; adjust volume to circumstances; adjust sensor to detect only close visitors

10.6.12 Whispering Headrests Experiment: Conclusions

We set up this experiment in the two galleries to test hypotheses that an audio label would prompt visitors to stop to investigate an object and that they would then investigate and find out more about it (the stages in our visitor–object interaction model).

The exhibits were very well received by visitors. While the audio label exhibits in themselves were not visually striking and so did not cause a visitor to divert towards them (unless they overheard the audio clip playing), once they heard the audio clip, it was very effective in persuading them that the object was interesting and worth hearing about. We learnt that usability is important: to indicate clearly which object is the subject of the label and to make sure that the audio is of good quality and directional so that it does not leak into the general exhibition environment.

10.7   SUMMARY

In this chapter we described three experimental exhibits installed in the Petrie and Horniman Museums in order to test the effects of certain display techniques. In Chapter 11, we analyse and compare the results more formally and draw conclusions.

CHAPTER 11

SOUND, COLOUR AND INTERACTION:
WHAT WE LEARNED

In Chapter 10, we described three experimental exhibits installed in the Petrie and Horniman Museums, which were designed to test the effects of certain display techniques with some Egyptian antiquities. A booklet explaining an ostracon (inscription) in the Petrie Museum tested colour, graphic information, the active involvement of the visitor and the use of touch, display that centred on the object and layered information. A geology display in the same museum investigated the effectiveness of multiple display elements using different senses. Audio labels for Egyptian headrests in the Petrie and Horniman Museums were designed to test the effectiveness or otherwise of this device in rendering the silent objects, the two unassuming ancient Egyptian headrests, communicative – in this case, literally giving them voices as whispering headrests. In this chapter, we present and analyse the findings from the studies, using the key concepts as our main tool (Figure 11.1 and Box 11.1). We then discuss them against the framework of the visitor–object interaction model (Figure 1.4).

We first revisit the findings from the three initial test galleries, in the British Museum, the V&A and the Horniman Museum (above 7.9).

```
KEY CONCEPTS
space syntax ... design idioms ... beauty + usability ... flow ...
learning styles ... object biographies
```

```
DISPLAY FACTORS
Line of sight and strong display elements
Strategic placing and effective exhibit design
Moving images
Colour
Sound
Graphic display of information
Active participation
Object-centred display approach
```

Figure 11.1   Schematic representation of the selected concepts and the design and interpretation factors identified during the evaluation of the three galleries (Chapters 6 and 7)

Source: © F. Monti/S. Keene.

11.1   IMPORTANT DISPLAY FACTORS

BOX 11.1   FACTORS THAT HAVE AN IMPORTANT INFLUENCE ON VISITORS' INTERACTION WITH EXHIBITS

Line of sight and strong display elements

Tracking exercises and analysis of visitor placings in relation to artefacts suggested that people tend to look at what is on their path, unless a strong element alerts their attention (above, 7.1). However, as the *Hands on* desks showed (above, 9.6.1), if an item is not striking, then placement in the path of the visitor is not sufficient to attract attention.

Strategic placing and effective exhibit design

Effective design and strategic positioning can draw visitors' attention to specific objects. The high level of visitor interest towards the centrally placed exhibits, such as the model of the Albert Memorial in Room 123 at the V&A and the popularity of the neatly and effectively arranged exhibits within the *Protecting new designs* display in the same gallery, are indications of this (above, 7.2.4).

Moving images

Videos can have a powerful attracting power on visitors, as noted at the V&A in Room 123 with the footage of Queen Victoria (above, 6.4.3) and in the *Music room* at the Horniman Museum (above, 6.5.1).

Colour

Equally commanding magnets for visitors are striking colours, as seen, for example, in the choice of objects viewed in the British Museum *Enlightenment* gallery (above, 6.3.4) and on the *Hands on* desks.

Sound

In the context of a multi-sensory environment, it has been found that *sound* enhances visual perception (Driver and Spence 2000), as demonstrated by the highly successful sound benches at the Horniman Museum *Music room* (above, 6.5.3).

Graphic display of information

Information presented in visually graphic terms (Robertson 2002) effectively attracts and holds visitor attention, as seen in the sound benches at the Horniman Museum *Music room* (above, 6.5.3).

Personal involvement

The reactions found to the *Hands on* desks in the British Museum (above, 9.6.4) and the sound benches at the *Music room* (above, 6.5.3) suggest that visitors welcome personal interpretative guidance, and yet they appreciate a certain degree of free agency and choice which stimulates their sense of wonder and personal discovery.

Object-centred display approach

The generally positive responses to the object-based displays in the three venues (above, 7.9) supports the view that, as we found above (7.9), object-centred exhibitions are more communicative than those which focus on abstract ideas (Jordanova 1989: 23 and 40; Peart 1984; Spalding 2002: 9). They encouraged a closer and deeper inspection of objects and promoted longer visits.

Multi-sensory and multimedia displays

It was also observed that displays employing a variety of interpretation media and artefact-based activities, such as the *Hands on* desk in the *Enlightenment* gallery (Chapter 9), the *Understanding objects* space within Room 123 at the V&A (above, 6.4.2) and the visual and audio experience offered by the sound benches at the Horniman Museum *Music room* promoted long interactions across a wide audience (above, 7.9). One reason is that they catered for a range of learning styles and different types of engagement.

11.2 THE THREE INTERPRETATIONS AT THE PETRIE MUSEUM COMPARED

We set up a study to directly compare visitors' reception of the three interpretative installations in the Petrie Museum – the booklet, the geology display and the whispering headrest. Visitors were approached and invited to try out the three temporary installations and to express their opinions in interviews (Appendix 10). The aims of this evaluation were to gather comparative information as to people's reactions to the three methods and to cross-check the results of the individual assessments.

11.2.1 Questionnaire-based Interviews with Visitors

Fifteen visitors agreed to partake in this research exercise. In the first part of the survey, people were shown the three installations; next they were interviewed about their impressions and about its best and worst features. These results are schematically shown in Table 11.2.

Overall, visitors thought that the three displays were successful in stimulating interest in the objects. In particular, five out of 11 comments on the booklet praised its ability to make the ostracon interesting; one visitor pointed out that the use of images and photographs in the geology display served the same purpose; and four out of 16 people were favourably impressed by the audio label's ability to convey the cultural richness of the headrest.

Also in common across the responses is the importance people ascribed to the recontextualisation provided by these interpretative solutions. Two individuals

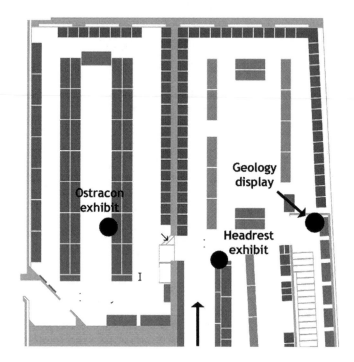

Figure 11.2   Petrie Museum: layout of the museum showing the location of the three experimental exhibits.
Source: © F. Monti/S. Keene.

appreciated the way in which the booklet reconstructed the original milieu of the ostracon; five visitors identified this specific quality in the map of Egypt in the geology display; and two respondents described the audio label as capable of conveying a feeling for the people and the past.

The evaluation of the three interpretative media suggested the relevance and potential contribution of the conceptual areas they were designed to test to the treatment of inconspicuous museum objects (Table 11.1). For example, the booklet was appreciated for its clear and effective delivery of information at different levels according to the visitors' choice, for its colour-coded information and for the user-friendly interface. With the geology display, the virtues of a multimedia and multi-sensory experience emerged. In particular, visitors enjoyed being able to touch the sample of rocks and thought that the use of photographs, illustrations and the map greatly added to their experience.

The whispering headrest was described as 'poetic', 'romantic' and 'an immersive and captivating experience that transports the user into the past', evoking images from the original cultural background of the object. These comments point to

Table 11.1   Petrie Museum: comparison of three exhibits. Reasons why people preferred certain interpretative media and different types of object

Interpretation medium: reasons for preference	Object: reasons for preference
Booklet The translation makes the object come to life Concise and comprehensive Good for all generations I enjoy learning by reading	*Ostracon* Reading the inscription brings it to life Written documents are very interesting The inscription is intriguing and aesthetically pleasing Gives an insight into daily life After having seen the Rosetta Stone at the British Museum, I appreciated this It was fascinating to find out what they ate
Audio label Creates a sense of the past beyond words and images Very atmospheric It grabs you to interact with a worthy object Love the way it sounds: very soothing It fires the imagination It gives you an insight into the object's life It created a back in time experience	
Handling box Touching things makes them interesting/relevant A novelty method I like to learn about things by myself rather than being told what to think	*Headrest* It makes you think about the people who used it Because of how it grabbed me Back in time experience Stone objects I appreciated the aesthetic merits of the stone vessels
Video It takes you to the original context of the objects It appears to many senses: sight, hearing	*Other* No interest in any, but interpretation brings them to life
Wall panel with map I enjoyed the use of pictures and map It is a medium I am familiar with	
Total responses 25	Total responses 17

the benefits of an interpretation strategy which uses sound to enhance visual experiences and to provide additional contextualisation for an object. The results also highlight the effectiveness of an 'object biography' approach to bring the headrests to life and to offer visitors different entry points into the narrative.

General comments, most liked and least liked aspects of all three displays are summarised in Table 11.2. Criticisms of the displays highlighted some of the limitations already found in the individual evaluation programmes. For example, from these comparative results, the booklet would benefit from a larger format; the geology display would be better if all its elements were together; and the whispering label would be improved if people could control it and if it were not unnecessarily activated so that it became obtrusive to others.

The interviews suggested that people are on the whole drawn to the type of interpretative medium that will engage the sense they personally favour (sight, touch, hearing) or which offers the style of learning most sympathetic to them. By the same token, it was inferred that visitors' preferences for theme or type of object influenced their reactions to these interpretative solutions. On a number of occasions, the respondents explained their likes or dislikes on the grounds of personal taste, sensibilities, preferred interaction media, socio-cultural background and life circumstances. For example:

> – *I love reading ... therefore I enjoyed the wordy panel.*
> – *I am a very visual person and I loved watching the video and examining the photographs of quarries.*
> – *I am a university lecturer and texts and books are pretty much my thing.*
> – *I am a potter and I am fascinated by ceramics and the tactile qualities of objects.*

This trend also emerged when people were asked which exhibit most stimulated their interest in the objects (Appendix 10, Q10; Table 11.2). Overall, the booklet received most preferences (eight out of 24) followed by the whispering label (seven), the handling box (five), the geology video (three) and, finally, one individual chose the geology wall panel with the map. Reasons for appreciating the booklet were not as varied and enthusiastic as the ones for the whispering headrest. For example, the ostracon's interpretation was described as 'a concise and comprehensive source of information', 'good for all generations' and 'being able to read its inscription brings the object to life', while with the whispering label:

- It recreates a sense of the past in a way which transcend words and images.
- It fires your imagination.
- It gives you an insight into the object's life and its people.

11.3   FINDINGS ON DISPLAY TECHNIQUES

An analysis of the findings of the experiments suggests that each of the display factors under investigation had a positive effect on audience engagement with silent objects.

Table 11.2 Petrie Museum exhibits: visitors' responses on the ostracon and booklet, geology display and whispering label. Comments, favourite and least favourite aspects

	General comments	Favourite aspects	Least favourite aspects
Booklet	A dull object comes to life	Finding out about the inscription	Nothing
Layered info	I love the translation	Concise and comprehensive	Too small
Active participation	Option of in depth information	Type of information colour coded	Booklet as a medium
Visual information	Content OK, but not medium	User friendly	Clarify object–booklet relationship
Colour coded	Childish design	Choice of amount of information	Better design
Tactile dimension		Original context of the object	Need a further information layer
Object-focused		Relevance to past people	Not interactive enough
	Total responses 11	Total responses 17	Total responses 15
Geology display	Very good/informative	Hands-on/tactile nature	Video at bad angle/too high/long
Visual information	Possibility to see and touch	Display with objects	Separation of hands on box and video
Object-centred	Not interested in stone/boring	Map puts things in context	Wrong location/space cramped
Moving images	Images bring dull subject to life	Wall panel on uses of stone	*Uses of stone* panel too long
Multi-sensory	Very useful – many objects of stone	Objects/labels/panels related	Boring objects
Multimodal	Mesmerising music of video	Pictures of quarries	Mirrors in the cabinet
Layout of objects	Like reading the long panel	Objects next to raw material	Add photos of objects on map
	Objects re-contextualised	Variety of media	Too quiet/needs to come to life
	Total responses 16	Total responses 16	Total responses 16
Talking headrest	Interesting/captivating/immersive	Very immersive	Nothing
Object-centred	Good to draw attention on dull object	Style brings the object to life	Not being able to control on/off loop
Sound enhances visual perception	Gives sense of people and past	Dream-like voice	A bit too long
Contextualisation by sound	Couldn't hear well/noise	Original	No direct information on label
Ability to bring object to life	Romantic/poetic experience	Poetic style of narrative	Pretentious
Object biography	Beautiful and moving experience	Nothing	Volume too low
	Mysteriousness of object	Truthful about object biography	Difficult to associate object and audio
		Relaxing way to learn	Add images for multisensory experience
	Total responses 15	Total responses 16	Total responses 16

11.3.1 Line of Sight and Strong Display Elements

The dual-venue whispering headrest study suggested that the audio label alone was not enough to draw attention to an inconspicuous object. Line of sight attraction is by definition visual, and even explanatory labels and panels were not sufficient. Especially in the Horniman Museum, we found that a strong visual element is necessary if visitors are to detour from their intended path.

11.3.2 Strategic Placing

The effect of positioning for exhibits that are only weakly visually attractive was underlined in all of these evaluations. Comparing the two venues for the whispering headrests was particularly useful. Besides the limitations of the poor sound at the Horniman Museum, the Petrie Museum audio-label installation attracted attention easily partly because of its prominent placing. At the Horniman Museum, visitors recommended a better design of the installation to improve its impact on gallery goers (above, 10.6.12).

In the geology display, the separation of the video and the handling box from the showcase was problematic, from which we learnt that within an exhibition system, all the elements need to be designed and integrated with consideration to usability and aesthetic requirements, as well as with an eye to content (above, 10.5.5).

11.3.3 Moving Images

Both positive and negative comments about the geology display's footage of quarries were useful in identifying some of the requirements for a successful implementation of this medium within a display. The video was criticised for its small screen and awkward placing on top of a tall cabinet, yet visitors positively commented on its interpretative contribution. When assessed for its communicative merits, the video was well received and indeed praised for its ability to recontextualise the objects, and for its evocative powers.

11.3.4 Colour

Colour can be employed for its differential impact in a visually monotonous exhibition where the objects on display are similar to each other in terms of shape, colour and material. The success of the red booklet in alerting people to something that might interest them indicated that if used in isolation, a bright colour, or a colour not used elsewhere in the display, can effectively draw attention to a weakly attractive element of the gallery (above, 10.4). Colour can also be used to differentiate types of information (above, 10.4, Figure 10.2) and to distinguish between various levels of communication.

11.3.5 Sound: Audio

The evocative, atmospheric and informative qualities of sound were tested in the whispering headrest experiment. Observations at the Petrie Museum indicated that the audio label encouraged deeper and longer interaction with the object (above, 10.6.7); visitors also agreed that they would have overlooked the object without the audio label (above, 10.6.10). During interviews, visitor descriptions of the headrest after listening to the audio clip were a mixture of visual observations and audio-derived information, suggesting that people did examine the object while listening to the label (Table 10.5).

In this comparative evaluation of the three installations, visitors interviewed praised the audio label for its immersive properties, for its ability to bring the object to life and for the poetic narrative style (above, 11.2.1).

11.3.6 Graphic Display of Information

The effectiveness of using photographs, drawings and maps in displays was suggested in the positive reception of the geology display (above, 11.2.1). The booklet experiment with the ostracon further indicated the power of visual information: visitors specifically appreciated the direct connection between object and interpretative medium created by the photograph of the ostracon on the front cover. They also enjoyed the translation of the inscription. This finding highlights the pivotal role of translations in the display of inscribed objects (above, 11.2.1 and Table 11.1; Slack, Francis and Edwards found the same: in the example of an inscribed cylinder, people wanted to know what it said).[1]

11.3.7 Active Individual Involvement

The booklet experiment further confirmed that visitors enjoy playing an active part and appreciate being able to choose the type and amount of information they access (above, 11.2.1). Similar positive results in relation to a hands-on flip-up label were recorded by Arndt et al. at an exhibit of a lion in a zoo study.[2] There, the hands-on label increased the percentage of visitors who stopped, the viewing time and how much they learnt. The *Medicine man* gallery in the Wellcome Museum of the History of Medicine has many text panels hidden behind small doors in the walls and these are very well used by visitors.[3] Bitgood agrees that this type of interpretation, when well designed, is capable of sparking considerable curiosity about the object.[4]

---

1   Slack, Francis and Edwards 2011: 162.
2   Arndt et al. 1993.
3   Informal observation in the Wellcome Collection of the History of Medicine Museum by S. Keene, 17 February 2012.
4   Bitgood 2000: 6.

The suggestions on introducing a switch for the whispering headrest to allow visitors to activate and pause the audio at will (above, 11.2.1, Table 11.2) also suggest a desire for a participatory role; however, this would eliminate the element of surprise that was a notable feature of this installation:

> *Whatever feelings I have in displays would be visual over verbal. If it were for me my ideal would be to find a way to avoid labels altogether. I favour the relation between visitor and object. This should be a journey of discovery, and a knowledge sharing opportunity. A two-way system.*[5]

11.3.8   Object-Centred Display Approach

The three experiments discussed here were all object-centred. The evaluation data repeatedly confirmed the favourable reception of this approach. In the context of the geology display, people expressed their liking for its presentation of things and the ease with which they could relate to them as opposed to abstract ideas (Table 11.2 – although at least one person thought the objects dull). The comparative results from the three exhibits indicated that an object-centred approach can be successfully achieved using several kinds of communicative media, as long as the connection between object and interpretation is clear to the viewer.

For example, from the audio label exhibits, we learnt the importance of clearly linking the object to the interpretative medium so that it can be easily identified. Visitors appraising the ostracon booklet mentioned especially the usefulness of the image of the ostracon on the front cover, which enabled them to easily identify the object.

11.3.9   Multi-sensory and Multimedia Displays

These multi-sensory displays using various media were successful in attracting and holding people's attention because, in the words of a visitor, 'by offering a variety of media you give everybody a chance to connect with the objects'. In such an environment, people are free to enter into a dialogue with an object at different levels, according to their interaction preference and learning style, as seen in the comparative results (above, 11.2.1).

11.4   CONCLUSIONS: THE VISITOR–OBJECT RELATIONSHIP

What can be concluded on the effectiveness of these measures in terms of the visitor–object encounter?

---

5   Interview with Stephen Quirke, Curator, the Petrie Museum.

11.4.1 Stage 1: The Visitor Stops to Look at the Object

This stage was investigated using the ostracon booklet and the audio-labelled headrests. About half the passing visitors stopped and investigated the striking red-coloured booklet and the nearby object. If they were in sight of the exhibit, then they were likely to stop and investigate this colourful item.

With the audio labels in the Petrie Museum, all passing visitors stopped to examine the installation when the audio was on; when it was off, none did so. However, the exhibit was on the main visitor path and it was difficult to avoid stepping close to it. Results in the Horniman Museum were not so clear-cut, but still, more people stopped when the audio label was operational. We chose settings that were as comparable as possible in the two museums, but they unavoidably differed in several respects.

We concluded from this that if people actually hear an unexpected audio clip, then they will stop to investigate; without it, they may have passed the object without stopping. If they do not pass it, they may still make a detour to investigate it if there is a visual sign.

The visitor having stopped, we found that it was essential to clearly indicate which object was the subject of the label, as several visitors missed the initial audio guidance or were confused by other objects in the same display.

11.4.2 Stage 2: The Visitor Becomes Aware that the Object is Interesting

The ostracon booklet was designed to make the user feel curious. It is hard to resist at least glancing to see what is in a booklet with coloured index tabs, which is not usually found in a museum display context. Once they saw what it was, most users spent quite a considerable time with the booklet and examining the object.

The geology exhibit, with its five components, did inspire curiosity among visitors – one commenting that they never usually looked at 'this sort of stuff', but had done so because of the variety of media used.

With the audio labels, most people who stopped did so because they were intrigued by the content at the start of the audio clip and wanted to hear more.

11.4.3 Stage 3: The Visitor Investigates and Learns about the Object

The ostracon booklet was particularly successful in allowing the user to visually appreciate the object while learning about it in a social context. It was observed that it prompted social interaction among people visiting the museum with a companion, friend or family member.

The ostracon results highlighted the power of visual imagery, the importance of an object-centred approach and the role that curiosity and novelty plays during the acquisition of information.[6]

When we checked how much information visitors had taken in about the ostracon with and without the booklet, without the booklet, people admitted that they knew little about the object, even though they said they were satisfied with, or even praised, the standard object label. Those who saw it with the booklet were able to give much more informative replies in the interview.

The geology display was successful in persuading people to investigate. The variety of media catered for a range of learning styles. However, we also learnt that in a multi-element exhibit, all the components need to be in close proximity and to be clearly identified as connected.

In general, the audio labels were successful in reinforcing people's desire to look at the object. Many of the visitors who we observed spent a considerable time with the exhibit. The audio clips played for just over 70 seconds; several (six out of 13) visitors listened for the full recording, some spending even longer after that looking at the object.

In the Petrie Museum, 18 out of 28 visitors looked closely and attentively at the headrest, as if trying to make sense of the narration they were hearing. Excluding those who failed to find the object, only three among those who listened to the recording showed no interest in the exhibit. In the Horniman Museum, the one person who did not listen to the whole recording explained that he lost interest because he wasn't sure he was looking at the right object and he didn't know for how long the recording was going to last. This comment highlights the importance of feedback at all stages of interaction to create meaningful experiences (usability and beauty concept) and to promote flow states.

11.4.4   Stage 4: The Visitor Feels that They Have Had a Rewarding Experience

Ostracon booklet: when interviewed, visitors registered a liking for the use of illustrations to convey information, for being able to choose the information they wanted, for the compelling qualities of flip-up covers and for the fact that the booklet made them look at an object that they would have otherwise missed. These results highlight the power of visual imagery, the importance of an object-centred

---

6   Bitgood 2000: 5; Griggs 1983: 120.

approach[7] and the role that curiosity and novelty play during the acquisition of information.[8]

Multi-component geology display: most visitors liked the photographs and the clearly presented map of Egypt best – demonstrating the power of graphically presented information. The handling box was also popular. The video suffered from poor usability – too high up to see easily and unconnected with the rest of the display. Nevertheless, visitors who viewed it liked the images and content.

Audio labels: most visitors had enjoyed the element of surprise inherent in the label installations. Immersive responses predominated in the Petrie Museum, as inferred from the nature and duration of engagement: 10 out of 28 visitors concentrated on the object and audio for longer than average and linked object and sound by listening and looking simultaneously (above, 10.6.7 and Figure 10.12). The low incidence of visual (two) and explorative (one) engagements suggested that once people found the headrest, they were keen to spend some time finding out about it.

This contrasted with the Horniman Museum, where people were not so absorbed and engaged, either because of the less favourable surroundings or because they knew they were part of an experiment.

Taking both museums together, in interviews most of the visitors felt that as a result of listening to the label, they had a good idea of what the object was and generally confirmed that they had learnt about it. This suggested to us that the installation had considerable holding power and was a good way to communicate with visitors.

A few adverse comments were annoyance due to hearing its repetition as the visit continued, that volume should be adjustable and about low usability at the Horniman Museum, including the sound quality there.

11.5   SUMMARY

The display factors that we had found important were summarised in Figure 11.1. The results of the experimental exhibits at the Petrie Museum and the Horniman Museum effectively tested the usefulness of a variety of display techniques in interpreting displays (summarised above, Table 10.1).

An exhibit that engages more senses than just that of sight is capable of addressing the challenges inherent in the four stages of interaction with an inconspicuous

---

7   Slack, Francis and Edwards 2011.
8   Bitgood 2000: 5; Griggs 1983: 120.

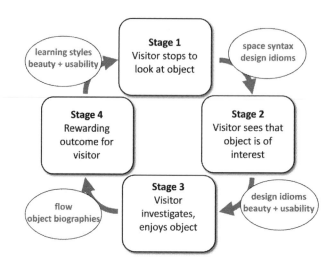

Figure 11.3   The influence of different display factors on the stages of the visitor–object interaction

Source: © F. Monti/S. Keene.

object. In one optimum scenario, an unassuming artefact would be positioned on a major gallery circulation route; colour or a movement-activated audio label could be employed to draw attention to it (Stage 1); photographs and illustrations could be a quick way to convey the object's rich content and context (Stage 2); a text booklet or a facsimile or duplicate artefact could be made available for handling (Stage 3); and an effective design and implementation of all the elements would create the right conditions for an enriching visitor encounter (Stage 4). The display of the Rosetta Stone (actual object rather than the replica) in Room 4 in the British Museum could be taken as an example of some of these principles. Intrinsically neither prepossessing nor eye-catching, the placement of the Stone in the main entrance from the Great Court, in a large, well-lit showcase supported by explanatory panels, enhances its attraction for a high proportion of visitors to the Museum. In fact, it is a victim of its own success, as constant crowds around it make it hard to see in any detail.[9]

Such an installation would not be suitable for every exhibition or gallery, or for every individual exhibit. To maximise benefits and reduce potential problems, these display techniques would need to be implemented sparingly, with an awareness of the design and spatial idiosyncrasies of the particular space and its usage patterns, and with a thorough understanding of the museum's audiences.

---

9   As many images from a Flickr search for British Museum Rosetta Stone show: www. flickr.com>British Museum Rosetta Stone. See also favourites for portico55.

Some of these techniques – colour and sound – would be effective only if they were an unexpected (possibly unique in the gallery) element of a display.

This set of observational studies also exposed how important it is to understand how people come across, approach and interact with museum objects, and how they receive and elaborate information about them.

PART 4

EFFECTIVE EXHIBITIONS

In this concluding part, we focus first on a gallery that we found to successfully exhibit dramatic and inconspicuous objects together. We then bring together our findings as a conceptual view of the qualities of galleries and exhibits. Finally, we discuss some of the wider implications of this work and present some guiding principles.

The *Tomb-chapel of Nebamun*, Room 61 in the British Museum, was chosen for our final study (Chapter 12) because it seemed that in it, silent and eloquent objects were displayed in harmony, so that it came close to representing the characteristics for our ideal exhibition. British Museum staff had already established that this gallery successfully engaged a high proportion of visitors in all of its exhibits. Our study aimed to revisit these findings and to use the assessment tools developed earlier to discover, if we could, what it was about the gallery's layout, design and different component exhibits, including a video reconstruction, that generated this desirable outcome. We also aimed to establish what messages and information visitors took from the gallery and how this related to the Museum's objectives for it.

In Chapter 13 we review our findings and our contribution to a better understanding of the characteristics that make exhibits attractive or unattractive to visitors. Visitor–object engagement at the atomic level (one object and one visitor) was defined by three key elements: *visitor*, *object* and *setting*. To comprehend these dimensions, the fields of *architecture, design, cognitive science* and *museology* were explored. A number of key concepts emerged from these theory domains for their potential contribution to this enquiry: *space syntax, design idioms, beauty and usability, flow, learning models* and *object biographies*.

We review our findings from the perspective of the four-stage model of visitor–object interaction: Stage 1: the visitor stops and looks at an object; Stage 2: they realise that the object is interesting to them; Stage 3: they investigate the object; Stage 4: they feel that they have had a rewarding experience.

We conclude in Chapter 14 by reflecting on visitors' approaches to the position of authority of the museum, their degree of awareness of exhibition mechanisms and their willingness and ability to acknowledge, question, and challenge what the museum proposes. The museum is the mediator between object and visitor, the connection through which messages and stories of the exhibition are inevitably filtered. It can be difficult for a museum professional to step outside their insider perspective. Museums are institutions that enjoy a high level of public trust and it is equally difficult for the visitor to remember that an exhibit – its design, interpretation, juxtaposition to other objects, and narratives – is the result of somebody's choice. By placing the visitor in the position to identify more actively what they want to see and by showing them how much lies hidden in each object, the museum performs its statutory and ethical responsibility of making collections available to all more effectively.

CHAPTER 12

HARMONY IN ANCIENT EGYPT

The *Tomb-chapel of Nebamun* gallery (Room 61) at the British Museum was chosen as a study because it seemed that the gallery might be a model for displaying silent objects together with striking ones in a way that resulted in very enjoyable experiences for visitors.

It came as a serendipitous revelation on a family visit to observe that here silent and spectacular objects do not compete for visitor attention, but rather work together to convey the exhibition's messages. Why was this so? This was the catalyst for undertaking research using our key concepts to understand the reasons behind this apparently symbiotic relationship.

12.1   THE GALLERY

Ancient Egyptian life and death: the Tomb-chapel of Nebamun is on an upper floor of the British Museum, at the west end of the sequence of ancient Egyptian funerary galleries and adjacent to Rooms 62 and 63 (the latter is reviewed in Chapter 8). The exhibition was designed to resemble the layout of a tomb-chapel. The walls and false ceiling of the gallery are of limestone to match the colour of the Theban hills where the Nebamun burial chamber is now lost; the walls are sky blue, as if under the Egyptian sun. The room's primary display is of 11 beautiful paintings from the ancient Egyptian tomb-chapel of Nebamun (approximately 1350 BC) depicting, for example, vivid scenes of Nebamun as a tall young man fowling in the marshes, stacks of food offerings and naked dancing girls. These are impressively presented in a showcase along the northern wall and in an adjacent free-standing display. The themes in the paintings (living conditions, work and survival, beauty, fashion and offerings from a tomb) are brought to life in three dimensions by 180 objects from the same period, some visually spectacular, others inconspicuous. Interpretative material, such as large photographs of Egypt, drawings and a 3D video reconstruction of the tomb-chapel, show how the structure would have appeared in its original setting and in pristine condition.

At the same time, the paintings and ancillary objects are deployed to demonstrate that the ancient Egyptians were as sophisticated as we are, to convey the extraordinary

Figure 12.1   The *Tomb-chapel of Nebamun* gallery at the British Museum: view from the east entrance from Room 62. After the dim lighting and often crowded conditions in Room 62, the *Nebamun* gallery lifted the spirits, with a more spacious layout, duck-egg blue walls and limestone-coloured floor and ceiling

Source: © S. Keene, courtesy of the Trustees of the British Museum.

artistic and aesthetic merits of the paintings and to invite reflection on how curatorial knowledge of this ancient culture is restricted to the material evidence currently available.[1] It was accepted that individual visitors may be reached by different facets of the messages; they are invited to take whatever they are ready for on the day.

12.2   RESEARCH OBJECTIVES AND QUESTIONS

Staff in the British Museum Interpretation Team generously made reports and data from their gallery evaluations available to us to use: tracking and visitor surveys and an evaluation of the video reconstruction of the tomb before it was installed in the gallery.[2] We made observations of visitors in the gallery and undertook a visitor interview survey on our own behalf; in addition, we also interviewed

---

1   Interview with R. Parkinson, gallery curator, 2009.
2   These internal reports have been referenced where appropriate.

British Museum staff to ascertain their views on to what extent their intentions for the gallery had been realised.

British Museum staff had already established that this gallery successfully engaged a high proportion of visitors in all of its exhibits and that they found their experience very rewarding. The objectives in our study were to use the analytical tools developed earlier to discover, if we could, what it was about the gallery's layout, design and different component exhibits that enabled spectacular and inconspicuous objects to work together to deliver the exhibition's messages without detracting from each other. We aimed to investigate the role and reception of the computer simulation in the context of the other elements of the exhibition. We also wished to establish to what extent the information and messages that visitors took from the gallery corresponded to the museum's objectives for it.

A series of research questions were addressed:

- How did people view objects and did they link them to create narratives?
- What was the role of the video in conveying such narratives?
- How did visitors receive the computer simulation in a British Museum permanent exhibition?
- Were the Museum's intentions successfully realised?

12.2.1 Research Method

The design of the evaluation programme stemmed from the three key dimensions of a visitor's encounter with objects: the setting, the visitor and the exhibit. The three dimensions are modulated by a number of factors and operate on many levels (above, 1.1).

The research methods employed were:

- preparatory desk-based research: visitor studies for the *Nebamun* gallery undertaken by the British Museum Interpretation Unit were reviewed. Some of their data were re-used in our analysis, and their results were compared to those from our similar surveys;
- analysis of space and visitor circulation patterns: the results from visitor circulation studies and observations conducted by the British Museum were drawn on so as to understand areas of interest and neglect within the gallery and the most common patterns of interaction in relation to space, design, display elements and objects;[3]
- gallery audit and assessment of the video against concept checksheets: the checksheets which employed the principles inherent in our key concepts

---

3   Interpretation officer: interview 2009.

(Appendix 2) were used to conduct a thorough audit of the visitors' experience of the exhibition. We extended this approach to analysing the gallery digital reconstruction of the tomb-chapel;

- visitor survey: randomly selected visitors were interviewed after their viewing of the gallery to understand how they chose, viewed and made sense of gallery exhibits. Data from the British Museum gallery survey were also taken into account;[4]
- interviews with museum staff: questionnaire-based interviews with the curator, interpretation officer and designer were conducted in order to understand what the Museum intended to communicate in the *Nebamun* gallery and the dynamics which created it.[5]

For interview questions, see Appendix 11; for data, see the website, www.ucl. ac.uk/silent-objects.

12.2.2 The Conceptual Framework for the Research

The key concepts developed in this research programme were used to comprehensively address the dimensions of visitor–exhibit–setting (above, 1.4).

We summarise the British Museum's results from their visitor-tracking surveys.[6] Design idioms – colour, light, text and the use of space – were used to analyse whether particular feelings were elicited in visitors and the extent of their appreciation of the objects: the attractive and holding power of exhibits.[7] Beauty and usability helped to gauge the potential of the exhibits to draw attention and to engage the viewer or user. Concepts from cognitive science helped to interpret responses to our questionnaire-based visitor survey. Concepts from the biography of things (the life trajectory of an object and its relationship with other objects and people) were checked to see how they had been incorporated to put across how different individuals (for example, audiences, curators and collectors) encounter objects and make sense of them.[8]

To assess the video, which showed a computer reconstruction of the tomb-chapel as it might have been prior to its discovery, we employed concepts from film and studies.[9]

---

4   Interview with the interpretation officer, 2009.
5   Interviews were held in 2009 with the gallery curator, the designer and the interpretation officer. Internal evaluation reports kindly made available to us are referenced in the bibliography.
6   Hillier and Hanson 1984.
7   Hall 1987.
8   Alberti 2005; Appadurai 1986.
9   Monaco 2000.

12.2.3   Analysis of Space and Visit Patterns

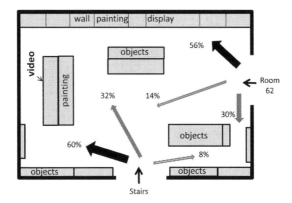

Figure 12.2   The *Tomb-chapel of Nebamun* gallery at the British Museum: the gallery layout showing the paths taken by visitors (per cent of visitors)

Source: © R. Miner/F. Monti/S. Keene.

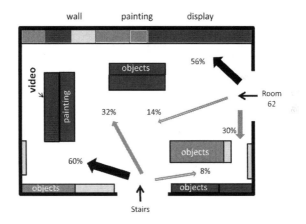

Figure 12.3   The *Tomb-chapel of Nebamun* gallery at the British Museum: the gallery layout showing the holding power of the displays. Darker = more visitors observed with level 3 or 4 engagement. Darkest: 91–100 per cent of visitors; medium – 81–90 per cent; lightest – 51–70 per cent (Figures 12.2 and 12.3 re-drawn from Miner 2009)

Source: © R. Miner/F. Monti/S. Keene.

Tracking and observation exercises were carried out by the British Museum in 2009.[10] Visitors were observed at various times of day on weekdays. Every third visitor to enter the gallery was tracked and the door of entry was changed after each tracking. The level of engagement was noted:

- Level 1: glance or very little interaction.
- Level 2: less than 10 seconds or only a basic level of interaction.
- Level 3: 10–40 seconds or a deeper level of interaction.
- Level 4: 40 seconds or more or a very deep level of interaction.

If a visitor walked away from an object and then returned to examine it, their level of engagement was taken as a 4.

Of 170 visitors in all, 70 simply walked through and 100 were tracked and their use of the gallery recorded.

This indicated the *attracting* and *holding power* of individual displays (Figure 12.3). The number of people that stop to look at an exhibit indicates its attracting power, while holding power refers to the amount of time visitors interact with it.

12.2.4 Gallery Use of Space

Although each display within the gallery could be viewed in isolation, the keen visitor would be able to quickly understand at least the primary level of conceptual organisation. From either entry point, the viewer had an overview of the whole exhibition and an uninterrupted vista of the wall-length display of paintings. When entering from the southern stairs, the gallery's introductory panel was immediately encountered, next to a large stela. Closer viewing could discover a video in an out-of-the-way area at the western end of the gallery (Figures 12.2 and 12.3).

As we observed in other case studies, visitors tended to view first what was nearest or in their path on entering the gallery: from the western stair entrance, the showcases on their left and then the wall paintings, and from the other entrance, the wall paintings and then the cases on the south side of the room. However, visitors spent longer in this gallery compared to many other British Museum galleries (a median time of 442 seconds) and stopped at many of the exhibits for a significant time (Level 3 or 4 engagement). Out of 19 cases and exhibits, only two encouraged fewer than 30 per cent of visitors to stop; these were cases situated almost out of sight from both entrances. The *Work and survival* display had the highest attracting power (77 per cent of visitors), followed by the painting depicting *Nebamun in the marshes* (above, Figure 3.7) and the *Feast scene*. The *Work and survival* display had high attraction power despite the mundane-looking objects exhibited in it,

10   Interview with the interpretation officer, 2009.

perhaps because it was located in the line of sight of visitors who turned left when entering from the west stairs (a tendency recorded during observations).

The degree of engagement with the gallery was also high. At least 60 per cent of visitors spent between 10 and 40 seconds (or more) with an exhibit; almost all of the 19 exhibits had a high level of holding power. The video recorded the highest level of interaction despite its obscure location: over 70 per cent of visitors used it, 97 per cent had a meaningful engagement with it and most stayed for its entire two-minute duration.[11]

12.3   ASSESSMENT AGAINST CONCEPTS

The gallery scored highly against all of the key concepts, especially for its potential to engender flow amongst visitors (Table 12.1). In responses to interview questions, many visitors said they had felt highly engaged emotionally as well as intellectually (12.3.3; Appendix 11; for a transcript of responses, see www.ucl. ac.uk/silent-objects).

Table 12.1   The *Tomb-chapel of Nebamun* gallery at the British Museum: concept checksheet scores (for data, see www.ucl.ac.uk/silent-objects)

Key concept	Score against maximum	
Space syntax	21/25	84%
Design idioms	70/85	82%
Beauty and usability	85/95	89%
Flow	48/50	96%

12.3.1 Space Syntax

A study of the spatial configuration of the gallery and of the way that individual exhibits complemented each other supported the curator's belief that the successful delivery of the messages was largely due to the visual design and to the carefully planned layout of the exhibits:

> as the design progressed we abandoned many of the possible intellectual themes, and we focused on representing the central theme of Dead and living (tomb-chapel) using the paintings and objects from the same period depicted in the paintings. We wanted to show the difference between the rich and the poor in two dimensions and three dimensions. To achieve this we planned the floor layout very carefully.[12]

---

11   These data are from Miner 2009, with permission.
12   Interview with R. Parkinson, gallery curator, 2009.

**Figure 12.4   The *Tomb-chapel of Nebamun* gallery at the British Museum: one
of the cases displaying the paintings. The visitor is looking at the
text panel below the case, which explains a detail in the painting,
as in Figure 12.5**

Source: © S. Keene, courtesy of the Trustees of the British Museum.

For example, items usually present in funerary scenes were displayed next to the
painting depicting a table of offerings. Observations of visitor behaviour indicated
that some individuals looked at the two displays in combination.

12.3.2 Design Idioms

The pale blue used for the walls and the case interiors and the creamy limestone
finish of the ceiling and floor generates a feeling of freshness and relaxation. Colour-
differentiated display was not used, but would tend to disrupt the impression of
design harmony. Light levels are generally high – considerably higher than in the
adjacent *Mummies* galleries. Lighting is not obtrusive but is even enough to see
the fine details of objects.

Figure 12.5 The *Tomb-chapel of Nebamun* gallery at the British Museum: painting: above, Nebamun's cattle, with below, an example of the explanatory text panels below the paintings that drew attention to details

Source: © Trustees of the British Museum.

The alternating colours and patterns of cattle create a superb sense of animal movement. The artists have omitted some of the cattle's legs to preserve the clarity of the design. The herdsman is telling the farmer in front of him in the queue:
'Come on! Get away! Don't speak in the presence of the praised one! He detests people talking … Pass on in quiet and in order … He knows all affairs, does the scribe and counter of grain of [Amun], Neb[amun].'
Wording of text panel accompanying the painting

Text clearly sets out the theme for each showcase or painting fragment and draws attention to details of interest. Especially effective are the graphic panels with the painting fragments, which explain and draw attention to details that might otherwise be overlooked. Visitors can frequently be observed looking at the paintings, the text and back to the paintings.

In terms of object layout, enough objects are displayed to make the exhibits enticing and clearly interesting (aided by the extraordinary survival of organic materials from this remote age), but not so many as to make the prospect of viewing the displays daunting.

12.3.3 Beauty and Usability

The gallery gives a clear impression of beauty: the harmonious colours, the spacious but convenient case layout and the beauty of the paintings themselves all contribute to this. At the same time, it scores highly on usability – it is easy to understand and appreciate the exhibits, objects can readily be associated with their text labels, while the graphic panels vividly explain and enhance the paintings (Figures 3.7 and 12.5). The video display also adds to the experience (12.4). Visitors' questionnaire responses support its high score against this concept.

The following key words relating to cognitive states were noted in responses to the unprompted Question 1: *what are your impressions of the gallery you just visited?*

Table 12.2   The *Tomb-chapel of Nebamun* gallery: types of engagement: words occurring in responses to questionnaire Q1: what are your impressions of the gallery you just visited? (n=25 visitors interviewed)

Emotional engagement Atmosphere, overwhelming, emoting, breathtaking, contemplative, magic, evocative, door to long gone culture, sense of the past	14
Aesthetic engagement Beauty, beautiful, superb, extraordinary, elegant, splendid	10
Intellectual engagement Interesting, informative, descriptions, engaging, difference	8

The word 'atmosphere/atmospheric' was used five times, while 'beauty/beautiful' was used six times.

Some typical responses (significant words emphasised) were as follows:

- I like the *atmosphere* created by the light. I had the impression that there was no barrier between me and the objects because of the type of showcases. Really enjoyed that.
- *Overwhelming.* Description *opened door to a long-gone culture* and *time and place.*
- Unbelievable – very *emoting. Breathtaking.*

- Extremely *interesting*, well displayed. Explanation clear. You can see how it was used. Everyday objects ...
- Really *interesting*. A lot of everything in it. It gives you a sense of the past.
- *Beautiful place* with some fantastic paintings.
- A very *atmospheric* and *contemplative* place, predominantly created to house the *beautiful* paintings.
- Good – clear layout of exhibits with *adequate descriptions*, centred round the *Tomb-chapel of Nebamun*.
- A modern approach to exhibition design compared to more object rich galleries. Very *beautiful* display of *extraordinary* paintings from Egypt. Shows *difference* of life between rich/poor.

And, somewhat less enthusiastic:

- Quite dark, hushed, with *interesting* paintings. Maybe more of a thoroughfare to the more popular exhibits? (Mummies, etc.) Different to the bright open space of the Parthenon Gallery we had just visited.
- A newish Egyptian gallery with a display of objects and paintings from a tomb-chapel. *Atmospheric*. Busy with school-kids.
- I thought it was going to be new, but not. Read about it.
- Would I have gone in there without being ... Uninspiring. Didn't excite me. No particular exhibit caught my interest. The video of the tomb was interesting but I found it *frustrating* the lack of ... to link video to artifact, how they were discovered and when. *How did they get here?*

We should note that one visitor found it uninspiring and dull, especially annoyed by the lack of information on how and when the painting fragments were discovered and how they were acquired by the British Museum. Nevertheless, this visitor had spent significant time in the gallery reflecting on it: 'The gallery was well designed and presents the pieces to their best advantage.' They suggested improvements: 'Egyptian music, Egyptian being spoken in the background, movies/stories of people behind the objects – how was it made? The whole story has not been told.' In other words, they would have enjoyed the gallery more if it had engaged senses in addition to sight, and wanted even more information from it.

12.3.4 Flow

Flow is an elusive state to measure.[13] Judging from the time (long compared to other British Museum galleries) that visitors spent in the gallery (below, Figure 14.6) and responses to the questionnaire survey, the gallery did enable a flow state of total concentration in visitors, at least at times when it was not busy with school

---

13   Csikszentmihalyi 1997.

group visits. Many visitors could be seen looking at paintings, objects and text panels and the video reconstruction with considerable concentration.

12.3.5 Object Biographies

Objects are displayed primarily as functional objects. There are clues at various points in the gallery as to the paintings' relationship with the tomb-chapel itself. Some expressed a wish for a more coordinated approach to the biographies of the paintings: for example, the text for one painting, *Surveying the fields for Nebamun*, tells us that there are related fragments in a Berlin museum. The excellent explanation in and around the video of the tomb-chapel itself is quite separate from this, but still does not deal with how the fragments came to be in the British Museum or where other fragments may be. One visitor in the survey commented on this lack.

Regarding the objects in the display cases, we have to assume that they are selected items of the appropriate date and context but unassociated with the tomb-chapel.

12.3.6 Personal Learning Styles

Objects are systematically arranged and interpreted via logical factual labels. This can be recognised as a didactic exhibition style suiting those who prefer analytical learning.

12.4   ASSESSMENT: THE VIDEO[14]

The presence of the three-dimensional digital reconstruction of the tomb-chapel (Figure 12.6) is significant because it was one of the first in a permanent gallery at the British Museum and constituted a digression from the Museum's traditional interpretation policies. The curator initially received the proposal to include the video in the gallery with trepidation, fearing that the video might distract from the objects. However, the exhibit's evident ability to contextualise the paintings without the need to physically reconstruct the building was recognised to be a significant asset.[15]

Visitors had provided an overwhelmingly favourable response in pre-installation testing, supporting its introduction in the gallery: they were attracted to the video, liked it and thought that it successfully conveyed a sense of the atmosphere within the tomb-chapel. But this formative evaluation also indicated that the Museum ought to be clear about the purpose of the resource and unambiguous about the

---

14   For a fuller assessment of the video and also of the version on the gallery website, see Monti 2009.

15   Interview with R. Parkinson, gallery curator, 2009; Wiley 2008.

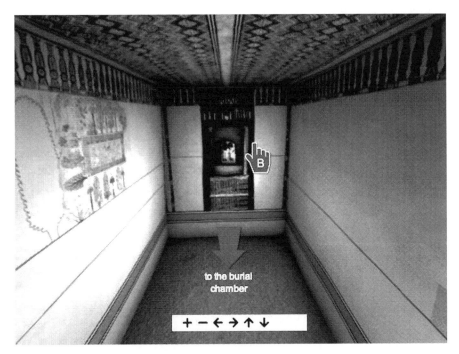

**Figure 12.6   The *Tomb-chapel of Nebamun* gallery at the British Museum:
scene from the tomb-chapel reconstruction video: the inner
chamber. Image from the online version**
Source: © Trustees of the British Museum.

reconstructive process.[16] These findings informed the design of the final version
of the digital screen.

The reconstruction is two minutes long. It consists of a sequence of three-
dimensional frames which takes the viewer on a journey of exploration from the
desert of Egypt, through the Nile Valley, to the West bank of the river and into
the tomb-chapel. Inside the edifice, the 11 paintings are shown in all their beauty,
located where it is believed they may originally have been and thus suggesting
what the tomb-chapel might originally have looked like when the paintings
were complete (Figure 12.6)[17] (the reconstruction can also be seen on the British
Museum web page for the gallery).

After considering a series of factors, such as visitor flow, costs and aesthetics,
the Museum had decided to locate the video in an out-of-the-way area of the

---

16   Wiley 2008.
17   The reconstruction can also be seen on the British Museum's web page for the gallery,
for which search 'Nebamun' at www.britishmuseum.org.

gallery (Figures 12.2 and 12.3) in order to neutralise its potential to distract visitors and ensure that the visitor flow is unobstructed even when large groups of schoolchildren gather around it.[18]

12.4.1 The Video Assessed Against Design Concepts

Despite the museum's hesitation over installing the video in the gallery, the video attracted and held the attention of a high proportion of visitors. In our interview survey, 12 out of 25 visitors had found it. Our survey responses showed that the digital medium was central to contextualising the paintings geographically and architecturally and to clearly linking paintings and objects (for detailed responses, see www.ucl.ac.uk/silent-objects):

- Image of village built on top of the tombs – view from balloon.
- Introduction from desert to tomb-chapel.
- You see what you would have seen as a tourist coming along from the mountain.
- Shows where they may have been.
- I like seeing it the way it first was and [the] general geographical/landscape context, then closes in on the site then enters the tomb-chapel.
- The curators' aspirations for the video, which they feel were successfully achieved, were 'We wanted to concentrate on creating the atmosphere … offer sense of colour and warmth'.[19]

In order to understand the reasons for its success, we analysed the video against some key concepts, assessing it by using a checklist just as we would other exhibits. This facilitated a focus on the video's design elements, the narrative approach and beauty and usability characteristics.

12.4.2 Design Idioms

The design strategy contributes to the successful realisation of the Museum's intentions through this medium.[20] The design of the reconstruction is evocative; the visual and textual information complements the gallery objects. The video is helpfully juxtaposed with an introductory panel and series of drawings showing the plan and side elevation of the tomb-chapel. The Museum chose not to use a soundtrack so as to maintain the contemplative and sombre atmosphere of an Egyptian tomb-chapel and to avoid intruding on other visitors' experience (a disadvantage of the whispering headrests, above, 10.6).[21] Each visual sequence has

18   Interview with R. Parkinson, gallery curator, 2009.
19   Interview with R. Parkinson, gallery curator, 2009.
20   Interviews with the gallery curator, designer and interpretation officer, 2009.
21   Interviews with the gallery curator, designer and interpretation officer, 2009.

a subtitle which explains what the viewer can see and the reconstructive process, and also distinguishes speculative from evidence-based information. The area is adequately lit, particularly on a bright day, when natural light seeps through the skylight.

12.4.3 Beauty and Usability

Through design consistency and an appropriate and eye-catching use of colour and space, the video achieves a harmonious effect. It tantalises the viewer with an evocative contextualisation of the paintings on display by means of a sequence of dazzling vistas. Besides this successful visual strategy, the video demonstrates a high degree of usability. The opening frame shows the duration and subject of the video and thereafter the subtitles provide clear conceptual and topographical orientation. The font is legible and the register of language is accessible to all. The video is placed at a height that is visible to children and wheelchair users. Its proximity to the paintings elicits a direct comparison between digital information and real objects.

12.4.4 Visual Communication Theories

The three-dimensional reconstruction video was analysed using a compositional interpretation method: framing, montage, sound and narrative structure.[22] Each individual image is clearly and eloquently framed, focusing the viewer's attention on the intended key messages without unnecessary clutter from visual information. Individual shots are seamlessly and coherently put together. The choice of silence rather than a soundtrack leads to a closer focus on the visual qualities of the exhibit. In general, the first level of the story, concerned with a contextual reconstruction of the paintings, comes across clearly. Other levels of the narrative, such as the theme of evidence-derived curatorial knowledge, are accessible to more discerning users.

12.4.5 Object Biographies

The video successfully conveys the original physical and socio-cultural context of the paintings and effectively communicates both the visual qualities and the original function of the paintings. Although the reconstruction highlights the beauty and the artistic merits of the fragments, their physicality and purpose also comes across. By highlighting gaps in knowledge and uncertainty in relation to the reconstructive process of the tomb-chapel, it invites reflection on the life of the paintings after they left Egypt, when they entered the museum collections. This narrative approach allowed some viewers to transcend the materiality of the objects and to consider notions of curatorial knowledge, absence and presence of evidence, and the unavoidable uncertainties inherent in reconstructive archaeology:

---

22   Monaco 2000.

- How much is here and how much lost. How was it lost? Where is it?
- Reconstructive process: shows how we gain knowledge from archaeology, and doubts and certainties.
- Gave you a sense of how much is preserved and how much is lost, and original context of the paintings.
- To show what is missed/damaged.

12.5   THE VISITORS AND THE VIDEO

For the purposes of this study, 25 people were interviewed by the researcher: 16 female and nine male (for the questionnaire, see Appendix 11; for detailed responses and data, see www.ucl.ac.uk/silent-objects). Age ranges were evenly distributed, with slightly more visitors being aged between 45 and 54. Fourteen out of the 25 visitors were visiting the Museum with a partner or friend, six with their family and five alone. In agreement with the results of the British Museum's survey, seven of the respondents had come to the Museum specifically to visit the *Nebamun* gallery on the wave of the marketing campaign for its opening in January 2009.[23] This may have impacted on the results of the evaluations and on visitors' perception, reception and recollections of the exhibition, since people who have invested time and effort in an experience are generally reluctant to feel that this has been wasted.

Twelve of the interviewed visitors had watched the video reconstruction. Among those who did not watch it, the most common reason was not having noticed its existence (10 responses) followed by time limitations (three responses). The segregated location of the digital exhibit was a deliberate strategy, but this issue might be reconsidered, as it seems regrettable that a proportion of visitors miss what others find adds to their enjoyment and understanding of the gallery. The screen could be signalled by means of an unobtrusive sign or mentioned in the gallery's introductory panel, which was observed to receive a high degree of visitor attention, despite other studies suggesting that such panels are ignored.[24]

The contextualising ability of the video and its contribution to the deliverance of the gallery's messages emerged from the findings. Visitors' favourite aspects were the video's ability to deliver the atmosphere of the original setting (five out of 15) and to convey a sense of the past through the full-colour reconstruction of the tomb-chapel (five out of 15). The role of the digital resource in the meaning-making process was also suggested in replies to Question 7: *how did you relate what you saw in the animation to the objects in this gallery?* According to six out of 16 interviewees, the most valuable aspect of the video was its ability to place the paintings in their original cultural, geographical and architectural context.

23   Miner 2009: interview.
24   Slack, Francis and Edwards 2011.

Figure 12.7   The introductory panel to the *Tomb-chapel of Nebamun* gallery is strategically situated opposite one of the main entrances, with lighting that draws attention to it

Source: © Trustees of the British Museum.

Four mentions were made to the reconstruction's role in offering a visual and straightforward representation of the relationship between the extent of paintings preserved and what had been lost. It was very significant that this higher-level message, which related to the limitations of object-derived knowledge and the representation of the past in academic institutions, was recognised and highlighted by visitors (12.4.1).

Overall, seven out of nine viewers thought that the video enhanced their understanding of the objects in the gallery. Two visitors who believed the contrary went on to explain that most of the information conveyed by the digital reconstruction had already been conveyed in other exhibits. This result can be interpreted positively, as an indication of the video's ability to visually corroborate some of the gallery's themes.

Finally, 16 interviewees were in favour of introducing similar digital resources into other galleries. In particular, visitors mentioned that such displays could provide a context, such as geographic location and links with countries of origin. Six respondents, however, added the caveat that they would welcome the introduction of other screens only if they were employed in moderation, if they added to the narrative and if they followed consultation with audiences, and six were either not interested or positively disliked them.

12.6   CONCLUSIONS

Visitors' responses to the gallery indicate that in general the experience was one of positive affect. This emotional response is not neutral: it is thought that it enhances cognitive processes as well, such as memory storage and retrieval, categorisation and analysis, associating ideas and more. This may help to explain the generally enthusiastic reception of the gallery by visitors and their feelings that they learned from it (12.3.3; above, 4.5).[25]

BOX 12.1   *NEBAMUN* GALLERY, YOUNG VISITORS

I heard them first, before I saw them, twittering like the birds in the *Hunting* painting. As I came round the corner, there was a lively group of five boys and girls about nine or 10 years old, with their teacher. They were looking at the introductory panel with the image of one of the paintings. Another visitor pointed out the original and they rushed over to look at it. 'That's the original one, thousands of years old.' 'Where's the cat?' 'I can see a butterfly.' 'There's a fish!'

Something even more enticing caught their eye 'Look! A computer!' and they rushed over to the video reconstruction.

'What's that big river?' 'Do you know what it's called?' 'Hey look that's what it was like inside the tomb.'

Attention was brief. Next they all moved over to one of the object cases. 'That's what they used to dig with.' 'Look at that pot.' 'Is that one of their houses?'

Then it was back to the paintings. As I left the gallery I could hear the excited chatter as they checked out the dancing girls and the desert hares with their brindled fur and whiskers, dangling from the hunters' hands.

12.6.1 The Methodology

The methodology, using visitor tracking, concept-based analysis checklists and structured visitor interviews, enabled us to evaluate the gallery in terms of visitor numbers and pathways and the ability of individual component exhibits to attract people and hold their attention. But, further, from this indepth and multi-perspective investigation, we were able to understand also how the gallery

---

25   Isen 1993: 263–4; Norman 2002: 39.

Figure 12.8   The *Tomb-chapel of Nebamun* **gallery at the British Museum:
visitors engrossed in one of the object display cases, *Fashion and
beauty*, which perhaps appeals to their personal interests**
Source: © S. Keene, courtesy of the Trustees of the British Museum.

succeeded in distributing visitors' attention evenly between silent and dramatic
objects. In contrast to *Egyptian death and afterlife: mummies* (Room 63), where
visitors interviewed expressed a positive dislike for inconspicuous objects, in
the *Nebamun* gallery, few people could think of anything they did not like much.
Visitors felt they had had an outstanding experience in the gallery, that all of
it had been worth their attention, and many took with them a greatly enhanced
understanding and appreciation of life in ancient Egypt.

12.6.2 The Gallery

The *Tomb-chapel of Nebamun* gallery essentially achieved what we would see
as ideal in a museum exhibition. The challenge of how to display inconspicuous
and spectacular objects together and avoid disparities in viewing was successfully
tackled. According to our findings, it illustrated the considerable advantages
for a museum in achieving this. Visitors spent significantly longer than normal
in the gallery and with the displays, with evident enjoyment. There was little
inconsistency between the Museum's communication intentions and visitors'
reception of them, which must surely be the aspiration of every exhibition curator
and designer.

The Museum's gallery design processes had been changed in the 10 years since the *Egyptian death and afterlife: mummies* gallery was opened in 1999 (above, 8.7). Even so, like most galleries and exhibitions, the *Tomb-chapel of Nebamun* gallery was created amidst stress and struggle with the inevitable imperatives and pressures of a complex project, with tensions between the processes of visual design, project management, academic concerns and creativity. The result is an outstandingly harmonious, beautiful and peaceful gallery.[26]

Each interpretative item and each object formed a piece in a wider picture of the deceased's world and was recognised as such by visitors. Thus, even in a space where the spectacular could easily have dominated, an even distribution of attention was achieved; visitors compared different sources of evidence and drew connections between the physical and the pictoral, the textual and the digital. The stories were conveyed by different media; the viewer was simultaneously storyteller and spectator.

Because each component exhibit was necessary to the gallery's narratives, visitors were enticed into a visual journey: an investigation of different sources in which they were gradually rewarded with additional pieces of the broader picture. This was achieved through a carefully planned layout, an effective design and interpretation strategy, an appropriate ratio between space and objects, and the creation of an atmospheric and evocative place.

In this scenario, the three-dimensional video reconstruction played a crucial role in unifying and contextualising. Although its obscure location could have been advertised more clearly, those visitors who did find the screen were rewarded with a clear, effective and evocative means of contextualising the paintings and an opportunity to reflect over the messages at the heart of the interpretation strategy. After the visit, the zealous visitor could plunge into an additional web-based virtual exploration of the ancient Egyptian monument to reach deeper and more detailed levels of understanding and to savour, once again, the evocative and moving atmosphere of the *Tomb-chapel of Nebamun* gallery.

---

26   Interview with R. Parkinson, gallery curator, 2009.

CHAPTER 13

REVIEWING THE FINDINGS

Silent objects, inconspicuous objects of humble appearance, often fail to engage the general public. Yet such objects are often intended as an important part of a museum exhibition. In this research project, our objective was to understand in some depth the reasons why they are overlooked and hence how to re-balance viewing patterns. Visitors would be rewarded with a better knowledge of objects and of the cultural contexts they represent.

All exhibitions to an extent comprise both visual and inconspicuous objects, but this study focused on displays of Egyptian collections where the dissonance between the two groups is particularly evident and where exhibitory practices have largely defined both the public perception and the scholarly understanding of ancient Egypt.[1]

13.1   THE FRAMEWORK OF THEORY AND CONCEPTS

Visitor–object engagement at the atomic level (one object and one visitor) was defined by three key elements: *visitor*, *object* and *setting*. To comprehend these dimensions, the fields of *architecture*, *design*, *cognitive science* and *museology* were explored. A number of key concepts emerged from these theory domains for their potential contribution to this enquiry: *space syntax*, *design idioms*, *beauty and usability*, *flow*, *learning models* and *object biographies*. We developed a four-stage model of visitor–object interaction and tested the validity of using these concepts by analysing galleries in the British Museum, the V&A and the Horniman Museum.

13.2   EVALUATION AND EXPERIMENTATION

We took our investigation further by investigating the dynamics of visitor encounters with 'glamorous' Egyptian objects in one of the most famous galleries in the British Museum – *Egyptian death and afterlife: mummies* (Room 63) – and went on to look at visitor engagement using the sense of touch in the *Hands on* desks in the Museum.

---

1   Moser 2006: 7–8.

These exercises supported the utility of these concepts and enabled us to isolate a series of design and interpretative factors which seemed to define positive visitor–object encounters. These factors were tested in an observational research exercise at the Petrie Museum and the Horniman Museum, where we designed, installed, implemented and evaluated three design and interpretative solutions.

Enriched by these findings, the research was taken to a different level when we applied our conceptual evaluation to a newly opened Egyptian gallery in the British Museum – Room 61, the *Tomb-chapel of Nebamun* – and found that in it the voices of silent objects were heard in harmony with those of the striking and beautiful, to the great enjoyment of the visitors we interviewed.

In two of the galleries we assessed, the *Tomb-chapel of Nebamun* and the *Music room* in the Horniman Museum, we found that visitors engaged with inconspicuous objects on a par with striking and conspicuous ones. In both these galleries, visitors spent significantly longer than they did in other galleries that we assessed (Chapters 6 and 12).

13.3   FINDINGS

The initial postulation that visitors generally overlook inconspicuous objects was strongly supported. For example, in the survey conducted at the six *Hands on* desks at the British Museum, when the actions of visitors were observed, it was visually striking objects that were in fact first selected even though respondents mentioned 'wanting to know what a curious looking object is' or 'the fact that an object looks very old' as their reasoned choice (above, 9.6.2). It seems that this mechanism operates in part unconsciously: although people attribute rational reasons for their attention, in actuality aesthetic qualities are a strong attraction. Alternatively, their claimed motives may simply reflect their desire to meet the intellectual standards they feel the museum expects of them, rather than citing what they fear may be judged as a shallow or inappropriate interaction with the objects.

Such sensitivity may increase or decrease according to the character of the gallery, the nature of the institution and the figure of the investigator. Despite aspiring to a 'technical neutrality',[2] the investigator cannot avoid influencing, through their questions, silences, mannerism and presence, the communication process; as such, the investigation was conducted across a range of national, local and university museums.

The role of visual qualities in the selection and preference of objects was further supported by the research at the British Museum *Egyptian death and afterlife: mummies*

---

2   Lynch 2004: 187.

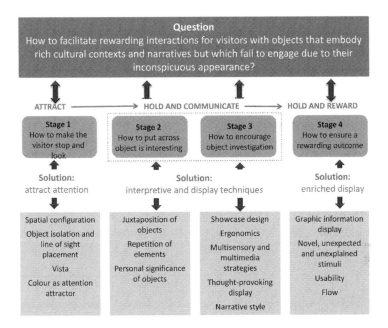

Figure 13.1   Schematic representation of the relationship between research questions, stages in the visitor–object interaction and key concept details

Source: © F. Monti/S. Keene.

(Room 63). When citing examples of things they found interesting in the gallery, visitors referred to them by recalling key visual characteristics, such as size, fine details, colourfulness and elaborate patterns (above, 8.5), or explained their attraction in terms of explicit aesthetic enjoyment: 'I aesthetically loved the contrast between the gold and the black of the wig', a woman said referring to the coffin of Henutmehyt. Visually enticing objects were observed to hold attention for a considerable amount of time by inspiring visual contemplation. Conversely, visitors were not well disposed towards small objects lacking a distinctive feature and they were not prepared to spend much time looking at them. These findings testify to the need to address the preconception, of which some visitors seem to be aware (above, 8.5.3), that inconspicuous objects are, in terms of the *value principle*, not worth much effort.[3]

13.4   MODELS FOR INTERACTIONS

The visitor–object interaction model was used as the basis for the research (Figure 1.4). An implementation of the proposed solutions should help the visitor to

---

3   Bitgood 2006: 464.

notice an object, become aware of its potential interest, investigate it and have a rewarding experience (Figure 13.1).

13.5   STAGE 1: THE VISITOR STOPS TO LOOK

Key factors that drew the visitor to look at an inconspicuous object were *patterns of visitor circulation, line of sight placement, vista* and *colour*. Given the predisposition of visitors to choose objects which they unconsciously judge will offer the most 'cost-effective' encounter, *spatial configuration* can be employed to draw attention to specific objects. As shown by the observational evidence, objects which are exhibited in isolation, in key positions and on the *line of sight* are likely to attract visitors' attention. However, strong exhibits can be used to alter circulation patterns within galleries and ultimately to re-balance the use of space. As such, it is suggested that the provision of an uninterrupted *vista* over the whole content of an exhibition puts the visitor in the position to mentally map their visit in an orderly way and increases the chances that inconspicuous objects will be attended to. Then, of the design elements investigated, *colour* emerged as the most effective way to attract and hold attention to a desired object.

13.5.1 Patterns of Visitor Circulation

The architectural characteristics of a museum gallery, the layout of the display cases and the arrangement of objects within the space are the dominant factors in determining visitor movement patterns and the dynamics of object encounters (above, Chapter 2). Other research has shown that visitor itineraries and exhibit attendance can be modulated by adjusting the syntactic properties of museum layouts. Choi's work indicates that people are initially drawn to what is in their path.[4]

Similar findings emerged from our study in the British Museum *Enlightenment* gallery, in the V&A's *Understanding objects* in the British Galleries and in the *Music room* at the Horniman Museum. In the British Museum *Egyptian death and afterlife: mummies* (Room 63), the tracking exercise showed that visitors move along the main east-west axes, on which the displays are aligned (above, 8.3).

We found, in common with other research, that the architectural characteristics of the gallery, the layout of displays and the location of objects defined the direction of visitor flow.[5] Bitgood suggests that 'patterns of visitor circulation are influenced by the general value principle': visitors show a propensity to decrease the effort

---

4   Bitgood 2006: 463; Bourdeau and Chebat 2001: 72; Choi 1999: 249.
5   Bitgood et al. 1992.

of circulation by choosing routes which involve fewer steps.[6] We did not find a tendency to turn right on entry and circulate anticlockwise as other studies have done,[7] and are in general sceptical about this suggestion. For instance, special exhibitions, which often have a planned visitor path, invariably assume a left turn on entrance.

13.5.2 Line-of-Sight Placement and Object Isolation

Two spatial factors that contribute to attracting visitor attention are placing an object on the visitor's line of sight and isolating it from surrounding displays. Evidence in support of the line-of-sight theory was found in *Egyptian death and afterlife: mummies* (Room 63) at the British Museum, where people most frequently interacted by following the central flow path of the gallery, distractedly glancing at the objects in sight (above, 8.3). Although large and striking specimens such as coffins and mummies were among the material remains that gallery goers were most frequently drawn to, less conspicuous exhibits in their line of sight also successfully caught their attention. The contrasting results from the comparative 'whispering headrests' experiment at the Petrie Museum and the Horniman Museum (above, 10.6.2) highlighted a considerable variation in visitor attendance between the centrally placed installation at the Petrie Museum and that at the Horniman Museum, which was in an area with less visitor traffic. Half of the visitors to the *Tomb-chapel of Nebamun* gallery missed the video reconstruction because it was not visible from the main gallery space. Objects in segregated areas risk being overlooked because circulation to less integrated spaces is generally limited; in such circumstances, an efficient arrangement of displays within a space can improve circulation patterns.[8] For example, because charming objects are capable of drawing visitors away from their path, as demonstrated by the sound benches at the *Music room* in the Horniman Museum (above, 6.5.1), they can be placed in less frequented places, thus encouraging a wider spatial exploration and promoting encounters with other objects on the route.

Once a better flow of visitors through a gallery is achieved, occasional inconspicuous objects could be centrally displayed to draw attention to them. An isolated object is likely to get the undivided interest of visitors unless there are other distracting stimuli in the vicinity, which will make it less noticeable, particularly if it lacks inherently salient factors.[9] The popularity of the centrally displayed model of the Albert Memorial in Room 123 at the V&A supports this proposal (above, 6.4.1), although besides being displayed in isolation and in a central position, the Victorian model is also a visually striking, large and sparkly

---

6   Bitgood 2006: 471.
7   Bitgood 2000; Dean 1994: 51; Underhill 2000: 76.
8   Psarra and Grajewski 2002; Glasgow Museum 2006.
9   Melton 1972; Bitgood 2002: 8.

artefact: all factors which contribute to draw people.[10] Another example is the sculptures of heads depicting James Watts, displayed together with normally unattractive tools and metal pieces, in a prominent position outside the James Watt workshop in the Science Museum (Figure 13.2). Isolated display needs to be employed in moderation as it relies on feelings of anticipation and surprise; if employed to excess, visitors will grow accustomed to it and will learn to ignore the humble objects, wherever they are positioned.

However, as observed in the British Museum *Egyptian death and afterlife: mummies* gallery, spatially prompted encounters do not necessarily result in long-lasting and indepth interactions (above, 8.4). Thus, additional procedures need to be implemented to encourage full appreciation. A centrally positioned object may lure the viewer into stopping by virtue of its location alone, but it risks being rejected if the viewer's attention is not held long enough for them to become aware of its potential interest. All things being equal, however, the very placing of inconspicuous objects in key positions makes a statement about the existence of interesting content (Stage 2) (above, 8.5.3). This feature relies on the visitor assumption that the museum authoritatively selects and highlights objects it thinks are worth seeing; the viewer thinks an object more valuable when it receives a special treatment. It is ultimately up to individual museums and curators to establish the extent to which to exert this authoritative touch.

13.5.3 Vista

Vista, or *isovist*, is an architectural term used to refer to the total area visible from one point.[11] It refers to a place where interconnected areas are visible to the viewer at all times, thus encouraging comparison and an extensive exploration of space.[12] A vista can be a means of drawing attention and of raising awareness of specific objects on display. The *Enlightenment* gallery at the British Museum to an extent exemplifies this concept: the grand, dramatic and uninterrupted vision over the whole gallery not only promotes a sense of wonder and surprise, but also enables comprehensive viewings and exploration of the exhibition, thereby encouraging balanced attention distribution among objects (Figure 6.1). The *Tomb-chapel of Nebamun* gallery in the same museum achieved this: almost all of the displays and the gallery were visible from either entrance (above, 12.2.4; Figure 12.1). Similarly, the component displays in the *Music room* in the Horniman Museum were easy to view from the entrance (above, 7.1; Figure 6.10).

If visitors are able to rapidly scan the gallery landscape, they can choose and define the pattern of their visit. Layout of space, lines of sight and visitors'

---

10   Dean 1994: 51.
11   Benedikt 1979.
12   Choi 1999: 249.

natural tendency to pursue the more effort-effective routes (in this instance, along the perimeters of the space) can be designed to encourage more thorough and purposeful viewings.[13]

13.5.4 Colour

Although colour proved to be a valuable tool in all the stages of the visitor–object encounter, a great deal of evidence suggested that its use was effective in Stage 1 in our visitor–object model: attracting attention. The experiments at the Petrie Museum, in particular the ability of the modest ostracon booklet to capture the eye of passing visitors and alert them to the object's presence, could largely be ascribed to the contrast between the booklet's bright red cover and the homogeneous and neutral background of the Museum's pottery gallery.

Colour can also facilitate the communication of broad themes.[14] It can be employed to evoke a general atmosphere and make the viewer aware of a potentially interesting cultural context (Stage 2) or to hold attention by enhancing certain characteristics of the object (Stage 3). Supporting observational evidence came from the research in the *Enlightenment* gallery and in the *Hands on* desks in the British Museum (above, 6.3.4 and 9.5.2). Colour can also be utilised to differentiate visually between types and levels of information, as in the ostracon experiment at the Petrie Museum, where people appreciated the sub-division of topics suggested by the booklet's colour-coded pages (above, 10.4).

13.6   STAGE 2: THE VISITOR BECOMES AWARE OF THE INTEREST OF THE OBJECT

The research suggested that *juxtaposition of objects*, *repetition of information* and *personal significance of objects* constitute effective strategies for alerting a visitor to the rich information and cultural connotations that an object embodies. Evidence showed that if an inconspicuous object is displayed *juxtaposed* with others which are better equipped to attract and hold the attention of visitors, the inconspicuous object is more likely to be considered. The James Watts busts in the Science Museum are a good example of this: the display of white heads surrounded by old tools, in the open in front of the workshop structure, attracts investigation out of surprise and curiosity (Figure 13.2). This is because visitors use the display context of the object in making assumptions on the cultural richness of the object. Despite some inherent difficulties, showing large *assemblages of similar objects* is an efficient way to attract attention, to allow the viewer to quickly and effectively draw comparisons within a large amount of information and to raise awareness

---

13   Bitgood 2006: 473.
14   Portas 1999: 80.

as to the existence of different types of object. The *Listen to order* display in the Horniman *Music room* exemplifies this (above, 6.5.3). The data suggested, further, that if the *personal significance* of an inconspicuous object is apparent to the visitor, it is more likely to attract attention (above, 8.5.5, 11.2.1), to convey the existence of cultural contexts and narratives of potential interest and to offer a positive and rewarding encounter.

13.6.1   Juxtaposition of Objects

Potential interest can be suggested to visitors if objects are arranged so as to offer visual clues that facilitate comparison and contrast.[15] This rationale informed the re-display of the geology collection at the Petrie Museum, where stone specimens were paired with artefacts of the same type of stone. It is more common to contrast appealing objects with less appealing ones: unexpected associations can create curious and intriguing vistas. In the *Enlightenment* gallery, for example, visitors were drawn to a copy of the Rosetta Stone (above, 6.3.1) because the object's presumed status made it attractive (not everyone realised that the exhibit is a facsimile). As a consequence, nearby displays also received high numbers of viewers in search of narrative links and further elucidation on the facsimile of the Egyptian document.

This principle works because visitors make assumptions on the potential interest of an object derived from its exhibitory context. Exhibits near a striking or glamorous object may or may not contribute to the nuances of the narrative, but they are unconsciously judged to be similarly worthwhile to examine.

13.6.2   Repetition of Information

In display design, it is believed that the meticulously planned massing of ordinary objects confers a special attraction.[16] This stratagem can be employed to draw the eye to an impressive display landscape, in the hope that the viewer's attention will turn next to individual items. This exhibition technique follows Gestalt theories of perception, where the whole effect (vista) is greater than the sum of its individual parts (single objects).[17] A successful outcome relies on an integration of design and interpretation procedures which need to work together to ensure that the whole effect does not overshadow the individual objects. Some advocate creating visual order in object-dense displays by leaving vacant spaces between groups of items to let the brain rest to record and interpret impressions in order to avoid overwhelming the viewer with excessive sensory stimulation.[18]

---

15   Wittlin 1971: 138.
16   Verlarde 1988: 93.
17   Behrens 1984: 49.
18   Wittlin 1971: 142.

Figure 13.2   Sculpted portrait heads of James Watt, by well-known eighteenth-century sculptors. Watt was very interested in the mechanical reproduction of scuptures, so these are arranged on a workshop bench with a selection of tools rather than as art objects

Source: © S. Keene, courtesy of the Trustees of the British Museum.

This is not done in *Listen to order* in the *Music room* in the Horniman Museum. In this extensive and striking display of musical instruments, the viewer is made aware of the great variety and abundance of objects and is subsequently invited to consider individual items by using the adjacent sound benches. Here, the eye tends to pay detailed attention to scanning and searching the array for changes in the shape and texture of the instruments – glittering metal versus delicately crafted wood, for example (Figure 3.3). Tufte argues that the repetition of small multiples of information technique is a desirable approach as it combines the benefits of offering macro (overview) and micro information (individual object).[19] The former delivers to the viewer the 'freedom of choice deriving from an overview, a capacity to compare and sort through detail', whereas the latter 'provides a credible refuge where the pace of visualisation is condensed, slowed and personalised'.[20]

Although the eye-catching benefits of large assemblages of objects are undeniable, this strategem is not guaranteed to be successful. Even when an assemblage of objects is carefully designed and strategically displayed, the benefits of an

---

19   Tufte 1990: 35.
20   Tufte, 1990: 35.

impressive vista can be overshadowed if the objects are visually monotonous. The spectacle can distract the viewer from the significance of the individual objects. And if the *en masse* display is perceived as one single item of information, once the initial visual excitement has worn off, the spectator may be inclined to move swiftly on. At the British Museum *Egyptian death and afterlife: mummies* gallery, for example, visitors reported that a display entirely dedicated to a group of funerary shabti failed to impress: instead of captivating their attention through an impressive vista, it caused visual boredom (above, 8.5.3). Another possible pitfall of this display technique is the potential for the visitor to assume that objects which are repeated are more common and are therefore less worthy of closer inspection (above, 8.5, 8.7). This rationale can apply even to visually enticing objects, as in the instance of the mummies in Room 63, which, according to some, were too numerous and created visual clutter (above, 8.6.5).

13.6.3   Personal Significance of Objects

Research has suggested that 'people commonly look for congruity, familiar patterns, connections, to be able to place their experiences into a context or a relationship they already know'.[21] The less communicative aspects of objects can be made evident by underlining the personal significance and possible points of contact between object and visitor (above, 10.5.2), thus raising awareness of the relevance of the object to the viewer. Csikszentmihalyi and Hermanson agree that if visitors are shown how specific exhibits are relevant to them and the connections between objects and the visitors' lives are enhanced, the experience will be more rewarding.[22] When interpretation is centred on themes which can be elaborated and assimilated at a personal level, each individual is offered a chance to appreciate, by affinity, even the most inconspicuous object. As an example, a visitor to the Petrie Museum explained how her appreciation of Egyptian ceramic production was the result of her occupation as a potter (above, 11.2.1).

This approach encourages people to draw parallels between their lives and the people behind the objects and to establish an active, critical and active participation and exchange with the artefacts. This emerged in visitor interviews in the *Egyptian death and afterlife: mummies* gallery at the British Museum (above, 8.5). Here, the universal theme of death connected people from all walks of life with variety of funerary objects and elicited recollections of personal experiences and personal beliefs on the subject. This was supported by the summative evaluation of the *Egypt reborn* long-term installation at the Brooklyn Museum, where visitors expressed interest in objects that had personal significance to them.[23] Object interactions fuelled by personal relevance are ongoing and, as seen in the

---

21   Hood 1993: 718.
22   Csikszentmihalyi and Hermanson 1995: 37.
23   Lindauer 2005: 52.

observation exercises at the V&A, are more long lasting and focused than those arising from visual appearance or central placing (above, 6.4.3). Positive object encounters enable visitors to build a sense of awareness and personal significance of previously unfamiliar artefacts. By being introduced to the original cultural context of an artefact, a person establishes an ease with its past which encourages future interactions as well. In the *Geology* display at the Petrie Museum, graphic information (photographs and moving images) was particularly effective in contextualising objects and making the viewer aware of their potential interest (above, 10.5.4). In general, the results of all the experiments at the Petrie Museum highlighted the importance that people ascribe to the contextualisation of the objects, whatever the interpretative means employed (Chapter 11).

13.7   STAGE 3: THE VISITOR INVESTIGATES THE OBJECT

This research suggests that the *ergonomics and design* of a showcase, *multi-sensory and multimedia strategies*, *thought-provoking* displays and the *style of the narrative* successfully promote object investigations. Good *display and exhibit design* induces closer inspection and draws the viewer in, as well as focusing the attention of the viewer on the existence of interesting content. Communication models which engage different senses (*multi-sensory*) and provide users with multiple modes of interacting with an object (*multimodal*) can foster rewarding encounters with inconspicuous objects at all stages of the interaction and among different visitor types. *Controversial* objects and topics can encourage investigation, although there is a risk of offence to certain visitors. The employment of an evocative or first-person *narrative style* can be an effective means of facilitating the investigation of an object's themes and engendering rewarding knowledge gains: it equips visitors with the intellectual and emotional understanding and awareness of an object that generate broader rewards from the experience.

13.7.1 Ergonomics and Showcase Design

From a design perspective, the physical characteristics of displays and interactives influence visitors' interrelation with them. The impact of ergonomics on the engagement process was underlined in Morris Hargreaves and McIntyre's summative evaluation of the V&A British galleries.[24] Supportive evidence repeatedly emerged from this research. Observational studies in the *Enlightenment* gallery at the British Museum documented that the table-top displays invited visitors to lean forward to closely examine their content (above, 6.3). This behaviour was in contrast with that elicited by the tall wall presses framing the entire perimeter of the same gallery. These dramatic display cabinets provided an

---

24   Morris Hargreaves McIntyre 2003: 13–14.

impressive vista over a wide array of objects, but the physical characteristics of these vitrines generally discouraged close-range viewings.

The popularity of the sound benches in the *Music room* at the Horniman Museum exemplified how excellent usability and ergonomics in an interactive can aid communication between visitors and objects. The easy connection with the objects, the clarity of the display format, its intuitive design and the immediate provision of audio, visual and textual information in response to visitor's actions all facilitated the exploration of the objects' cultural contexts (above, 6.5). Conversely, when some of these qualities were lacking, for instance, in the computer interactive on registration marks in *Understanding objects* (Room 123) at the V&A, it was difficult for communication to be established and the visitor remained oblivious of the potential interest of the objects (above, 6.4.3).

13.7.2 Multi-sensory and Multimedia Strategies

Our brains have a natural propensity to draw on a range of sensory inputs when perceiving the external environment, with various modes of perception weighted more heavily during the processing of information procedures according to circumstantial and individual variations.[25] For this reason, allowing visitors to use various senses can offer a richer experience and engage a wider range of users. For example, the Petrie Museum experimental *Geology* display, designed to explore visual and tactile interactions through video, photographs, a map and a hands-on box, showed that people favoured the sensory stimulation and communication channel that they preferred or that related to the learning style that they found most congenial (above, 11.2.1). By providing a choice of visual inputs for the visual thinker, the possibility of a tactile exploration to the hands-on visitor or audio for the sonically inclined, multi-sensory exhibitions offer a variety of tools to investigate objects and set the conditions for rewarding knowledge gain (Stage 4), as in the sound benches at the Horniman Museum (above, 6.5.3). The inclination of visitors to seek the mode of communication they found most congenial was supported in the findings from the comparative evaluation of the three installations (above, 11.2.1):

> – *I am a very visual person and I loved watching the video and examining the photographs of quarries* or
> – *I am a university lecturer and texts and books are pretty much my thing.*

A critical but thoughtful interviewee in the British Museum *Tomb-chapel of Nebamun* room would have liked to have used their sense of hearing – 'Egyptian music, Egyptian being spoken in the background' – to complement the visual spectacle in the gallery (above, 12.3.3).

---

25   Driver and Spence 2000: 731; Ernst and Bülthoff 2004: 162.

The particular benefits of tactile and hands-on participation was strongly suggested in the evaluation of the object-handling sessions at the British Museum (Chapter 9), which visitors welcomed as opportunities to become familiar with objects which seen in a traditional display case they would have otherwise ignored. Equally, the chest of drawers in *Understanding objects* (Room 123) at the V&A raised awareness, through hands-on use, of the rich interest of its content (above, 6.4.3).

Displays providing for different senses and involving different modes also have implications for accessibility.[26] People with physical and mental disabilities benefit from a well-designed multimodal exhibit; visually impaired users rely upon tactile elements, hearing impaired users are more inclined to visual inputs and those who normally feel excluded from traditional display strategies can, through hands-on activities, find ways to participate.

13.7.3 Thought-Provoking Displays

Choosing communication strategies and themes which are divisive, novel or potentially shocking is a possible tactic that may encourage object investigation. Museum research suggests that visitors welcome written information and resources that raise contentious questions and points of view that differ from their own.[27] The decision to display controversial objects is in itself a means of provoking intellectual engagement. For example, the display of human remains is a contentious issue. As we found in the study conducted in the *Egyptian death and afterlife: mummies* gallery at the British Museum, such display does not meet with unanimous approval (above, 8.5.5), yet in general the presence of human remains encouraged reflection on critical issues, centred attention on the objects and raised people's awareness of cultural context (also found by Kelly).[28] The British Museum, however, recognises that this is a controversial area and the decision to re-exhibit human remains was taken after extensive research which concluded that the vast majority of visitors were comfortable with the display of such material and that its careful and contextualised presentation would constitute one of the most direct and insightful sources of information about different cultures.

A cautious and research-supported display and representation of controversial objects can be valuable. It can raise awareness of interesting cultural issues embodied in unassuming objects and hence successfully trigger some of the stages of the visitor–object interaction model, it can be a way of making visitors more aware of debates among museum professionals, offering them a chance to play a more active role, and it avoids museums patronising the visitor by assuming that they are 'the baby bird waiting with its beak open for the careful museum to feed

---

26   Davidson, Heald and Hein 1991: 290.
27   Rodari 2005: 4.
28   Kelly 2010.

it with pre-digested information' as Weil puts it so well.[29] For example, the *Silence* exhibition in the Karl Ernst Osthaus Museum in Hagen, Germany consisted of an empty gallery from which all the objects had been removed, yet people walked through the bare space recalling the absent exhibits, as if the memory of the museum and its collections 'crept out of its walls'.[30]

13.7.4 Narrative Style

The style of the narrative, for example, the evocative, first-person talking label used in the whispering headrests experiment (above, 10.6, Box 10.3), can be used to intrigue the viewer. Csikszentmihalyi and Hermanson stress the importance of intrinsic motivation which can be fostered by intellectual and also emotional connections with objects. They observe that the use of diaries and personal letters in exhibitions attracts visitors because they connect us with another's feelings.[31] The poetic register of the whispering headrest audio labels operated on the same principle. As reported in the visitor interviews, the audio interpretation was appreciated for 'recreating a sense of the past in a way which transcends words and images', for 'firing the imagination' and for 'giving an insight into the object's life and its people' (above, 10.6.10).

13.8   STAGE 4: THE VISITOR HAS HAD A REWARDING EXPERIENCE

A variety of experiences with an object may feel rewarding to the viewer: personal, cultural or temporal connections; aesthetic enjoyment; surprise or shock; humour; and gain in knowledge. This research identified four particularly effective ways to promote such an involvement. These are: *graphic display of information, novel and unexpected stimuli, usability* and *flow*. The results of the ostracon booklet experiment, the *Geology* display and the study in the British Museum *Egyptian death and afterlife: mummies* gallery suggested that the provision of *graphic information* can communicate complex concepts succinctly, inspiringly and in memorable ways. The responses to the audio-label experiment exemplified the benefits of introducing a *novel* means of interpretation within a gallery. The different impact of the audio labels effectively drew attention to the headrests (above, 10.6.4). By breaking up the pace of the visit, they succeeded in holding visitors' attention and thus offered them an opportunity to discover the object's potential (above, 11.3.5). The experiments showed that all the individual elements of a display need to be accessible, *usable* and coherently and cohesively integrated if a visitor is to experience an enriching object interaction.

---

29   Weil 2002: 65.

30   Fehr 2000: 43.

31   Csikszentmihalyi and Hermanson 1995: 59.

Finally, the studies pointed to the positive contribution of *flow* conditions to visitor–object encounters; it was observed that when the right conditions were in place, the displays were capable of engaging the visitor in highly focused and prolonged object interactions.

13.8.1   Graphic and Visual Display of Information

The evidence we found supported other studies that suggest that exploiting the visual potential of objects and using graphic interpretation enhances visitors' cognitive and emotional experiences of objects.[32] The four main principles at the core of a graphic and visual approach to exhibit design have great potential benefits for exhibit design (above, 3.1.4).[33] In general, presenting information in visually intuitive ways tends to offer museum goers tools to decode objects, thus placing them in a position to gain knowledge.

In the re-display of the geology collection at the Petrie Museum, the map and photographs used to explain them were instrumental in people's appreciation of the significance of the subject matter. Juxtaposing objects (also effective in Stage 2; see 13.6) can also offer visual stimuli: in the same exhibit, stone specimens were paired with artefacts of the same type of stone and the evaluation results suggested that this was another key element of the display (above, 10.5).

13.8.2   Novel, Unexpected and Unexplained Stimuli

Novel or unexpected sensory stimulation can be utilised to focus and retain the viewer's concentration on an object, 'a loud noise, an unexplained association, a mysterious object'.[34]

Visitor studies have demonstrated that stimuli which contrast with others positively contribute to the average holding time of a visitor at an exhibit.[35] The difficult task is to strike a balance between sensory overload and sensory monotony in order to achieve the required conditions for distinctiveness without nullifying its effect through repetition.[36] As Wittlin explains, sensory monotony may occur in a display in spite of, as well as because of, an overload of information.[37]

---

32   Robertson 2002.

33   Tufte 1990: 35.

34   Csikszentmihalyi 1995: 36.

35   Sandifer 2003: 121; Bitgood 2002: 8.

36   Bitgood 2002: 8.

37   Wittlin 1971: 143.

13.8.3 Usability

The notion of usability was borrowed from the practice of design. We mean by this term the actions that a user perceives an object being capable of performing (above, 4.5).[38] Usability can apply to the characteristics of an exhibition environment as a whole (*macro* usability) or to individual exhibits (*micro* usability). On a macro level, good usability results from a coherent and symbiotic relationship between the individual elements of an exhibition. On a micro level, it is manifested as intuitive design. Although form (appearance) may attract attention, high usability is an important holding factor for an exhibit.

Observational evidence of the importance of macro usability emerged, for example, from the *Geology* display at the Petrie Museum, where the physical separation between objects, the video and the handling box created confusion among visitors. They found it difficult to understand the communication scheme and the separated interpretation tools as a whole (above, 10.5.5). The reactions to the whispering headrests brought further indications to support this principle; in this context, visitors expressed their frustration at not being able to easily associate the audio and the headrest (above, 10.6.11). The results of evaluations of the interactives in the V&A British gallery by McManus and Morris Hargreaves McIntyre supported these findings.[39] They concluded that a full integration of interactives into the display and a clear object-interactive connection enhance the visitor's experience with objects. The usability of individual interpretative elements was demonstrated to be one of the main factors contributing to holding the visitor's attention.

Usability can also assist the visitor to decide on the further development of their object encounter. The high usability of the sound benches at the Horniman Museum engendered long in-depth interactions, often encouraging subsequent closer examination of the musical instruments on display (above, 7.3). The video in the British Museum *Tomb-chapel of Nebamun* gallery encouraged visitors to look more closely at the many inconspicuous objects displayed there and contributed to its high usability and visitors' enjoyment of it (above, 12.4).

13.8.4 Flow

Flow is a state of deep mental involvement, of complete immersion in an activity or an experience, which is assisted if four preconditions are met: a clear set of goals, unequivocal feedback, challenge of activity matches user's skills and ability to promote deep focus (above, 4.7).[40]

---

38   Norman 2002.

39   McManus 2003: 10; Morris Hargreaves McIntyre 2003: 310.

40   Csikszentmihalyi 1997: 29–31.

The comparative evaluation of the three galleries described in Chapter 7 shows a correlation between flow-type experiences and duration of interaction (above, 7.4). The assessment of the flow potential of the *Music room* at the Horniman Museum suggested that the exhibition's high flow-inducing qualities derived from the conceptual and topographical guidance offered throughout the space, the provision of interpretation tools matching the skills of its audiences (above, 4.7) and the immersive activities on offer. In other words, people here spend a long time with the objects because they are clear on what is available and on what they can do, and the interpretation matches their level of skill and stimulates their affective and cognitive systems. At the same time, they can easily focus on the displays.

The provision of topographic and conceptual guidance, which operates both on a large (museum and the exhibition) and small (individual display) scale, can equip the visitor with the necessary skills and information to engage with a gallery, one of the requisites for a flow state (above, 4.7.1). It also constitutes a form of feedback for visitors on their interactions with objects. Conceptual assistance with the structure and thematic sub-division of an exhibition can be supplied by explicit explanations on introductory panels, by the layout of routes and cases and by design strategies such as differentiating themes by colour. Guides to the topographic layout of an exhibition facilitate and direct people's movement within the space. McManus agrees that communicative organising principles should be explicitly indicated.[41]

However, this is not necessarily easy to implement effectively. The British Museum, since our studies, has instigated the concept of *gallery gateways*. Evaluation of the classic 'hierarchy of wall panels introducing the gallery and its sections and subsections, and object labels giving detailed information on the objects' had shown that fewer than 10 per cent of visitors stopped to read gallery introductory panels and, similarly, found that between 30 and 50 per cent of visitors were oblivious to text panels in cases.[42] The British Museum is now developing the idea of using striking objects to introduce galleries instead of text panels: *gateway objects.*

However, this is complicated because visitors still expect to find panels and miss them if they are not there (possibly these are different visitors from those who did not read them?). In our survey interviews, we found that visitors felt that the lack of clear and visible explanations about the conceptual layout of the *Egyptian death and afterlife: mummies* gallery (Room 63) at the British Museum was one reason for the difficulty they found in easily grasping the layout of the exhibition, in associating objects and ideas and in linking displays as a narrative (above, 8.6.2). A very high proportion of visitors did study the overview panel for the *Tomb-*

---

41   McManus 2003: 10.
42   Slack, Francis and Edwards 2011; 157–8.

chapel of Nebamun gallery (Figure 12.3, the case opposite the stairs entrance; Figure 12.7).

If they are to have a rewarding engagement with an object, the visitor needs to be at ease in the environment. Level of crowdedness, temperature and noise should be controlled to set the right conditions. This was well demonstrated by the survey results in the *Egyptian death and afterlife: mummies* gallery at the British Museum (above, 8.6.4), where crowds and noise levels are recurrent criticisms and were singled out as major reasons for visitors' lack of deep involvement. By the same token, interactives also need to be unobtrusive to other gallery viewers. In the British Museum *Tomb-chapel of Nebamun* gallery, the video was shown without audio for this reason, while the whispering headrests audio label experiment (above, 10.6) attracted disapproval from some for disturbing other people's enjoyment of the collections (above, 10.6.10).

13.9   SUMMARY

The evidence we found in this research supported our hypotheses that the appearance of museum objects influences our behaviour towards them and results in many being overlooked. The key concepts that we derived from our theory review proved to be the basis for tools that were useful in assessing exhibitions and exhibits, and in understanding visitors' reactions to them. By using them, we were able to identify a number of possible solutions to the treatment of inconspicuous objects in the four stages of visitor–object interaction (Figure 13.1). In particular, to persuade a visitor stop and look (Stage 1) spatial configuration, object isolation, line-of-sight placement and colour were identified (13.5). To convey the existence of interesting cultural contexts and content (Stage 2) juxtaposition of objects, repetition of information and personal significance were discussed (13.6). Ergonomics, multi-sensory solutions, thought-provoking displays and the style of the narrative were proposed as ways to engender an object investigation (Stage 3) (13.7). Finally, visual display of information, novel and unexpected stimuli, usability and flow (13.8) were isolated for their contribution to setting the conditions for knowledge gain and visitor enrichment (Stage 4). Besides these practical guidelines, this research also contributed to understanding the museum experience on other levels. This will be discussed in the final chapter.

CHAPTER 14

CONCLUSIONS: EFFECTIVE EXHIBITIONS

Objects which are visually striking imply of their nature the existence of interesting stories, and thus generally attract and hold visitor attention more successfully than those that are less immediately attractive. This common experience was supported in our research. Bitgood suggests that in museums, the value of an encounter with an object is calculated, usually unconsciously, as the ratio between the effort involved and the assumed pay-off, and that 'when confronted with two exhibited objects, one perceived as more attractive and the other less attractive, visitors approach the more attractive one and ignore the other'.[1] This is unsatisfactory because it encourages uneven viewing patterns centred on visually magnetic objects and accidental encounters with prominently placed exhibits at the expense of experiences that are potentially more rewarding for the visitor.

The pursuit of optimum interpretation and display techniques is a very current preoccupation. In our investigation of a number of galleries, the two that offered the best visitor experience were both ones that engaged the audience with both silent and spectacular objects alike: the *Music room* in the Horniman Museum and the *Tomb-chapel of Nebamun* gallery in the British Museum. These galleries attracted and held visitors for comparatively long periods of time, and generated enthusiasm about the experience. By employing the new tools that we had developed to use in analysing and evaluating museum exhibitions and exhibits, we were able to understand some of the factors that lay behind their success. These tools offer a new understanding of some of the major exhibition features that influence visitor satisfaction.

14.1   THE RESULTS OF THE RESEARCH PROGRAMME

This research project has contributed a better understanding of the characteristics that make exhibits attractive or unattractive to visitors (above, Chapter 13); a set of methodology tools for assessing the potential of an exhibition to engender rewarding visitor experiences (14.4); guidelines to specifically address the four stages of the ideal visitor encounter with an inconspicuous object (above,

---

1   Bitgood 2006: 464.

13.5–13.8); and general guiding principles to inform rewarding visitor–object encounters (14.5).

Stemming from the copious studies which, since the early 1900s, have explored the dynamics of visitor–object interactions, we employed concepts from different fields of theory to investigate actual concerns in museum practices. Using as its focus the display and interpretation of objects in Egyptian collections, the investigation allowed us to develop a set of methodology tools which can be employed to assess an exhibition's potential to engender rewarding visitor–object encounters and practical guidance on how best to address individual stages of the visitor–object encounter. It also promoted a reflection on the principles at the heart of visitor experiences with museum objects. In so doing, it paved the way for future research.

14.2   WIDER IMPLICATIONS

The investigation also stimulated reflection on its wider implications. In particular, the ethics of museum authority versus genuine choice for visitors emerged as an issue. Is it satisfactory to accept visitors' rejection of some objects or should the museum exert its authority and manipulate visitors into encounters with things it considers to be particularly worthy of attention? Where shall we draw the boundary between public benefit and neglect as the result of free will? If a museum decides to forgo ways to persuade visitors to interact with a worthwhile object, is it depriving them of the chance to choose how to use their time and attention or would it be respecting the their right to decide?

It can be argued that the museum's authoritative selection starts with choosing which objects to exhibit. It is well known that in general only about 10 per cent of the objects in the collections are ever exhibited: the rest remain truly silent in store.[2] Once selected to form part of an exhibition narrative, objects may as well be exhibited in a way that makes their role clear. Still, it must be acknowledged that some of the ways that we have found to direct and hold the viewers' attention are not likely to be apparent to them. Therefore, museums should use these techniques in the awareness that they could be considered to be manipulative.

There is no universal answer to this issue; rather, it is the moral and ethical responsibility of each museum to establish the degree of intervention they wish to exercise for the good of the visitor.

An important aspect of the visitor–object connection is visitors' approach to the position of authority of the museum, their degree of awareness of such mechanisms

---

2   Keene 2002: 14–15; 2005: 1–2; Stevenson 2008: 18.

and their willingness and ability to acknowledge, question and challenge what the museum proposes. The museum is the mediator between object and visitor, the filter through which exhibition messages and stories must inevitably pass. It can be difficult for a museum professional to step outside their insider perspective. It is hard for them to objectively observe how the visitor receives and perceives their work, and how messages are assimilated once viewed through the viewer's set of assumptions on museums in general and on that particular museum. Museums are institutions that enjoy a high level of public trust, and it is equally arduous for the visitor to remember that an exhibit – its design, interpretation, juxtaposition to other objects and narratives – is the result of somebody's choice. Choices are subject to a series of forces and limitations related to museum contingencies and to the inevitable incompleteness of any individual's knowledge and expertise.

The divide between authorship and authority is often blurred in the eyes of both visitors and museum advocates. As highlighted by MacDonald, museum staff often refer to an exhibition by the name of its makers, but the official author of an exhibition is ultimately the museum, which approves specific gallery implementations and hence accepts ownership of these choices.[3] This anonymity and lack of clarity are in part responsible for people's reluctance to take a critical and analytical stance when visiting a museum. A clearer and more explicit expression of the role and contribution of staff members, in particular the exhibition director and curators, to museum display would help visitors to draw a distinction between author and authorship. In this scenario people would be invited to attribute ideas and display choices to specific individuals; such a connection might promote a more healthy critical approach, since visitors would not feel they were challenging the museum's authority, but rather were entering into a dialogue with the authors of what they see.

14.3   PRACTICAL SOLUTIONS

In practical terms, this research project showed that there are many solutions that are available to solve our problem, but to be effective, they need to be attuned to the individual and specific circumstances of the museum, the cultural setting, the exhibition and exhibit, and its audiences. The characteristics and condition of the objects, visitor profiles, the museum's mission statement and financial circumstances, together with a variety of practical and logistic concerns, inform the chosen approach. Any chosen path will never be universally acclaimed across all audiences: even within one visitor group, variations are to be expected due to individual preferences. In other words, despite laudable efforts to render inconspicuous objects interesting to visitors' eyes, inevitably a few will remain mute presences to some who will choose to turn their backs on them.

---

3   MacDonald 2004: 162.

Since museums are full of inconspicuous objects, the repetition of the same successful solution for all silent objects would not be equally effective: a variety of media and approaches need to be used. The challenge is therefore to utilise a range of techniques, avoiding transforming the exhibition into a funfair of lights and special effects to which people may soon grow indifferent.

14.4   METHODOLOGY FOR A DEEPER UNDERSTANDING OF VISITOR EXPERIENCES

We produced a set of practical techniques that constitute tools for analysis of visitor movement patterns: a count of visitor flow within a space, tracking visitor movements and static snapshots of visitors; placement in relation to gallery features; observation sheets to determine the depth and characteristics of a visitor–object interaction; and checksheets derived from the key concepts. The four-stage model of the visitor–object encounter (Figure 1.4) can also be used as an instrument for a better understanding of its individual interrelated stages.

This set of tools could also be used in creating new exhibitions in the awareness of the various factors necessary for effective visitor–object encounters. Ultimately, it can lead to a deeper understanding of the visitor experience. We were encouraged that, of all the galleries we analysed, the two that we found to generate the deepest interest in silent objects were also those in which visitors spent longest and seemed to enjoy the most.

14.5   GUIDING PRINCIPLES TO IMPROVE VISITOR–OBJECT ENCOUNTERS

We found that the effective implementation of certain specific display and interpretation strategies could suggest to visitors the interesting content of inconspicuous objects. As a consequence, visitors' reception and perception of the objects was positively affected. As a visitor said of the hieratic ostracon exhibited with its booklet (above, 10.4):

> It is amazing how dull it is at first, and how interesting it looked after I could read its text. It was not just a piece of stone with some scribbles anymore, but a fascinating snapshot from the past.

We offer the following principles as relevant to good practice in promoting visitors' communication with objects, with emphasis on the treatment of inconspicuous objects. As well as those that we found, there are undoubtedly many other principles and techniques available to achieve this.

Space, through its Physical and Immaterial Properties, Shapes the Dimension and Parameters of the Visitor Encounter with Objects

Figure 14.1   The beguiling vista of music in the *Music room* in the Horniman Museum

Source: © S. Keene, courtesy of the Trustees of the British Museum.

The broad design strategy and visual effect of an exhibition, as opposed to the individual physical characteristics of things, can encourage satisfying and lasting experiences for visitors (Figure 14.1). On a different level, it can be argued that the atmosphere and the visual qualities of a gallery deeply influence visitors, affecting their cognitive and emotional processes, and altering their predisposition to the displays (above, 4.5). The visual impact of both an exhibition and its content fundamentally shape the visitor experience (as we found in the *Music room* in the Horniman Museum and the *Tomb-chapel of Nebamun* gallery in the British Museum). In particular, visitors who cannot establish conventional object and text interactions, for example, because of language barriers, can enjoy a visual dialogue with things or can engage with the gallery's architectural and design features.

Visitors Operate on an Attention, Time and Energy Budget which Defines and Deeply Affects the Dynamics of their Visits and their Object Encounters

Figure 14.2   The Great Court at the British Museum: a place for resting, meeting and social interaction

Source: © Trustees of the British Museum.

To maximise visitor experiences, museums need to take account of the existence of these mechanisms. Because of limitations of attention, time and energy, visitors are often reluctant to 'invest' in objects that they do not think will provide sufficient reward in terms of enjoyment, inspiration, learning, recall of memories, opportunity for social interaction or aesthetic experience. Instead, when people perceive from the physical attributes of an object that satisfactory returns are not likely, they rely on the objects highlighted by the museum, on the assumption that these are where it is worthwhile spending their time and effort. If they are to be able to provide rewarding experiences, museums need to understand the factors that drive object selection and attraction, and consciously use their knowledge to guide visitors in their investment of resources.

Displays that Focus on Objects Presented in Imaginative and Stimulating Ways have a Strong Attracting, Holding and Communicating Power for Viewers

Figure 14.3 Object-focused displays like this in the *Making the modern world* gallery in the Science Museum, London, can interest visitors through unexpected juxtapositions

Source: S. Keene, courtesy of the Trustees of the British Museum.

Paradoxically, communication strategies of this type, which openly suggest new possible contexts for the objects through bold and novel juxtapositions, offer a remedy to the de-contextualisation processes of the modern period, when objects were regarded as sources of knowledge, which 'through their proper arrangement would reveal the basic structures of natural history, history, science, and art'.[4] If visitor–object encounters are channelled through the physical qualities of objects rather than through the words of the museum, the gallery goer can assume an active role and is less reliant on predigested information. The viewer is here in the position to draw from the natural capacity of things to trigger and make thinkable otherwise elusive ideas and, in ideal conditions, to gain a sense of personal achievement which will, in turn, confer positive long-lasting connotations on the experience.[5]

Sensory Variety, rather than a Hierarchical Domination of Sight over other Senses, Delivers a Wider Selection of Objects to Broader Audiences

Figure 14.4   Examining an object at the *Hands on* desk in the Roman Britain gallery in the British Museum
Source: © S. Keene, courtesy of the Trustees of the British Museum.

The standard museum exhibit is most likely to rely exclusively on the sense of sight. A display that engages more of the senses is capable of engaging a wide range of audiences, including non-native language speakers, those with disabilities

---

4   Hooper-Greenhill 2000: 127.
5   Packer and Ballantyne 2002: 185.

and others. Multi-sensory experiences mean that the individual maximises and integrates the inputs from different senses (vision, hearing and touch) and can facilitate learning and memory because more areas of the brain are involved. Such exhibits are particularly good at engaging attention with silent objects, and indeed may even enable them literally to speak.

Current practices are developing the provision of sensory and interactive experiences. However, such provisions are often criticised for 'dumbing down' the museum experience. This can be worryingly reminiscent of early museum attitudes which separated visitors (with regard to touching objects) into two categories: on the one hand, the respectful and unobtrusive touch of the upper classes; and, on the other, the dirty, unnecessary and unruly contact of the masses. In our experimental audio labels, some visitors thought them to be intrusive to others even though they themselves had enjoyed hearing them (above, 10.6.11).

Clearly, many galleries and exhibitions are best appreciated as places of quiet contemplation and visual enjoyment, but the *Music room* music benches in the Horniman Museum, the British Museum's *Hands on* desks and the video integrated into the *Tomb-chapel of Nebamun* gallery there demonstrate that it is possible to combine the best of both experiences.

A Visitor–Focused Approach Needs to be Informed by a Comprehensive Understanding of the Synergistic Components of the Visitor–Object Encounter

Figure 14.5   The three elements of the visitor experience
Source: © F. Monti/S. Keene.

Our findings illustrate the *synergistic* nature of a visitor experience:[6] the product of the combination of spatial arrangement, display design, selection of objects and

---

6   Falk 1993: 145.

visitor-related factors, such as prior knowledge of a subject, predisposition and the level of influence exerted by the museum.

Although most museums claim to be visitor-focused, the comprehensive understanding of the visitor experience necessary to truly identify and understand visitor needs is often lacking. Thus, visitor–object encounters are often reduced to a standardised, universal, one-way system of knowledge transmission, where the visitor is supposed to assimilate a range of predigested notions about the things in the showcases.[7] A truly effective visitor-focused approach needs not to be a frame of mind which privileges quantifiable processes of knowledge gain, but, rather, one which favours personal satisfaction, self-progression, enjoyment, awareness of the potential cultural context and the narratives intrinsic to the collections, and which enables the visitor to select what they really want to attend to.

This paradigm requires an awareness of the objects and themes that visitors pursue, the web of stories and episodes relevant to them in varying degrees of harmony and discord, and the reasons behind individual viewing patterns. Within this new modus operandi, aesthetic appeal, curiosity, glamour and iconicity are subordinated or ancillary to visitors' personal desire to know more about the objects most relevant to them or simply to what they feel like exploring on the day. By the same token, visitors will still be free to choose aesthetic appeal, glamour, otherness and familiarity; we must not demonise such qualities by defining them popular in an elitist manner. In practical terms, this can be achieved through an implementation of some of the display and interpretation techniques described in this book.

A Deeper Understanding of the Requirements of Rewarding Visitor Encounters with Inconspicuous Objects Leads to Visitor Choice

This is a critical point to consider if we accept that a major way in which museums control what visitors attend to is by emphasising one object over another through displays. The very act of exhibiting a selection of objects is an inevitable imposition of the exhibitors' choice and constructions on the viewers.[8] Encouraging visitors to truly identify and pursue their interests would enable the museum to re-balance, to an extent, such an imposition. Our results supported the initial assumption postulated in the introduction that it is not realistic to aim for all visitors to engage with all objects on one occasion, because of limited attention span, the progression of mental and physical resources during the visit, and the idiosyncratic differences inherent in individuals (above, 1.4). Moreover, we observed that there was, predictably, a general predisposition for people to engage and pursue objects within their realm of interest, familiarity and expertise. This suggests that

---

7   Hooper-Greenhill 2000: 136; Weil 2002: 65.
8   Baxandall 1991: 34.

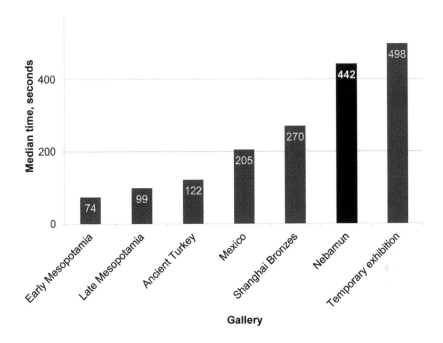

Figure 14.6   Median times (seconds) that visitors spent in the *Tomb-chapel of Nebamun* gallery compared to other galleries in the British Museum (survey in 2009). Visitors stayed longer in the *Nebamun* gallery, where humble objects are integrated with the spectacular paintings
Source: © R. Miner/F. Monti/S. Keene.

some types of artefacts will probably never be of interest to every type of visitor, whatever the efforts of the museum.

In this scenario, the museum has two goals: firstly, by raising visitors' awareness that some inconspicuous objects are potentially interesting, to enable them to find objects with themes of potential significance to them; and, secondly, to help people to discover not only new objects, but new ideas too. For example, a museum could use a collection from ancient Egypt to stimulate curiosity about issues of contemporary history or other messages. This opens the door to two-way museum communication in which curators (who cannot escape being human and having interests themselves) contribute their vision, knowledge and new thinking, and the public (who in this society expect museum staff to share their expertise through exhibitions) are offered different degrees of active interaction. The benefit would be a reciprocal and more rewarding experience.

In pursuit of these goals, it was reassuring to discover that it is possible, through carefully designed modes of communication, to alert visitors to the existence of inconspicuous objects and their richness of content. Once all the required conditions for an ideal encounter with an object are in place, the museum's mission is successfully accomplished. It will then be up to the individual to decide whether to develop their awareness of an object's existence into different types of interaction or whether to invest their time and resources somewhere else. By placing the visitor in the position to identify more actively what they want to see and by showing them how much lies hidden in each object, the museum performs more effectively its statutory and ethical responsibility of making collections available to all.

In short, the museum needs to give thought and imagination to the display of each of the objects in an exhibition or gallery, not just those that will attract attention anyway. Otherwise, why exhibit those that will be little more than interior decoration as far as viewers are concerned?

14.6   FUTURE DIRECTIONS

Like the Roman god Janus, with one face on the past and one towards the future, this work is a portal between previous visitor research and its future direction.

14.6.1 Continuity between Past and Present

The importance of understanding how visitors move through exhibitions, what they see, where they focus their attention and ultimately what they gain from their experience has been a preoccupation for many from the early twentieth century to the present day. Because of such a wealth of information, this research has been able to take a more detailed and investigative approach and use our developing understanding of the reasons and mechanisms behind visitor behaviour to isolate key factors to the visitor encounter with inconspicuous objects.

Some of the findings in this research were reported in previous studies to different extents. Having withstood the test of time, they are still being probed in current museum research. For example, in the late 1920s and early 1930s, Robinson and Melton observed visitors' movements through the gallery in relation to the exhibits and showed, essentially, 'that where and how objects and interpretative information where placed in a gallery determined whether it was viewed by the average visitor'.[9]

Museum research and evaluation have expanded and evolved since Robinson's and Melton's times, yet the pursuit of ideal interpretation and display techniques is still a very current concern. The British Museum, for instance, besides having an ongoing evaluation programme aimed at improving its permanent galleries,

---

9   Robinson 1928; Melton 1935; Korn 1989: 220.

has staged a series of self-contained exhibitions in one of its galleries to test visitors' reactions to different display and communication solutions and has set up experimental displays to ascertain how visitors use (or do not use) text panels. These studies suggested interesting parallels with our research results. For example, they showed that visitors spend longer in an exhibition with fewer objects, that they prefer shorter labels, that they are attracted to moving exhibits, that they tend to browse around galleries in the least strenuous fashion, and that there are 'star' objects (exhibits, which through their visual characteristics attract the visitor) and 'gateway' objects (large, bright, iconic, isolated artefacts that attract visitors and lure them into an exploration of the cultural contexts related to the object and the surrounding displays).[10]

The knowledge gained from their research informed the refurbishment of the British Museum Japanese Gallery. In this object-focused exhibition, the development of Japanese culture from prehistory to modern times is traced through 'gateway objects' to which are attached large and informative labels with explanations about the exhibits and their related cultural contexts.[11] Early observational evidence has suggested that this display strategy is preferred by visitors.

14.6.2 Future Research

Our investigation suggested various areas for further examination, for example, an assessment of visitor–object interactions in different types of museum, in a social context and across various different visitor groups.

Using the methodology presented here, large-scale replication of studies in different venues would enable the further exploration of findings that are site-specific as contrasted with results that are generally applicable. Research could be extended to different venues and collection types. The dynamics of multiple object encounters and the ways in which people link objects to create personal narratives, one of the key objectives of the British Museum *Egyptian death and afterlife: mummies* gallery study (Chapter 8), could also be further researched in other venues to clarify some of the findings observed in that museum. Such a strategy would detect different trends among visitors to various types of museums (such as archaeology, ethnography, fine arts and science) and results could be compared for a range of objects, displays and interpretative solutions in different contexts.

---

10   Slack, Francis and Edwards 2011.
11   This type of label is called 'pebble', halfway between object labels and display panels. Divided in three vertical sections, on the left is a photograph of the gateway object, in the centre an explanation of it (about 100 words) and on the right an account of the broader cultural context (about 100 words).

With a comprehensive understanding of the dynamics of single-visitor interaction, rapport with inconspicuous objects in the context of a social visit could be assessed. Such a line of research would make it possible to investigate the extent to which social interaction introduces new variables to consider when dealing with the display of inconspicuous objects. The investigation could be extended to scrutinise the dynamics of object interaction among different visitor groups so as to offer a comprehensive understanding of all museum audiences.

These new research directions would provide a complete picture of the optimal treatment of inconspicuous objects in a range of museums, in relation to the full spectrum of museum audiences.

ACKNOWLEDGEMENTS

Francesca Monti writes:

I would like to acknowledge the financial support of the Arts and Humanities Research Council, without which the doctorate research would have not been carried out. During the research for my PhD, my supervisors, including Stephen Quirke, Curator at the Petrie Museum, provided invaluable advice and assistance without which it could not have been successfully completed. I am greatly indebted to them and to the many others who offered me their invaluable assistance throughout this project.

I also wish to thank the museum professionals who made the research possible: at the V&A, Juliette Fritsch and David Judd; at the Petrie Museum, Tracy Golding, Judy Joseph and Hugh Kilmister; at the Horniman Museum, Hassan Arero, Louise Bacon, Maria Regan, Dina Sharp and Finbarr Whooley; at the British Museum, Joe Cribb, Brendan Moore, Sam Moorhead, Richard Parkinson, Kim Sloan, Ian Leins and Kusuma Barnett, Volunteer Coordinator. A special thank you to all the volunteers who greatly illuminated me on the dynamics and secrets of the *Hands on* desks. Rhea Miner and Kate Wiley generously shared their findings on the *Tomb-chapel of Nebamun* gallery. Sarah McDaid provided invaluable help with the text, in particular with the introductory chapter.

I am grateful to Rhiannon Johns, Elizabeth Bloxam, Elizabeth Corey-Pearce, Clive Orton and David Wengrow who generously shared their expertise on subjects relevant to this enquiry.

Very great thanks are due to Brian Smith and his colleagues at FeONIC, who designed and installed the equipment for the whispering headrests experiments, and to Debra Low, who lent her voice to the ancient Egyptian headrests.

Finally, my deepest gratitude goes to those who indefatigably sustained me with their encouragement and inspiration. In particular to my husband, Richard, to my friends Silvia, Maureen and Zoe, to my family beyond the sea, and to Lily-Rose and Henri, my precious baby twins.

Suzanne Keene writes:

I would like to thank and express my gratitude to a number of people who assisted with the later stages of the preparation of the book. At the British Museum, Richard Parkinson gave much further assistance; Stuart Frost made important contributions to the manuscript and to other relevant work. Stephen Quirke and Sally MacDonald at the Petrie Museum, UCL, Finbarr Whooley at the Horniman Museum and Xerxes Mazda at the British Museum kindly gave permission to publish the research on their museums, and Stephen Quirke, as ever, provided much further encouragement and information. At the Science Museum, Andrew Nahum contributed a voice for some eloquently silent objects for the cover image text.

I would like also to especially thank the museums and people who kindly permitted the use of images: Christopher Sutherns at the British Museum, Tim Boon and Jeremiah Solak at the Science Museum; Roxanne Peters at the V&A, and the Petrie, Horniman and Winchester City Museums.

BIBLIOGRAPHY

Albers, J., 2006. *Formulation: Articulation*. Facsimile edn of original portfolio published in New Haven: Ives-Sillman; New York: Harry N. Abrams, 1972. London: Thames & Hudson.

Alberti, S., 2005. 'Objects and the museum'. *Isis*, 96(4): 559–71.

Alexander, J., Crompton, T. and Shrubsole, G., 2011. *Think of Me as Evil? Opening the Ethical Debates in Advertising*. Machynlleth: Public Interest Research Centre/World Wildlife Fund.

Alt, M.B. and Shaw, K.M. 1984. 'Characteristics of ideal museum exhibits'. *British Journal of Psychology*, 75: 25–36.

Appadurai, A. (ed.), 1986. *The Social Life of Things: Commodities in Cultural Perspective*. Cambridge: Cambridge University Press.

Arigho, B., 2008. 'Getting a handle on the past: the use of objects in reminiscence work', in H. Chatterjee (ed.), *Touch in Museums: Policy and Practice in Object Handling*. Oxford: Berg, pp. 205–12.

Arndt, M.A., Screven, C., Benusa, D. and Bishop, T., 1993. *Behaviour and Learning in a Zoo Environment under Different Signage Conditions. Visitor Studies: Theory, Research, and Practice*. Jacksonville, AL: Centre for Social Design, Jacksonville State University.

Ascherson, N., 2004. 'Pharoahs still rule … in Las Vegas. Encounters with Ancient Egypt (review)'. *The Observer*, review section, 4 January, p. 15.

Ashby, F., Isen, A. and Turken, U., 1999. 'A neuro-psychological theory of positive affect and its influence on cognition'. *Psychological Review*, 106: 529–50.

Atkinson, R. and Shiffrin, R., 1968. 'Human memory: a proposed system and its control processes', in K. Spence and J. Spence (eds), *The Psychology of Learning and Motivation*. London: Academic Press.

Bailey, M., 2011. 'BP to give £10m to four UK arts institutions', *The Art Newspaper*, 19 December, http://www.theartnewspaper.com/articles/BP+to+give+%C2%A310m+to+four+UK+arts+institutions/25299 [accessed 3 July 2012].

Baudrillard, J., 1968. *The System of Objects* (trans. J. Benedict from *Le système des objects*. Paris: Editions Gallimard). London: Verso.

Baxandall, M., 1991. 'Exhibiting intention: some preconditions of the visual display of culturally purposeful objects', in I. Karp, and S. Lavine (eds), *Exhibiting Cultures: The Poetics and Politics of Museum Displays*. Washington DC and London: Smithsonian Institution Press, pp. 33–41.

Bazin, G., 1967. *The Museum Age* (trans. J. van Nuis Cahill). New York: Universe.

Beard, M., 1992. 'Souvenirs of culture: deciphering (in) the museum'. *Art History*, 15: 305–32.

Beardsley, M., 1982. *The Aesthetic Point of View*. Ithaca, NY: Cornell University Press.

Bechtel, R., 1967. 'Hodometer research in museums'. *Museum News*, 45: 23–6.

Behrens, R., 1984. *Design in the Visual Arts*. Englewood Cliffs, NJ: Prentice Hall.

Belcher, M., 1991. *Exhibitions in Museums*. Leicester: Leicester University Press.

Bellamy, K. and Oppenheim, C. (eds), 2009. *Learning to Live: Museums, Young People and Education*. London: National Museum Directors' Conference.

Benedikt, M., 1979. 'To take hold of space: isovists and isovist fields'. *Environment and Planning B*, 6: 47–65.

Bennett, T., 1995. *The Birth of the Museum*. London and New York: Routledge.

Bennett, T., 2006. 'Civic seeing: museums and the organisation of vision', in S. Macdonald (ed.), *A Companion to Museum Studies*. Oxford: Blackwell, pp. 282–301.

Berg, B., 2004. *Qualitative Research Methods for the Social Sciences*. London: Allyn & Bacon.

Billings, S., 2009. 'Second life'. *Museum Practice*, Autumn, 47.

Birley, M., 2002. *The Rhythms of Life*. London: Jarrold Publishing and the Horniman Museum.

Bitgood, S., 1994. 'A primer on memory for visitor studies professionals'. *Visitor Behaviour*, IX: 4–8.

Bitgood, S., 1995. 'Visitor circulation: is there really a right-turn bias?' *Visitor Behaviour*, 8: 15–16.

Bitgood, S., 2000. 'The role of attention in designing effective interpretative labels'. *Journal of Interpretation Research*, 5: 31–45.

Bitgood, S., 2002. 'Environmental psychology in museums, zoos, and other exhibition centres', in R. Bechtel and A. Churchman (eds), *The Environmental Psychology Handbook*. New York: Wiley.

Bitgood, S., 2006. 'An analysis of visitor circulation: movement patterns and the general value principle'. *Curator*, 49: 463–75.

Bitgood, S. and Cleghorn, A., 1994. 'Memory of objects, labels and other sensory impressions from a museum visit'. *Visitor Behaviour*, IX: 11–12.

Bitgood, S., Dukes, S. and Abbey, L., 2006. 'Interest and effort as predictors of reading: a test of the General Value Principle', *Current Trends in Audience Research*, 19: 1–6.

Bitgood, S. and Patterson, D., 1988. 'Some evolving principles of visitor behaviour', in S. Bitgood, J. Roper and A. Benefield (eds), *Visitor Studies: Theory, Research, and Practice, Volume 1*. Jacksonville, AL: Centre for Social Design, pp. 40–50.

Bitgood, S. and Patterson, D., 1993. 'The effects of gallery changes on visitor reading and object viewing time'. *Environment and Behaviour*, 25: 761–81.

Bitgood, S., Benefield, A. and Patterson, D., 1989. 'The importance of label placement: a neglected factor in exhibit design'. *Current Trends in Audience Research*, 4: 49–52.

Bitgood, S., Hines, J., Hamberger, W. and Ford, W., 1992. 'Visitor circulation through a changing exhibits gallery', in A. Benefield et al. (eds), *Visitor Studies: Theory, Research, and Practice, Volume 4.* Jacksonville, AL: Centre for Social Design, pp. 103–14.

Black, M. (ed.), 1950. *Exhibition Design.* London: Architectural Press.

Boast, R. and Evans, C. 1986. 'The transformation of space: two examples from British prehistory'. *Archaeological Review from Cambridge*, 5: 193–205.

Borgmann, A., 1995. 'The depth of design', in R. Buchanan and V. Margolin (eds), *Discovering Design: Explorations in Design Studies.* Chicago: University of Chicago Press, pp. 13–22.

Borhegyi, St F., 1968. 'Space problems and solutions, in St F. Borhegyi and J. Hanson (eds), *The Museum Visitor: Selected Essays and Surveys of Visitor Reaction to Exhibits in the Milwaukee Public Museum.* Milwaukee: Milwaukee Public Museum, pp. 40–44.

Borun, M. and Miller, M., 1980. 'To label or not to label?' *Museum News*, 58: 64–7.

Bourdeau, L. and Chebat, J., 2001. 'An empirical study of the effects of the design of the display galleries of an art gallery on the movement of visitors'. *Museum Management and Curatorship*, 19: 63–73.

Bourdieu, P., 1984. *Distinction: A Social Critique of the Judgement of Taste.* London and New York: Routledge.

British Museum, 2005. 'The British Museum Gallery Evaluation Project – Enlightenment Gallery Research Findings'. Unpublished internal report.

Brookfield, S., 1986. *Understanding and Facilitating Adult Learning.* San Francisco: Jossey-Bass.

Brooks, J. and Brooks M., 1993. *The Case for Constructivist Classrooms.* Alexandria, VA: Association for Supervision and Curriculum Development.

Buchanan, R. and Margolin, V. (eds), 1995. *Discovering Design: Explorations in Design Studies.* Chicago: University of Chicago Press.

Caldwell, N., 2001. '(Rethinking) the measurement of service quality in museums and galleries'. *International Journal of Nonprofit and Voluntary Sector Marketing*, 20: 161–71.

Carl, W., 1994. 'Flow – the psychology of optimal experience: history and critical evaluation'. Unpublished paper: Rochester Institute of Technology, http://www.dac.neu.edu/w.carl/PDFs/flowpaper.pdf [accessed 16 July 2012].

Chatterjee H. (ed.), 2008. *Touch in Museums: Policy and Practice in Object Handling.* Oxford: Berg.

Chatterjee, H. and Noble, G., 2009. 'Object therapy: a student-selected component exploring the potential of museum object handling as an enrichment activity for patients and hospitals'. *Global Journal of Health Science*, 2: 42–9.

Choi, Y., 1999. 'The morphology of exploration and encounter in museum layouts'. *Environment and Planning B: Planning and Design*, 26: 241–50.

Clark, D., 1999. 'Yerkes-Dodson Law of Arousal', http://www.nwlink. com/~donclark/hrd/history/arousal.html [accessed 3 July 2012].

Cotton Dana, J., 1929. 'The museum as art patron'. *Creative Art: A Magazine of Fine and Applied Art*, 4: xxiii–xxvi. Reproduced in B. Messias Carbonell (ed.), *Museum Studies: An Anthology of Contexts*. Oxford: Blackwell, Chapter 40.

Creative Research. 2002. 'Summative Evaluation of the British Galleries: Overview of Findings'. Internal report, http://www.vam.ac.uk/files/file_upload/5872_ file.pdf [accessed 3 July 2012].

Csikszentmihalyi, M., 1975. *Beyond Boredom and Anxiety*. San Francisco: Jossey-Bass.

Csikszentmihalyi, M., 1978. 'Attention and the holistic approach to behaviour', in K. Pope and J. Singer (eds), *The Stream of Consciousness: Scientific Investigations into the Flow of Human Experience*. New York: Plenum.

Csikszentmihalyi, M., 1988. 'The flow experience and its significance for human psychology', in M. Csikszentmihalyi and I. Csikszentmihalyi (eds), *Optimal Experience: Psychological Studies in Flow of Consciousness*. Cambridge: Cambridge University Press.

Csikszentmihalyi, M., 1990. *Flow: The Psychology of Optimal Experience*. New York: Harper and Row.

Csikszentmihalyi, M., 1993. 'Why we need things', in S. Lubar and W. Kingery (eds), *History from Things*: *Essays on Material Culture*. Washington and London: Smithsonian Institution Press, pp. 20–29.

Csikszentmihalyi, M., 1995. 'Design and order in everyday life', in R. Buchanan and V. Margolin (eds), *Discovering Design: Explorations in Design Studies*. Chicago: University of Chicago Press, pp. 118–26.

Csikszentmihalyi, M., 1997. *Finding Flow*. New York: Basic Books.

Csikszentmihalyi, M. and Hermanson, K., 1995. 'Intrinsic motivation in museums: what makes visitors want to learn?' *Museum News*, 74: 35–7.

Csikszentmihalyi, M. and Robinson, R., 1990. *The Art of Seeing: An Interpretation of the Aesthetic Encounter*. Los Angeles: The J. Paul Getty Museum.

Davidson, B., Heald, C. and Hein, G., 1991. 'Increased exhibit accessibility through multi-sensory interaction'. *Curator*, 34: 273–90.

Davies, C., 2006. 'Cashing in'. *Museums Journal*, 106: 37–9.

Dean, D., 1994. *Museum Exhibitions: Theory and Practice*. London and New York: Routledge.

Dewey, J., 1938. *Experience and Education*. Terre Haute, IN: Kappa Delta, PI; New York: Simon & Schuster, 1997.

Driver, J. and Spence, C., 2000. 'Beyond modularity and convergence'. *Current Biology*, 10: 731–5.

Driver, J. and Spence, C., 1998. 'Cross-modal links in spatial attention'. *Philosophical Transactions: Biological Sciences*, 353: 1319–31.

Duncan, C., 1995. *Civilizing Rituals: Inside the Public Art Museums*. London and New York: Routledge.

Durbin, G. (ed.), 1996. *Developing Museum Exhibitions for Lifelong Learning*. London: The Stationery Office.

Durbin, G., 1990. *Learning from Objects: A Teacher's Guide*. English Heritage.

Durbin, G., 2002. *Interactive Learning in the British Galleries, 1500–1900*. Conference Proceedings: Interactive Learning in Museums of Art, http://www.vam.ac.uk/vastatic/acrobat_pdf/research/gail_durbin.pdf [accessed 3 July 2012].

Economou, M., 2004. 'Evaluation strategies in the cultural sector: the case of the Kelvingrove Museum and Art Gallery in Glasgow'. *Museum and Society*, 2: 30–46, http://www2.le.ac.uk/departments/museumstudies/museumsociety/documents/volumes/economou.pdf [accessed 3 July 2012].

Ekuan, K., 2002. *The Aesthetics of the Japanese Lunchbox*. Cambridge, MA: MIT Press.

Ernst, M. and Bülthoff, H., 2004. 'Merging the senses into a robust percept'. *TRENDS in Cognitive Science*, 8: 162–9.

Eysenck, M., 2001. *Principles of Cognitive Psychology*. Florence, KY: Psychology Press.

Falk, J., 1993. 'Assessing the impact of exhibit arrangement on visitor behaviour and learning', *Curator*, 36: 133–46.

Falk, J., 2002. *Lessons Without Limits: How Free Choice Learning is Transforming Education*. Walnut Creek, CA: Altamira Press.

Falk, J. and Dierking, L., 2000. *Learning from Museums: Visitor Experiences and the Making of Meaning*. Walnut Creek, CA: Altamira Press.

Falk, J., Koran, J., Dierking, L. and Dreblow, L., 1985. 'Predicting visitor behaviour'. *Curator*, 28: 249–57.

Fehr, M., 2000. *A Museum and its Memory*. Stanford, CA: Stanford University Press.

FeONIC website: http://www.feonic.com [accessed 3 July 2012].

Filep, S., 2008. 'Applying the dimensions of flow to explore visitor engagement and satisfaction'. *Visitor Studies*, 11(1): 90–108.

Fisher, S., 2000. *What is the Appeal of Ancient Egypt? Qualitative Research with the Public*. Susie Fisher Group: unpublished report for the Petrie Museum of Egyptian Archaeology, University College London.

Fleming, D., 2005. 'Creative space', in S. MacLeod (ed.), *Reshaping Museum Space: Architecture, Design, Exhibitions*. London and New York: Routledge, pp. 53–61.

Frank, B., 2000. 'Ceramics as testaments to the past: field research and making objects speak', in S. Knell (ed.), *Museums in the Material World*. London and New York: Routledge, pp. 60–64.

Frascara, J., 1995. 'Graphic design: fine art or social science?', in V. Buchanan and R. Margolin (eds), *The Idea of Design*. Cambridge, MA: MIT Press, pp. 44–55.

Frost, S., 2011. 'In touch with the past: Hands on at the British Museum'. *Social History in Museums*, 35: 25–34.

Gardner, H., 1985. *Frames of Mind: The Theory of Multiple Intelligence*. New York: Basic Books.

GCI, 2011. 'Museum lighting research', http://www.getty.edu/conservation/our_projects/science/lighting/index.html [accessed 3 July 2012].

Gibson, J., 1979. *The Ecological Approach to Visual Perception*. Hillsdale, NJ: Lawrence Erlbaum Associates.

Gilman, B., 1923. *Museum Ideals of Purpose and Method*. Cambridge, MA: Harvard University Press.

Glasgow Museum, 2006. *The Kelvingrove New Century Project (KGNCP): Aims*. The Glasgow Museum, http://www.glasgow.gov.uk/en/Visitors/MuseumsGalleries [accessed 3 July 2012].

Griggs, S., 1983. 'Orientating visitors within a thematic display'. *International Journal of Museum Management and Curatorship*, 2: 119–34.

Hall, M., 1987. *On Display: A Design Grammar for Museum Exhibitors*. London: Lund Humphries.

Handsman, R., 1987. 'Stop making sense: towards an anti-catalogue of woodsplint basketry', in A. McMullen and R. Handsman (eds), *A Key into the Language of Woodsplint Baskets*. Washington, CT: American Indian Archaeological Institute, pp. 144–63.

Harvey, M., Loomis, R., Bell, P. and Marino, M., 1998. 'The influence of museum exhibit design on immersion and psychological flow'. *Environment and Behaviour*, 30: 601–27.

Hein, G., 1995. 'The constructivist museum'. *Journal of Education in Museums*, 16: 21–3.

Hein, G., 1998. *Learning in the Museum*. New York: Routledge.

Hillier, B., 1996. *Space is the Machine*. New York: Cambridge University Press.

Hillier, B., 2007. *Space is the Machine: A Configurational Theory of Architecture: Space Syntax*. Electronic edition, London: Space Syntax. http://eprints.ucl.ac.uk/3881/ [accessed 3 July 2012].

Hillier, B. and Hanson, J., 1984. *The Social Logic of Space*. Cambridge: Cambridge University Press.

Hillier, B. and Tzortzi, K., 2006. 'Space syntax: the language of museum space', in S. MacDonald (ed.), *A Companion to Museum Studies*. Oxford: Blackwell, pp. 282–301.

Hirshi, K. and Screven, C., 1990. Effects of questions on visitor reading behaviour, *ILVS Review: A Journal of Visitor Behaviour*, 1: 50–61.

Holden, J., 2006. *Cultural Value and the Crisis of Legitimacy: Why Culture Needs a Democratic Mandate*. London: Demos.

Honey, P. and Mumford, A., 1982. *Manual of Learning Styles*. London: P. Honey.

Hood, M., 1993. 'Comfort and caring: two essential environmental factors'. *Environment and Behaviour*, 25: 710–724.

Hooper-Greenhill, E., 2000. *Museums and the Interpretation of Visual Culture.* London and New York: Routledge.

Hooper-Greenhill, E., 2001. *The Museum as Teacher: The Challenge of Pedagogic Change.* Paper delivered to Volgt de Gids? Nieuwe perspectiven voor educatie en gidsing in kunstmusea. Konig Boudewijnstichting, Brussels, 28 March.

Hooper-Greenhill, E., 2008. *Museums and Education: Purpose, Pedagogy, Performance.* London and New York: Routledge.

Hopkins, R., 2004. 'Painting, sculpture, sight, and touch'. *British Journal of Aesthetics*, 44: 149–66.

Horniman Museum. Website: http://www.horniman.ac.uk.

Hoskins, J., 1998. *Biographical Objects.* London and New York: Routledge.

Ingold, T. (ed.), 1996. *Key Debates in Anthropology.* London and New York: Routledge.

Intelligent Space Partnership, 2003. *The Impact of the Built Environment on Care within A&E Departments.* Norwich: The Stationery Office (NHS Estates), www.intelligentspace.com [accessed 3 July 2012].

Isen, A., 1993. 'Positive affect making and decision-making', in M. Lewis and J. Haviland (eds), *Handbook of Emotions.* New York: Guilford, pp. 261–77.

Jacob, G., 2009. *Museum Design: The Future.* North Charleston, CA: Booksurge.

Jordanova, L., 1989. 'Objects of knowledge: a historical perspective on museums', in P. Vergo (ed.), *The New Museology.* London: Reaktion Books, pp. 22–40.

Keene, S., 2002. *Managing Conservation in Museums.* London: Butterworth-Heinemann.

Keene, S., 2005. *Fragments of the World: Uses of Museum Collections.* Oxford: Butterworth-Heinemann.

Keene, S. with Monti, F. and Stevenson, A., 2008. *Collections for People: Museums' Stored Collections as a Public Resource.* London: UCL.

Kelly, L., 2010. 'Engaging museum visitors in difficult topics through social-cultural learning and narrative', in F. Cameron and L. Kelly (eds), *Hot Topics, Public Culture, Museums.* Newcastle upon Tyne: Cambridge Scholars Publishing, pp. 194–210.

Kingery, W. (ed.), 1996. *Learning from Things: Method and Theory of Material Culture Studies.* Washington DC and London: Smithsonian Institution Press.

Kolb, D., 1984. *Experiential Learning: Experience as the Source of Learning and Development.* Englewood Cliffs, NJ: Prentice Hall.

Kopytoff, I., 1986. 'The cultural biography of things', in A. Appadurai (ed.), *The Social Life of Things: Commodities in Cultural Perspective.* Cambridge: Cambridge University Press, pp. 64–91.

Korn, R., 1989. 'Introduction to evaluation: theory and methodology', in S. Mayer (ed.), *Museum Education, History, Theory and Practice.* Reston, VA: National Art Education Association, pp. 219–38.

Lakota, R. and Kantner, J., 1976. *The National Museum of Natural History as a Behavioural Environment.* Washington DC: Offices of Museum Programs, Smithsonian Institution.

Lamb, T. and Bourriau, J. (eds), 1995. *Colour: Art and Science.* Cambridge and New York: Cambridge University Press.

Leach, E., 1978. 'Does space really constitute the social?', in D. Green, C. Haselgrove and C. Spriggs (eds), *Social Organisation and Settlement: Contributions from Anthropology*, volume 471 of the *International Series.* Oxford: British Archaeological Reports, pp. 38–72.

Legrenzi, L. and Troilo, G., 2005. *The Impact of Exhibit Arrangement on Visitors' Emotions: A Study at the Victoria and Albert Museum.* Paper presented at the 8th International Conference in Arts and Cultural Management at HEC Montreal, Canada, http://neumann.hec.ca/aimac2005/PDF_Text/LegrenziL_TroiloG.pdf [accessed 3 July 2012].

Levine, M. 1982. 'You-are-here maps: psychological considerations'. *Environment and Behavior*, 14(2): 221–37.

Lindauer L., 2005. 'From salad bars to vivid stories: four game plans for developing "educationally successful" exhibitions'. *Museum Management and Curatorship*, 20: 41–55.

Litwak, J., 1996. *Label Length and Title Type as Determinants in Visitor Learning.* Paper presented at the Annual Meeting of the American Educational Research Association, New York, 8–12 April.

Lord, B., 2005. 'Representing enlightenment space', in S. MacLeod (ed.), *Reshaping Museum Space: Architecture, Design, Exhibitions.* London and New York: Routledge, pp. 146–57.

Lugli, A., 1996. *Dalla meraviglia all'arte della meraviglia.* Limited publication from the Science and Merveille/Les Cabinets de Curiosités Conference, Louvre, Paris. Modena: Fondazione Collegio San Carlo di Modena.

Lynch, B., 2004. *Access to Collections and Affective Interaction with Objects in the Museum.* Unpublished doctoral thesis submitted to the University of Manchester.

MacDonald, S., 2003. 'Lost in time and space: ancient Egypt in Museums', in S. MacDonald and M. Rice (eds), *Encounters with Ancient Egypt: Consuming Ancient Egypt.* London: UCL Press.

MacDonald, S., 2004. 'Authorizing science: public understanding of science in museums', in A. Irwin and B. Wynne (eds), *Misunderstanding Science? The Public Reconstruction of Science and Technology.* Cambridge: Cambridge University Press, pp. 152–71.

Markus, T., 1987. 'Buildings as classifying devices'. *Environment and Planning B: Planning and Design*, 14: 467–84.

Mazda, X., 2006. *Interpretation at the British Museum.* Lecture for the British Museum Studies Group, London, 26 January.

McManus, I., Jones, A. and Cottrell, J., 1981. 'The aesthetics of colour'. *Perception*, 10: 651–66.

McManus, P., 1989. 'Oh, yes, they do! How museum visitors read labels and interact with exhibit texts'. *Curator*, 32: 174–89.

McManus, P., 1993. 'Memories as indicators of the impact of museum visits'. *Museum Management and Curatorship*, 12: 367–80.

McManus, P., 2003. 'Lots of ways of finding out. Love that! A qualitative account of visitor experiences in the displays, film rooms and study areas of the British Galleries at the V&A'. Internal report, http://media.vam.ac.uk/media/website/uploads/documents/legacy_documents/file_upload/5876_file.pdf [accessed 3 July 2012].

Melton, A., 1935. *Problems of Installation in a Museum of Art.* Washington DC: American Association of Museums (reprinted 1988).

Melton, A., 1972. 'Visitor behaviour in museums: some early research in environmental design'. *Human Factors*, 14: 393–403.

Michalski, S., 1990. 'Towards specific lighting guidelines', in *Proceedings, Ninth Triennial Meeting, ICOM-CC, Paris*. Paris: ICOM, pp. 583–5.

Miho Museum. http://www.miho.or.jp/english/index.htm [accessed 3 July 2012].

Miner, R., 2009. 'Evaluation of Gallery 61: Ancient Egyptian Life and Death: The Tomb Chapel of Nebamun (1350 B.C.)'. Unpublished internal report, Interpretation Unit, Department of Learning and Audiences. London: British Museum.

Minolta, 1998. *Precise Color Communication: Color Control from Feeling to Instrumentation*. Minolta, Japan: Minolta.

Museums, Libraries and Archives Council, 2004. *Inspiring Learning for All. Current Thinking: Learning Styles and Alternative Learning Approaches.* The National Archives: UK Government Web Archive. http://webarchive.nationalarchives.gov.uk/*/http://www.inspiringlearning.gov.uk [accessed 3 July 2012].

Monaco, J., 2000. *How to Read a Film: Movies, Media and Multimedia.* Oxford: Oxford University Press.

Monbiot, F., 2011. 'Advertising is a poison that demeans even love – and we're hooked on it'. *The Guardian*, 25 October, p. 29.

Monti, F., 2004. 'Evaluation of the British Museum Hands On Programme'. Internal report to the British Museum.

Monti, F., 2008. 'Digital issues', in S. Keene with F. Monti and A. Stevenson, *Collections for People: Museums' Stored Collections as a Public Resource.* London: UCL, pp. 57–64.

Monti, F., 2009. 'The tomb-chapel of Nebamun at the British Museum: the digital, the spectacular, and the inconspicuous under one limestone roof', in A. Seal, S. Keene and J. Bowen (eds), *EVA London 2009: Electronic Visualisation and the Arts: Conference Proceedings.* London: BCS, pp. 94–106, http://ewic.bcs.org/content/ConWebDoc/27694 [accessed 3 July 2012].

Morphy, H., 1992. 'Aesthetics in a cross-cultural perspective: some reflections on native american basketry'. *Journal of the Anthropological Society of Oxford*, 23: 1–16.

Morphy, H., 1996. 'For the motion', in T. Ingold (ed.), *Key Debates in Anthropology.* London and New York: Routledge, pp. 255–75.

Morris Hargreaves McIntyre, 2003. 'Engaging or Distracting? Visitor Responses to Interactives in the V&A British Galleries'. Internal report, http://www.vam. ac.uk/files/file_upload/17659_file.doc [accessed 3 July 2012].

Morris Hargreaves McIntyre, 2005a. 'Visitor Insight Digest'. Report to inform West Midlands hub business planning, http://www.renaissancewestmidlands. org.uk/local/media/downloads/WM%20digest.pdf [accessed 14 December 2006].

Morris Hargreaves McIntyre, 2005b. *Never Mind the Width, Feel the Quality.* Paper presented at the Museums and Heritage Show, May, http://www.visitors. org.uk/events/andrew.pdf [accessed 3 July 2012].

Morris Hargreaves MacIntyre, 2008. 'Touching history: an evaluation of Hands On desks at the British Museum', http://www.britishmuseum.org/research/ visitor_research.aspx [accessed 3 July 2012].

Morris Hargreaves MacIntyre, 2011. 'Visitor insight monitor 2010/11: annualised findings of the British Museum rolling survey April 2010 to March 2011 (April 2011)'.

Moser, S., 2006. *Wondrous Curiosities: Ancient Egypt at the British Museum.* Chicago: University of Chicago Press.

Neate, R., 2011. 'Ad men use brain scanners to probe our emotional response'. *The Observer*, 15 January, p. 29.

Norman, D., 1988. *The Psychology of Everyday Things.* New York: Basic Books.

Norman, D., 2002. 'Emotion and design: attractive things work better'. *Interactions Magazine*, 9(4): 36–42.

Norman, D., 2004. *Emotional Design: Why We Love (or Hate) Everyday Things.* New York: Basic Books.

O'Hara, M., 2004. 'British Museum Interpretation Audit: The Roxie Walker Galleries of Egyptian Funerary Culture'. Unpublished internal document.

Ohta, R., 1998. "My eyes have seen the glory": visitor experience at a controversial flag exhibition', in *Current Trends in Visitor Studies and Evaluation*, vol. 11. Los Angeles: American Association of Museums, pp. 48–58.

Orna-Ornstein, J. (ed.), 2001. *Development and Evaluation of the HSBC Money Gallery at the British Museum.* British Museum Occasional Paper no. 140. London: British Museum Press.

Ortony, A., Norman, D.A. and Revelle, W, 2005. 'The role of affect and proto-affect in effective functioning', in J. Fellous and M. Arbib (eds), *Who Needs Emotions: The Brain Meets the Machine.* New York: Oxford University Press.

Packard, V., 1957. *The Hidden Persuaders.* New York: David McKay Company.

Packer, J. and Ballantyne, R., 2002. 'Motivational factors and the visitor experience: a comparison of three sites'. *Curator*, 45: 183–98.

Parry, R. and Sawyer, A., 2005. 'Space and the machine', in S. MacLeod (ed.), *Reshaping Museum Space: Architecture, Design, Exhibitions.* London and New York: Routledge, pp. 39–52.

Pearce, S., 1992. *Museums, Objects and Collections.* Washington DC: Smithsonian Institution Press.

Peart, B., 1984. 'Impact of exhibit type on knowledge gain, attitude, change, and behaviour'. *Curator*, 27: 220–237.

Peponis, J. and Hedin, J., 1982. 'The layout of theories in the natural history museum'. *9H*, 3: 21–6.

Pepper, S., 1981. *World Hypotheses: A Study in Evidence*. Berkeley, CA: University of California Press.

Perry, D., 1993. 'Beyond cognition and affect: the anatomy of a museum visit', in D. Thompson et al. (eds), *Beyond Cognition and Affect, Visitor Studies: Theory, Research, and Practice*. Jacksonville, AL: Center for Social Design, pp. 43–7.

Pevsner, H., 1976. *A History of Building Types*. Princeton, NJ: Princeton University Press.

Popova, A., 2001. *Spatial Patterns of Knowledge Transmission*. Unpublished thesis, MSc in Advanced Architectural Studies. The Bartlett School of Architecture, UCL, London.

Portas, M., 1999. *Windows: The Art of Retail Display*. London: Thames & Hudson.

Preziosi, D., 1996. 'Brain of the earth's body: museums and the framing of modernity', in P. Duro (ed.), *The Rhetoric of the Frame: Essays on the Boundaries of Artwork*. Cambridge: Cambridge University Press, pp. 96–110.

Psarra, S. and Grajewski, T., 2002. 'Track record'. *Museum Practice*, 19: 36–42.

Psarra, S., 2005. 'Spatial culture, way-finding and the educational message', in S. MacLeod (ed.), *Reshaping Museum Space: Architecture, Design, Exhibitions*. London and New York: Routledge, pp. 78–94.

Psarra, S., 2009. *Architecture and Narrative: The Formation of Space and Cultural Meaning*. Abingdon: Routledge.

Punch, K., 2005. *Introduction to Social Research: Quantitative and Qualitative Approaches*, 2nd edn. London: Sage.

Pye, D., 1978. *The Nature and Aesthetics of Design*. London: Barries and Jenkins.

Pye, E. (ed.), 2007. *The Power of Touch: Handling Objects in Museum and Heritage Contexts*. Walnut Creek, CA: Left Coast Press.

Robertson, I., 2002. *The Mind's Eye*. London and New York: Bantam Books.

Robinson, E., 1928. *The Behaviour of the Museum Visitor*. Washington DC: American Association of Museums.

Robinson, J., 1858. *On the Museum of Art, No. 5 in a Series of Addresses*, 1857. London: Chapman and Hall. Reproduced in B. Carbonell (ed.) [2004], *Museum Studies: An Anthology of Contexts*. Malden, MA: Blackwell, pp. 225–30.

Rodari, P., 2005. 'Learning in a museum: building knowledge as a social activity'. *Journal of Science Communication*, 4: 1–5.

Sachatello-Sawyer, B. et al., 2002. *Adult Museum Programs: Designing Meaningful Experiences*. Walnut Creek, CA: Altamira Press.

Sandell, R., 2005. 'Constructing and communicating equality', in S. MacLeod (ed.), *Reshaping Museum Space: Architecture, Design, Exhibitions*. London and New York: Routledge, pp. 185–200.

Sandell, R., 2007. *Museums, Prejudice and the Reframing of Difference*. Abingdon: Routledge.

Sandifer, C., 2003. 'Technological novelty and open-endedness: two characteristics of interactive exhibits that contribute to the holding of visitor attention in a science museum'. *Journal of Research in Science Teaching*, 40: 121–37.

Screven, C., 1969. 'The museum as a responsive learning environment'. *Museum News*, 47: 7–10.

Serrell, B., 1996. *Exhibit Labels: An Interpretative Approach*. Walnut Creek, CA: Altamira Press.

Shettel, H., 1973. 'Exhibits: art form or educational medium?' *Museum News*, 51: 32–41.

Skolnick, L., 2005. 'Towards a new museum architecture', S. MacLeod (ed.), *Reshaping Museum Space: Architecture, Design, Exhibitions*. London and New York: Routledge, pp. 118–30.

Slack, S., Francis D., and Edwards, C., 2011. 'An evaluation of object-centred approaches to interpretation at the British Museum', in J. Fritsch (ed.), *Museum Gallery Interpretation and Material Culture*. London and New York: Routledge, pp. 153–64.

Sloan, K., 2003. *Enlightenment. Discovering the World in the Enlightenment Century*. London: British Museum Press.

Sloan, K., 2004. *Enlightenment Study Day*. Notes to the paper presented at the British Museum Enlightenment Study Day, 20 March.

Space Syntax. http://www.spacesyntax.com [accessed 3 July 2012].

Spalding, J., 2002. *The Poetic Museum: Reviving Historic Collections*. Munich, London and New York: Prestel.

Stein B. and Meredith M., 1993. *The Merging of the Senses*. Cambridge, MA: MIT Press.

Stephens, S. (ed.), 1989. *Building the New Museum*. New York: The Architectural League of New York.

Stevenson, A., 2008. 'Museums and collections in England and Wales', in S. Keene with F. Monti and A. Stevenson, *Collections for People: Museums' Stored Collections as a Public Resource*. London: UCL, pp. 13–20.

Stevenson, J., 1992. 'The long-term impact of interactive exhibits'. *International Journal of Science Education*, 13(5): 521–31.

Stiftung Jüdisches Museum Berlin, 2001. *Discovering the Jewish Museum Berlin*. Berlin: Stiftung Jüdisches Museum.

Sullivan, L., 1956. *Autobiography of an Idea*. New York: Dover Publications.

Sun, W., 1987. *Flow and Yu: Comparison of Csikszentmihalyi's Theory and Chung-Tzu's Philosophy*. Paper presented at the meetings of the Anthropological Association for the Study of Play, Montreal.

Thomson, G., 1978. *The Museum Environment*. London: Butterworth-Heinemann.

Thompson, D., 1990. 'An architectural view of the visitor-museum experience', in S. Bitgood, A. Benefield and D. Patterson (eds), *Visitor Studies: Theory*,

Research and Practice: Volume 3. Jacksonville, AL: Centre for Social Design, pp. 72–84.

Thompson, J. (ed.), 1993. *Manual of Curatorship: A Guide to Museum Practice.* London: Butterworth/The Museums Association.

Throsby, D., 2001. *Economics and Culture*. Cambridge: Cambridge University Press.

Tufte, E., 1990. *Envisioning Information*. Cheshire, CT: Graphics Press.

Turner, D., 2007. 'The secret of Apple design'. *Technology Review*, May, http://www.technologyreview.com/printer_friendly_article.aspx?id=18621 [accessed 3 July 2012].

Tzortzi, K, 2007. *Museum Building and Exhibition Layout: Patterns of Interaction.* Paper to the 6th International Space Syntax Symposium, Istanbul, July.

Ucko, P. (ed.), 2003. *Encounters with Ancient Egypt* (8 vols). London: UCL Press.

Underhill, P., 2000. *Why We Buy: The Science of Shopping.* New York: Thomson Texere.

Vaughan, R., 2001. 'Images of a museum'. *Museum Management and Curatorship*, 19: 253–68.

Velarde, G., 1988. *Designing Exhibitions.* London: The Design Council.

Vergo, P., 1989. 'The reticent object', in P. Vergo (ed.), *The New Museology.* London: Reaktion Books, pp. 41–59.

Vroomer J. and de Gelder, B., 2000. 'Sound enhances visual perception: cross-modal effects of auditory organisation on vision'. *Journal of Experimental Psychology*, 26(5): 1583–90.

Wacquant, L., 2007. 'Pierre Bourdieu', in R. Stones (ed.), *Key Sociological Thinkers.* London and New York: Macmillan.

Wagensberg, J. et al. (eds), 2006. *Cosmocaixa, The Total Museum Through Conversation Between Architects and Museologists.* Barcelona: Sacyr.

The Week, 2006. 'Exhibition of the week: Jameel Gallery of Islamic Art'. *The Week*, 29 July, 573.

Weil, S., 2002. *Making Museums Matter.* Washington and London: Smithsonian Institution Press.

Welch, R. and Warren, D., 1986. 'Intersensory interactions', in K. Boff, L. Kaufman and J. Thomas (eds), *Handbook of Perception and Performance, Vol. 1, Sensory Processes and Perception.* New York: John Wiley & Sons.

Wiley, K., 2008. 'Nebamun AV testing'. Unpublished internal report, Interpretation Unit, Department of Learning and Audiences. London: British Museum.

Wittlin, A., 1971. 'Hazards of communication with objects'. *Curator*, 14: 138–50.

Zaccai, G., 1995. 'Art and technology: aesthetics redefined', in R. Buchanan and V. Margolin (eds), *Discovering Design: Explorations in Design Studies.* Chicago: University of Chicago Press, pp. 3–12.

GALLERY OBSERVATION RECORD SHEET

Points to observe	Observations
a) *Overall and initial response to the exhibition*	
Visitor coming from… Initial interaction with the exhibition What do they look at first? What next?	
b) *Objects and displays*	
Exhibits looked at (visually pleasing)? Are they *fully absorbed* in interaction, or aware of the environment? Do they *read labels*? Comfortable viewing of objects? Do they *return* at a display already viewed? Do they stay at a *display/s* longer than others?	no briefly yes extensively
c) Interpretation, interaction and interactives	
Interaction type (audio guide, guide, looking, labels, interactives) Level of interaction with displays[1] Do they use interactives? Engagement type with interactives Do they understand how to use them? Do interactives reinforce looking at objects?	visual explorative discovery immersive visual explorative discovery immersive
d) Other observations	
Do they sit down? What after viewing this gallery/section?	

Other:

DATE AND TIME: CONDITIONS:
VISITOR (AGE, SEX):   DURATION of VISIT:

[1] *Visual* – looking only; *explorative* – briefly finding out what it is; *discovery* – finding out something about the object; *immersive* – longer engagement, making links.

APPENDIX 2
CONCEPT CHECKSHEET

SPACE SYNTAX

The layout of exhibition elements in a space and the configuration of space influences the behaviour of visitors

Vista over all areas of gallery	5	1	Some parts not visible from entrance/all areas
Spaces in gallery integrated			Separate spaces, secluded corners
Clear intended viewing path			No clear intentional viewing path
Visitors follow intended viewing pattern			Visitors ignore/don't follow intended path
Attention is spread among exhibits			One or more large prominent exhibits dominates the exhibition
Totals			/25

DESIGN IDIOMS

Colour can be employed to accentuate a desired effect, to draw people's attention and to delimitate a space

Colour used to highlight sections	5	1	Sections are not colour themed
Evokes feelings/impressions			Not evocatively used
Draws attention to collection features			Not related to collection features
Totals			/15

Lighting can be employed to highlight quality, texture, shape and specific features of objects

Appropriately lit	5	1	Too dark/too bright
Objects enhanced by lighting			Object viewing obscured by lighting
Additional lighting tools			No additional lighting tools used
Light emphasises atmosphere			Light does not contribute to atmosphere
Totals			/20

Text (exhibition titles, introductory labels, group labels, object labels) should be readable, legible and enrich the visitor's experience

Key themes and messages are clear	5	1	Key messages don't come across
Information graphically displayed			No information graphics
All text clearly legible – colour, font, positioning			Some or all text illegible

Positive	5				1	Negative
Appropriate language register						Inappropriate register
Appropriate use of terminology						Excessive use of specialist terminology
Appropriate text length						Text too long/too concise
Totals						/30

Object positioning and layout: objects should be harmoniously laid out with regard to grouping and juxtaposition, and positioned so that they are clearly visible

Positive	5				1	Negative
Objects are clearly visible	5				1	Objects are too high/low/hidden
Objects are at the correct inclination						Poorly positioned, key details not visible
Juxtaposition of objects increases interest						Inappropriate object juxtaposition
Objects laid out with sufficient space						Objects too crowded/sparse to appreciate
Totals						/20

BEAUTY

The overall visual and physical dimension of a design system affects the visitor experience

Positive	5				1	Negative
Harmonious	5				1	Incongruous
Welcoming						Unwelcoming
Relaxing atmosphere						Solemn and overwhelming
Consistent design						Inconsistent design
Visually appealing						Visually dull
Colour coordinated or themed						Colour use confusing
Attention to details						Details overlooked
Vista over whole exhibition						Fragmented view
Well maintained						Run down
Appropriately lit						Inadequately lit
Appropriate number of visitors						Overcrowded/empty
Comfortable temperature						Cold/hot/stuffy
Totals						/60

USABILITY

Usability is also crucial - is the exhibition an awkward or a relaxing and stimulating experience?

	5				1	
Clear topographical orientation						Absence of topographical orientation
Conceptual guidance						Absence of conceptual guidance
Objects can be connected with interpretive medium						Object separated from interpretation
Exhibits at comfortable height/distance						Too high/low/far
Engaging						Not engaging
Intuitive to visit						Difficult to visit due to unclear topography
Totals						/30

FLOW

The exhibition has clear themes and structure

	5				1	
Aims of the exhibition/exhibits are clear						Aims unclear
Clear description of exhibition structure						No guidance on exhibition structure
Extent of exhibition is clear						Can't tell extent of exhibition
Progress through exhibition is evident to visitor						No feedback on progress
Totals						/20

The skills of the visitor are well matched to the exhibition

	5				1	
Relaxed						Anxious/uneasy
Sense of achievement/progress						Inadequacy
Engagement						Boredom
Enjoyment						Frustration
Totals						/20

The person is completely focused because of the demands of the mental activity

	5				1	
Fully absorbed in the exhibition						Distracted, looking around, chatting
Prolonged time spent with exhibits						Brief time spent with exhibits
Totals						/10

OBJECT BIOGRAPHIES

Objects have life histories just like people. Are key moments, changes in status, ownership, use or socio-economic context shown?

Key moments conveyed	5			1	Not conveyed
Changes of status put across					Not conveyed
Significant timescales conveyed					No information on timescales
Reference to other relevant objects					Other objects not referenced
Overview of socio-political contexts					No mention of socio-political context
Totals					/25

Are objects exhibited as themselves or are they used as symbols?

The object arouses/excites/moves the viewer	5			1	The object leaves the viewer indifferent
The object narrates the past					The past is not conveyed by the object
Object not a symbol but a part of the past					Object used as symbol in an exhibit story
Multi-sensory experience (e.g. touch)					Only experienced through sight and text
Totals					/20

Objects are both art and artefact and may be exhibited for both

The physicality of objects comes across	5			1	An abstract meaning comes across
Displays convey agency/effects of objects					Solely elicit admiration of beauty
Cultural contexts of origin are conveyed					No cultural contexts come across
Both visual qualities and uses conveyed					Bias on art or artefact side of the object
Totals					/20

PERSONAL LEARNING STYLES

Each visitor has a particular learning style preference (or may combine them) and different types of museum exhibition and exhibit will appeal to those with the relevant style

Criteria: didactic exhibition style/analytical learning

Objects are systematically arranged in displays	5			1	
Interpretation is mainly facts and sequential ideas					

	5					1	
Logical theories invite comparison and thinking							
Specialist language is used							
No allowance for personal interpretation							
Topics progress from simple to complex							

Criteria: behaviourist exhibition style/common-sense learning

	5					1	
Displays designed to motivate viewers							
Interpretation gives a linear set of goals							
Visitor physically respond to stimulus (e.g. press a button, tick a box)							
Feedback from one action used to create next stimulus							
Positive/negative feedback is provided for responses							
Interactives removed from the exhibition space to avoid distractions							

Criteria: discovery exhibition style/experiential learning

	5					1	
Exhibits and activities lead to a gradual understanding of exhibition narrative							
The visitor plays an active role							
The displays are interactive, with clear feedback							
Hands-on activities offered to promote first-person discovery							
Interactives are integrated in the exhibition space							
Appeals to children for its participatory nature							
The gallery is a lively place							

Criteria: constructivist exhibition style/imaginative learning

	5					1	
Exhibits not in linear, predetermined sequence							
Exhibits offer different entry points							

Information offered via various media, more than one sense						
Social interaction is promoted						
Listening and sharing of ideas is important in the search for meaning						
Visitors can make connections with familiar concepts and objects						
Independent thinking is encouraged						
Places for contemplation encourage time with the exhibits						

CHAPTER 8: MUMMIES, OBJECTS, VISITORS AND STORIES: DATA FROM OBSERVATIONS

Visitor interactions with gallery	No.	%
Not stopping/passing through	32	12
Walking by slowly, while distractedly glancing at the objects	96	36
Stopping just to take the odd picture	26	10
Stopping to read wall panel/s and briefly looking at objects next to it/them	12	5
Stopping to find out about the odd object (less than 3 mins)	44	16
Looking at some objects and briefly reading text (3–5 mins)	46	17
Looking at most objects + labels + looking carefully again (5 mins +)	10	4
Total visitors observed	266	100

Age distribution of visitors (by observation)

Under 18	0
18–24	0
25–34	8
35–44	6
45–54	5
55–64	4
65–74	4
75+	0

CHAPTER 8: MUMMIES, OBJECTS, VISITORS AND STORIES: VISITOR SURVEY QUESTIONNAIRE

PART 1: YOU AND THE THINGS IN ROOM 63

1. What are your impressions of the gallery you just looked at?
2. Which things did you find the most interesting? Why?
3. What did you find less interesting? Why?
4. If you think of the objects you have just seen in the gallery, do any images/ ideas/feelings come to mind?
5. Did you find out anything new about Ancient Egypt?

PART 2: ABOUT YOU

6. Have you been to Egypt?

7. Are you visiting the museum:	8. Gender	9. Age:
Alone	M F	Under 18
With a partner/friend		18–24
With your family		25–34
With your school/college		35–44
With a tour group		45–54
Other		55–64
		65–74
		75+

10. Additional comments (if any)

CHAPTER 8: MUMMIES, OBJECTS, VISITORS AND STORIES: INTERVIEW RESPONSES AND DATA

DEMOGRAPHICS

Number of interviewees: 30

Age distribution of interviewees		Nature of visit		Have you visited Egypt?	
Under 18	0	Alone	19	No	28
18–24	3	With partner/friend	9	Yes	2
25–34	8	With family	1	(1 scuba	
35–44	6	School/college	0	diving, 1	
45–54	5	Tour group	0	for heritage	
55–64	4	Other	1	reasons)	
65–74	4	Total	30		
75+	0				
Total	30	Gender	19		
		Male	11		
		Female			

INTERVIEW QUESTIONS

These were open questions and multiple replies were recorded.

Q1 What are your impressions of the gallery you just looked at?	No. of responses
Excellent; very impressive; wonderful; fantastic; overpowering; atmospheric	10
Well displayed and well presented; I really enjoyed text panels	7
Informative	4
Wonderful objects; I didn't expect to see so many beautiful mummies	4

A lot of objects in proportion to the space; overwhelmed by amount of objects; can't understand the organisation of the displays; too much to take in	4
It made me feel funny to see dead people on display – I would like to see what an Egyptian person feels about it	3
Very surprised by the degree of preservation of objects from a long time ago	3
Too much to read (panels, labels); written interpretation takes the attention away from the objects; not clear connection between labels and objects	2
It saddened me to think of colonisation and how much Britain took from other countries – I don't need to travel to Egypt now, it is all here; surprised to see how much from all over the world is in the British Museum	2
Pity objects are out of context, not *in situ* and separated one from the other	2
Too crowded and difficult to appreciate at busy times, otherwise adequately spaced out	2
It highlights the importance of visual arts in the past	1
Makes me want to read more on the subject	1
Total responses	45

Q2   Which things did you find the most interesting? Why?

Choice	Reasons	No. of responses
'Mummies' (mummified bodies and anthropoid coffins)	Morbid side; well preserved; good to see typological variations; personal interest on the subject; good to see it in real life after TV; they are beautiful and amazing objects; objects demonstrate fascinating afterlife beliefs; labels and text brings them to life; presented in a very approachable way (you can look closely, good wall panels); it is what the Egyptians are famous for; lavish and visual feast	18
Tomb models	Show snapshot of daily life; make me feel closer to the people; never seen one boat with mast still in place; I love to look at the details and their conditions; I had never seen them before	6

Human skull in display What we learn from human remains	I like trying to gain information myself rather than being spoon-fed	3
'The coffins' (burials at Deir el-Bahri)	So many; size; colourful and elaborate decorations; just like seen on TV	3
Detailed explanations of methods of mummification	Explained in words and illustrations, and exemplified by the objects	3
Plain gold coffin with black hair	Aesthetically loved the contrast between the gilded coffin and the black of the wig	2
Reconstruction of life/death of woman	Brings exhibits to life; I can identify with it	2
Jewellery	Beautiful; ladies like jewellery	2
Burial and afterlife rituals	Personal interest	2
Real old organic objects (e.g. hair, rope, sandals)	Amazed by preservation	1
In G65 five pebbles used for grinding pigments.	They made me think of one object (from Zimbabwe) on the *Hands on* desk downstairs; so they came to life	1
Paintings of black people (G65)	They are relevant to me (being black)	1
Coptic objects	It shows another side of Egypt	1
Objects from Ethiopia	Reminded me that Egypt is part of Africa	1
Painting inside wooden coffins	Beautiful	1
Development of written language (G61)	So much part of their life	1
Bread and food	It places you closer to the ancient people	1
The beaded shroud	I have never seen one before	1
Labels, even if many	Not too boring to read; concise although quite a few	1
Total preferences		51

Q3　What did you find less interesting? Why?

Choice	Reasons	No. of responses
Small objects, objects of daily use, and shabtis	I looked at them in the past; today I was in for a sensory interaction I know they are important, but there is not a big story behind them It takes too long to look and understand them I can't read the inscriptions on them Manufacture is not so good – anyone could have made them Too many of them, they are small and look all the same Common implements, pottery is not interesting because any civilisation can achieve	10
Hardly anything	I find all interesting Some things are less fabulous looking but I know that if they are here they must be important, so I try to look at them There are interesting message in any object Some are more interesting than others, but all interesting overall	9
Coffins and mummies	It is the side of Ancient Egypt that we always see Too many of them, so you don't look at any	5
Things not really from the 'old times'	Not of interest if it is not really old Very different from 'true Egyptian'	2
Human remains and mummies	I can't stop thinking that it is somebody's father, son, mother, etc.	2
Perhaps too object-rich	Today's museums choose to display less but more in detail. Accustomed to that style When there is too much you don't pay attention to anything	2
Large wooden statues of pharaohs	I love trees and nature and made me thing of waste of resources	1
I can't remember because I didn't look at it	n/a	1

Statuettes of gods with animal heads	Difficult to keep track of them all	1
Different type of mummies according to economy	Difficult to follow	1
Things with writings that I can't read	I don't understand the writings, so they are boring	1
Paintings	Can't relate to them	1
	Total responses	36

Q4 If you think of the objects in the gallery, do any images/ideas/feelings come to mind?	No. of responses
Compassion for the dead; crucial role of death and afterlife; our mortality; I hope they don't mind being on display like this: sadness for them: they went through all those effort for the Afterlife; is it necessary to show them like this?; violated	8
People are very creative in all historical time; so many original ideas 4,000 years ago; their lives were not too dissimilar from ours – they were very advanced in many areas; they suffered illness just like us; material culture testifies similarities with us (e.g. cups, utensils); it made me feel close to them and moved	7
Achievements in terms of craftsmanship and artistry; gilded coffin frightened me – I am used to art from the Middle Ages and this style is frightening	3
Make me feel like going back to that period and experiencing it all; triggers sense of the past	2
Mankind's futile expenditure on funerary practices and provision for immortality – still very applicable today	2
Not really	2
How much British people have stolen from everybody else; how do Egyptian people feel when they see their heritage here?	2
It is nothing new, I have been seeing this for 30 years now, and it does not provoke any fresh feelings	1
It makes me think of how the cult and care for the dead (in many different forms) has always existed	1
Each object evokes different feelings and creates different images (e.g. mummies I was scared of and uncomfortable with)	1
Everything is so old here (from the USA)	1
It seems to reinforce the stereotype of Egypt as a place of wonders and mysterious things	1
Pictorial details on wooden coffins made me think to their natural environment	1
Beauty of objects from so long ago	1

It made me consider how much human beings can learn about the past from material culture, history and archaeology	1
Symbolism found in all the small details	1
So difficult to really think of those people as real – they are so far away … one wonders if the depiction in museums reflects reality or if is all speculation	1
Total responses	**36**

Q5 Did you find out anything new about Ancient Egypt?	No. of responses
Not really; I already knew a lot; I had seen a lot on the subject on TV	6
Yes, a lot, but can't think of anything in particular; yes, because I was very ignorant	6
It was a very complex and advanced society	4
Not today, I came for a sensory immersion	1
Details about wrapping of mummies; historical variations in terms of mummification processes and coffin styles	6
Past links between Egypt and other African countries (e.g. Ethiopia); map and timeline; reminded me that Egypt is part of Africa, close to Ethiopia and Sudan	3
They treated all dead with respect and care regardless of their social and economic background	2
Shabtis, although small and of unassuming appearance, have interesting stories to tell	2
No, but objects can be used as visual illustrations to the jigsaw pieces of knowledge which I have been collecting through the years	1
My knowledge has been expanded a little bit by individual objects (pebbles, mast on boat, seeing a real mummy), but overall it tells us nothing new or challenging	1
Total responses	**32**

CHAPTER 9: *HANDS ON* THE PAST AT THE BRITISH MUSEUM: VISITOR SURVEY QUESTIONNAIRE

NOTE: Data are available on http://www.ucl.ac.uk/silent-objects/

PART 1: ABOUT YOUR VISIT

1. Is this your first visit to the Museum?_

    Yes   No

1a. (If *no*) How many times have you previously visited the museum?

    1-5   More than 5

2. Are you visiting the Museum:

    Alone

    With a partner/friend

    With your family

    With your school/college

    With a tour-group

    Other

PART 2: FINDING THE DESK

3. How did you come across the desk?

    Walking by

    Information desk

Leaflet

Internet

Recommendation from someone

Other (please specify)

4. (If *not walking by*) Was the desk easy to find?

Yes   No

5. Is it clear what this desk is about when you first approached it?

Yes   No

6. Did you notice the signboard next to the desk?

Yes   No

PART 3: YOUR EXPERIENCE WITH OBJECT HANDLING

7. Have you taken part in similar object-handling activities before, either here or somewhere else?

Yes   No

7a. (If yes) Could you tell me where?

8. Do you know that there are other five object-handling desks in the British Museum?

Yes   No

9. How likely do you think you are to use another desk in the Museum today?

Very likely   Likely   Not likely   Not sure

10. How likely do you think you are to use a desk in a future visit to this Museum?

Very likely   Likely   Not likely   Not sure

11. Can you remember which object on the desk *first* attracted your attention?

    Yes   No

11a. (If yes) Could you tell me which one?

12. Could you tell me how many objects did you look at or touch?

    1–3

    3–5

    5+

13. What makes an object interesting to you?

    The way it looks (e.g. colour, shape, size, etc.)

    Personal interest in that type of object

    Having seen it before

    The fact that it is very old

    It looks very curious and wanting to know what it is

    Other (please specify)

14. If you could choose, what other type of object would you like to handle at the desk?

15. What was your favourite aspect of this experience?

    Touching the objects

    Being able to ask questions about the objects whilst holding them

    Having somebody to tell me about the objects

    Being able to compare a range of objects

    Being able to look at details of the objects

    Other (please specify)

16. What was your least favourite aspect of this experience (if any)?

    I wasn't sure what I was supposed/allowed to do

    The conditions at the desk: too crowded, badly lit, too noisy, etc.

    I felt uncomfortable with the person behind the desk

    Difficulty in understanding the language

    I wasn't sure when it was OK to go

    I felt awkward approaching the desk

    Other (please specify)

    None

17. Do you have any additional suggestions that could help us to improve this service?

PART 4: A FEW QUESTIONS ABOUT YOU

18. Gender		19. Age	20. Nationality
M	F	Under 18 18–24 25–34 45–54 55–64 65+	

CHAPTER 10: OSTRACON AND BOOKLET: VISITOR SURVEY QUESTIONNAIRE

NOTE: Data are available at www.ucl.ac.uk/silent-objects

A. OBJECT AND LABEL

I would like to show you *one* object from the museum (UC39630). I would like you to have a look and read the label, and tell me when you are ready to talk about it.

1. Could you tell me in a couple of sentences what do you think of the display and label of the inscribed stone?

2. Do you think you have a good idea of what the object is after having looked at it?

Very good   Good   A bit poor   Very poor

B. OBJECT AND BOOKLET

I would like you to look at the same object again, in combination with this small booklet to see what you think of this. Tell me when you are ready to answer some questions about your new experience.

3. Do you think the amount of information on the booklet is:

Too much   A bit too much   About right   Too little

4. Each page gives different types of information: was that clear to you?

Yes   No

5. Did you look at the booklet:

Selectively

Page by page

Randomly

Just the first page(s)

Other

6. Which page did you find the most interesting? (Please point to ONE page of the booklet)

6a. Could you tell me why you found that page interesting?

7. In the next set of questions you are presented with a statement.

Please indicate your level of agreement or disagreement with each statement

	Strongly agree	Agree	Disagree	Strongly disagree
The booklet made me look at the object carefully				
Booklets like this one are more appropriate for children and young visitors				
I think it is too colourful				
The illustrations were useful in putting the information across				
I don't think the booklet is the sort of thing I would be interested in				
I think it is a good idea to allow visitors to choose the information to read about an object				
During a museum visit there is not enough time to look at similar booklets				
I was compelled to lift the flip windows to know more				
The booklet would make me stop and look at an object which I would otherwise miss out				
I couldn't find the information I wanted				

8. Do you have any suggestions to improve the booklet?

Yes   No

8a. (If yes) please elaborate

C. PERSONAL BACKGROUND

I would like to conclude with a couple of questions about you.

9. Which of the following aspects of the Egyptian culture are you most interested in? (Please choose ONE answer)	10. Which of the following best describes you?
Funerary customs Writing Trade War Ceramics Other Daily life Religious beliefs	Curious General interest Friend of the Petrie Museum Long-standing interest Studying for a qualification in Egyptology/archaeology Other
11. Gender M F	

12. Age

Under 18

18–24

25–34

45–54

55–64

65+

CHAPTER 10: GEOLOGY DISPLAY: VISITOR SURVEY QUESTIONNAIRE

NOTE: Data are available on www.ucl.ac.uk/silent-objects

PART 1: THE GEOLOGY DISPLAY

1. Could you tell me what are your overall impressions of the geology display?

2. Which of the following elements of the display did you look at:

Objects in the display cabinet

Labels next to objects

Explanatory information on panel with map

Map of Egypt

'The uses of stone' wall panel

Handling box

Video of ancient Egyptian quarries

3. How do you rate the following elements of the display (please tick the appropriate box)?

	Very good	Good	Acceptable	Poor	Very poor
Arrangement of objects					
Amount of objects on display					
Object labels with colour-coded information types					
Amount of information on object labels					

Lighting
Use of colour
Wall panel with map of Egypt
Map of Egypt
Photographs
'The uses of stone' wall panel
Handling box
Video of Egyptian quarries

4. What did you find the most interesting element of the display (please choose one)?

Groups of objects in the display cabinet

Labels next to the objects inside the display cabinet

Information on panel with map of Egypt

Map of Egypt showing the location of a selection of quarry sites

Information on 'the uses of stone' wall panel

Photographs and illustrations

Handling box

Video of ancient Egyptian quarries

Other (please specify):

5. In which order did you look at the display (please choose one)?

(1) Objects in the display cabinet (2) Wall panel with map of Egypt (3) (1) Wall panel with map of Egypt (2) Objects in the display cabinet (3) 'Uses of stone' wall panel

(1) 'Uses of stone' wall panel (2) Wall panel with map of Egypt (3) Objects in the display cabinet

I alternated looking at objects and wall panels

I looked only at (please complete):

Other (please specify):

PART 2: Wall panel with map OF EGYPT

6. In the next set of questions you are presented with a statement. Please indicate your level of agreement or disagreement with each statement.

	Strongly agree	Agree	Disagree	Strongly disagree
The map made me look carefully at the objects on display				
I would have liked more photographs				
The photographs of the ancient quarries offer much information difficult to convey by words				
I prefer the 'the uses of stone' wall panel which has more text to read				
The map is an effective way to offer information about the objects on display				
It was difficult to relate the information on the wall panel to the objects on display				
I like visual information as it is easier to remember than text				
I thought the map was confusing				
The design of the panel is clear				
The wall panel with the map does not have all the information I want				

7. The map with the location of ancient quarry sites in Egypt is useful (please choose one answer):

To give an indication of important ancient quarries sites in Egypt

To explain where the stone types in the display may have been quarried

To offer a general idea of the geography of Egypt

To convey the importance of stone in Ancient Egypt

To stimulate interest on the subject of stone as a material

Other (please specify):

8. Do you have any suggestions to improve the geology display?

Yes   No

8a. (If yes) Please elaborate

PART 3: ABOUT YOU

9. Which of the following aspects of the Egyptian culture are you most interested in?

(Please choose ONE answer)

Daily life

Religious beliefs

Funerary customs

Writing

Trade

War

Ceramics

Other

10. Which of the following best describes you?

Curious

General interest

Friend of the Petrie Museum

Long-standing interest

Studying for a qualification in Egyptology/archaeology

Other

11. Gender M F	12. Age
	Under 18
	18–24
	25–34
	45–54
	55–64
	65+

CHAPTER 10: HEADRESTS WITH AUDIO LABELS: VISITOR INTERVIEW QUESTIONNAIRE

NOTE: Data are available at www.ucl.ac.uk/silent-objects

PART 1: INITIAL REACTIONS

1. How did you come across the talking object?

> The talking label started when I passed by

> I was walking towards the display to look at the objects and the audio started

> I was attracted by the audio which was already playing

2. What were your initial reactions when the talking label started to play?

3. How easy was it to find the headrest on display?

> Very easy   Easy   Difficult   Very difficult

PART 2: CONTENT AND STYLE OF THE TALKING LABEL

4. Do you think the amount of information of the talking label is:

> Too much   About right   Too little

5. Do you think the first-person narrative style of the talking label is:

> Evocative

> Informative

> Absorbing

> Pretentious

Confusing

Other

6. Do you think you have a good idea of what the object is after having listened to the talking label?

Very good   Good   Poor   Very poor

7. How would you describe the object in your own words?

8. Is there anything else you would like to know about the headrest?

Yes   No

8a. If yes, could you please tell me what?

PART 3: YOU AND THE TALKING OBJECT

9. Did you listen to the entire talking label?

Yes   No

9a. If you listened only to part of it, could you tell me why?

10. What were you doing whilst the audio was playing?

Listening carefully without looking at anything in particular

Listening whilst looking around

Listening whilst looking at the headrest in the display case

Not really listening

11. What did you most like about the talking label?

It made me look closely at an object which I may otherwise have missed

It stimulated my curiosity about this object and similar ones

It brought the object to life

It broke up the pace of the museum visit

The music

Other

12. What did you least like about it?

I think it is obtrusive

I wasn't sure what it was about

I wasn't sure whether I had to do something to switch it on/off

I do not like audio information

The clip is too long

The clip is too short

Other

13. Do you have any additional comments or suggestions?

PART 4: ABOUT YOU

14. Which of the following best describes you?

Curious

General interest

Friend of the Petrie Museum

Long-standing interest

Studying for a qualification in Egyptology/archaeology

Other

15. Gender M F	16. Age
	Under 18
	18–24
	25–34
	45–54
	55–64
	65+

CHAPTER 11: THE PETRIE MUSEUM: OSTRACON BOOKLET, GEOLOGY DISPLAY AND WHISPERING HEADREST VISITOR SURVEY QUESTIONNAIRE FOR COMPARATIVE EVALUATION

PART 1: THE TALKING LABEL

The exhibit I would like you to look at is a wooden headrest, which is explained by means of an audio label. Once you have looked at the object and listened to its label, I will ask you three more questions.

1. What are your impressions of the object and its talking label?

2. What do you like *best* about the talking label?

3. What do you like *least* about the talking label?

PART 2: THE GEOLOGY DISPLAY

Now I would like you to look at the stone objects in this cabinet, the two wall panels, the object-handling box and the video with footage of ancient Egyptian quarries. When you are ready, I will ask you three more questions.

4. What are your impressions of the geology display?

5. What do you like *best* about the geology display?

6. What do you like *least* about the geology display?

PART 3: THE RED BOOKLET

Please look first at an inscribed stone fragment and then at the booklet with information about it. When you are ready, I will ask you a couple of questions about your experience.

7. What are your impressions of the object and the booklet?

8. What do you like *best* about the booklet?

9. What do you like *least* about the booklet?

PART 4: COMPARATIVE REACTIONS

Finally, I would like to ask you about the comparison between the three displays.

10. Which was the most successful way to stimulate your interest in the objects (please choose no more than two)?

Colour-coded booklet for the inscribed stone

Talking label for the headrest

Wall panel with pictures and map of Egypt

Video of ancient quarries

Handling box with rock samples

Other

11. Please explain the reasons behind your answer

12. Which of the following objects did you find the most interesting?

Inscribed piece of stone

Wooden headrest in the shape of a hare

Group of stone objects

13. Please explain the reason for your preference

14. Do you have any suggestions to improve any of the three installations we looked at today?

CHAPTER 12: TOMB-CHAPEL OF NEBAMUN GALLERY VISITOR SURVEY QUESTIONNAIRE

NOTE: Further data and transcripts of responses are available on http://www.ucl. ac.uk/silent-objects/

DATE: TIME: NUMBER:

Hello, my name is Francesca Monti. I am a researcher in Museum Studies at University College London. I am currently asking people about their experiences in the room you just looked at (*Tomb-chapel of Nebamun* gallery). I would be grateful if you could help me with my research by answering a few questions. It will only take five to 10 minutes. Thank you ... Please do not feel pressured to answer in any particular way.

General data	About the video reconstruction
25 visitors interviewed	Of 25, 12 watched the video, 13 didn't
14 visiting with partner or friend	Why not?
6 with family	10 Not aware of it
5 alone	3 short of time
7 visiting this specific gallery	

PART 1: YOU AND THE THINGS IN THE *TOMB-CHAPEL OF NEBAMUN* GALLERY

What are your impressions of the gallery you just looked at? Could you describe it?

Which things did you find the most interesting? Why?

What did you find less interesting? Why?

If you think of the objects you have just seen in the gallery, do any images/ideas/feelings/memories come to mind?

Did you find out anything new about Ancient Egypt?

After spending time in the gallery, what would you say you got out of the experience? Please choose all that apply (show card):

I saw beautiful, awe-inspiring objects

I learnt something that I didn't know

It brought up memories from my life

It transported me to a different place or time

It improved my knowledge of Ancient Egypt

I felt completely absorbed in the viewing

I enjoyed watching the video

I had an emotionally moving experience

I thought the gallery was a beautiful place

I gained a better understanding of other people/cultures

It made me reflect on how different life can be for different people

I felt very stimulated by the stories presented in the gallery

PART 2: THE VIDEO ANIMATION

7. Did you watch the animation?

7a. If yes, what did you see? What was your favourite part of it?

7b. If no, why?

8. How did you relate what you saw in the animation to the objects in this gallery?

9. Did the animation help you to understand the objects in the gallery, or the story/ stories behind the objects?

9a. If yes, how?

9b. If no, how could it be improved?

10. Do you know that there is an online interactive version of the animation?

11. Would you like to see more screens of this type around the museum's rooms? Anything in particular?

PART 3: ABOUT YOU

I would like to conclude with a couple of questions about you.

12. What was your reason for coming to the museum today?

   To see a specific gallery or exhibit (if so please specify) – the *Tomb-chapel of Nebamun* gallery

   For a general visit to the museum

   To attend a talk, a tour or a special event

   To meet friends

   Other

7. Are you visiting the museum: Alone With a partner/friend With your family With your school/college With a tour group Other	8. Gender M F	9. Age Under 18 18–24 25–34 35–44 45–54 55–64 65–74 75+

Additional comments (if any):

Thank you very much for your help

INDEX